LOUIE'S WIDOW

LOUIE'S WIDOW

ONE WOMAN'S VENGEANCE
AGAINST
THE UNDERWORLD

by *Cecile Mileto*
with
DAVE FISHER

P❦P

A PLAYBOY PRESS BOOK

The facts related in this book are all true. Some names, identities and locations have been changed, in part because of pending litigation.

Published simultaneously in the United States and Canada by Playboy Press, Chicago, Illinois. Printed in the United States of America. Library of Congress Catalog Card Number: 75-17266. ISBN 87223-443-6. First edition.

To Operation Re-Entry and The Village South
for saving my children's lives

Q: *"Mrs. Mileto, do you have trouble remembering times of the year?"*
A: *"I am trying to forget this whole life."*

—Cecile Mileto, DECEMBER 20, 1973

LOUIE'S WIDOW

PART
I

I had a man once who was like nobody else's man. He made me laugh, and he taught me how to love, and meanwhile he was stealing the rest of the world blind.

His name was Louis Mileto. Louie. My Louie.

— I —

On New Year's Eve 1958, my sister went into our basement, put a shotgun under her chin and blew her face off.

She was 17 years old, married, pregnant and desperately unhappy. I knew exactly what she was feeling. I was married, the mother of three young children and desperately unhappy too. And I was 18 years old.

We were each other's very best friend. Our parents split up when we were young and we spent what there was of our childhood being shipped back and forth across the country. Our real father had a terrible temper, and he used to beat up my mother badly. When she left him, she kept herself locked in an apartment because she was terrified he would come and beat her again. My sister Louise and I had a special buzzer signal to get into the building.

My father was never mean to us, he just didn't seem to care that we existed. He worked as a waiter at resort hotels and moved with the seasons. When I was with him he would buy me the very best clothes, and give me all the money I needed. Then he'd put me away in some boarding school. I always ended up stealing whatever I could from him, hocking everything and running back home to my mother.

My mother was a very beautiful woman. She was about five feet seven inches tall, weighed 117 pounds and had long, flowing blond hair. Her second marriage was exactly the opposite of her first. This time she did the beating up. Everything she couldn't do to my father, she did to my stepfather. He was a tall, stocky, good-natured man who always wore suspenders. I remember whenever my mother got mad she'd grab those suspenders and pull back as far as she could before snapping them. He never got mad, he never raised his voice. "That's all right, babe," he kept saying, "that's all right, babe."

He had four children of his own from a first marriage, and very little money. He was always a hard worker, and later would do very well, but at first we were poor. At one point he had to sell his blood to feed us. My mother made Louise and me feel very guilty about that, making us feel that it was all our fault because we weren't his children.

They loved each other very much, and had a wonderful relationship. But it was a relationship with only enough room for the two of them. Louise and I were excluded. My mother kept telling us, "It's just the four of us," but it wasn't. It was them and us. She wouldn't let him be our father. She kept us separate from him. She made it very clear that we were her children, and he wasn't to hit us or yell at us. In fact, we didn't even talk to the man. I wasn't able to look him in the eye and talk to him until I was married and had three of my own children.

My sister and I tried to commit suicide for the first time when I was 11 years old. We ate a bottle of 100 aspirins, then we went to sleep. When we woke up the next morning our ears were ringing and we were sick to our stomachs, but we didn't die. We never told anybody about it.

I tried it again when I was 13. I was living in Chicago with my father, and he was always working and leaving me alone. I took a knife and made a deep cut in my wrist, and but it didn't bleed enough, and it hurt too much, so I stopped cutting and put Band-Aids over the cut. No one noticed.

I don't think Louise actually planned her suicide. My stepbrother had just gotten out of the Navy and brought home an Italian rifle. We celebrated New Year's Eve in the new house my stepfather bought for my mother. After we all went to sleep, Louise went into the basement, found the bullets hidden in a pair of ice skates and killed herself.

My stepfather found her and at first he thought it was my mother, even though he had just left her upstairs. But he got so crazy when he saw Louise's body in my mother's pajamas and with no face, that he started screaming, "Somebody's murdered my wife, somebody's murdered my wife." He even called the police and told them that.

I was very jealous at Louise's funeral. She had a lot more courage than I did.

I missed her greatly. All we ever really had was each other, and boys. We both really wanted to be wanted, and there were always boys around who wanted us. I had sex for the first time when I was 12 years old. My family was living over a television store in Astoria, Queens. A 16-year-old neighbor that I had a real crush on lived nearby and he was always hanging around the apartment. One rainy afternoon we were left all alone and we started experimenting. We laid on a rug in the living room— it was a very clean rug, everything in that house was always absolutely clean and in place—and began playing with each other. There was really nothing to it. I didn't feel excited, I didn't feel like something important had happened, I just felt really good.

Sex never had any real meaning for me, it was just something to do, something that made you feel good—until I met Louie. But that didn't take place for ten years. First there was David.

David Watson was my first husband. I met him when I was 13 years old. He was my sister's boyfriend and I idolized him. He was the leader of the local hot rod club. They weren't Hell's Angels types, they just liked to take their engines apart, rebuild them and then race. David was the best mechanic and he had the fastest car and also the fastest mouth.

After a few months he broke off with Louise to go steady with another girl. She came home crying one afternoon, really upset about being thrown over. "We can't let him do that to us," she told me, "not to the Hartman sisters!" Her plan was for me to take him away from this other girl and then give him back to her. Taking him away wasn't hard—at 13 I had the body of a sexy 18-year-old and a pretty face—and he came running as soon as I started flirting with him. But once I had him I didn't want to give him back. He was my own status symbol. He was the leader of the whole gang, and I was his girl. I never realized that Louise cared about him as much as she did.

David was good to me all the time we were going out. He was working as a tool and dye maker and making $120 a week, which was a lot of money in 1955. He was always buying me gifts, rings and pins and bracelets. And when I was 15 he asked me to marry him.

I really wanted to. I wanted to do anything to get out of that house. This was an offer to escape. I thought it would be a lot of fun to be married and have children and play house. At worst, it still had to be better than what I had. I said yes. My mother said no.

"Either you give me permission to marry him," I warned her, "or I'll make you!" She still refused.

Two months later I deliberately got pregnant. My mother offered to take my baby and raise it as her own, but I wouldn't let her. So she had no choice. She cried when she signed the permission papers. She hated David. She felt I was too young. And she hated the fact that I was taller than he was.

My wedding was very funny. We went to the same justice of the peace in Brooklyn who had married my friend Margy a year earlier. I was so pregnant I had no clothes that fit, so I wore a beige skirt and loose-fitting green blouse. Margy was my maid of honor. She came to the wedding in pin curlers. Our best man had a long beard, and this was when crew cuts were the style. The justice of the peace took one look at all of us and said he didn't want to perform the ceremony.

"But you married me last year," Margy said.

He looked at her very carefully, then he seemed to remember. "That's right, that's right, I did. And how is your marriage going?"

"Oh," she told him, "I'm getting a divorce."

David had to do some very fast talking to convince him to marry us, but eventually he performed the quickie ceremony. We spent our wedding night at my mother's house. I was very happy. I was married, I was pregnant, I was going to have a life of my own. And I didn't have to go back to eighth grade.

The marriage was a disaster. At first we moved back and forth between my mother's apartment and the places we would rent, but finally we bought a house in Syosset, out on Long Island. My job was to provide sex and children. It was never a real relationship. He would grab me whenever he felt like it and force me to make love. He was always the aggressor, always trying to make deals. "If I paint the ceiling, will you make love with me in the afternoon?" "If I buy you a coat will you . . ." It didn't take me long to realize I had made a mistake, but it was too late. We were married and had children. We were both trapped.

Paige was born in 1956. David really wanted a son, and blamed me when I gave birth to a daughter. He used to tell me it was my fault that we had a girl. That didn't bother me; she was a beautiful baby and I loved her. I wanted her for myself.

I didn't know the first thing about babies. I cried the whole day we brought her home from the hospital, "She's gonna die, she's gonna die, I don't even know how to make formula." My sister did everything for me. There was always somebody doing everything for me. Always.

A year later our second daughter, Nancy, was born. David was so ashamed that we'd had another daughter he just hung his head and didn't say a word. Eighteen months later he finally got his son, Philip.

He liked keeping me pregnant. He was terribly jealous and thought that the more children I had, the more I would stay home. Not that I was allowed to go anywhere by myself. I was practically confined to the house. I wasn't allowed to do anything—play cards, go to the movies, visit girl friends. But even then he was always accusing me of cheating on him.

Who had time for cheating? My life consisted of keeping the house clean, raising the children, cooking the meals, watching television and being available for sex when he wanted it. I was 18 years old, the mother of three children, and the wife of a man I hated.

I tried suicide again, but I still wasn't as brave as Louise. The best I could do was swallow a bottle of aspirin tablets. That turned out to be a total failure. My ears started ringing, I couldn't hear and I was sick to my stomach. But I knew I wasn't dying. I was disappointed.

I couldn't stand living with him, and I was afraid of suicide, so that left only one alternative. One afternoon while he was at work I packed my bags, took the kids and moved out. I didn't leave a note, I just left. I found an apartment in Long Beach, locked the door and hid out. Just like my mother had done when she left my father.

It didn't take him long to find me. I heard him come banging up the stairs. He smashed the front door open and started beating up on me. He just kept hitting me. He broke three of my ribs, then threw me down on the bed and ripped my clothing off. He wanted me and he was going to take me. I had no say. When he finished with me he just said, "Let's go," and that was it. I went. There was no choice.

Things got a little better after that. He let me get my driver's license. He let me go to the movies by myself, and he let me out to play canasta with the other girls on the block. But he still controlled me totally. I had a penny jar with about 300 pennies in it, and that was all I had in the world. If I needed money for an ice cream cone, or a pack of cigarettes, I had to dig into that jar. That was my life savings, 300 pennies.

David never stopped being jealous of me. He was so insanely jealous he even quit his job, brought a machine home, and started working in the basement so he could keep an eye on me. I was such a nervous wreck that my doctor prescribed some pills to calm me down.

I loved those pills! They calmed me down, they relaxed me, they made me happy. I discovered that I could be even happier if I took double the prescribed amount of pills. From that point on life became much easier, mainly because I was always speeding on my pills.

I also started seeing other men. I figured why not? David kept accusing me of it, so I decided that as long as I was being blamed for something, I might as well be doing it. My girl friends helped cover me, and David never really knew about them. The men had no meaning. They were all just people who happened to be around the neighborhood.

It was at this point I met Louie Mileto.

I remembered Louie vaguely from Queens. His mother owned apartment houses. I never knew exactly what his father, who was separated from his mother, did to make a living. Actually, no one *knew* Louie, they just knew about him. He was always moving too fast for anyone to know him. In-and-out Louie. First he was there, then he was gone.

He was known around the neighborhood as the local thief. He didn't have to steal, his parents had money, but for him it was the excitement. It was always a game with him. He stole fireworks from his father and blew up the family garage behind the house. He robbed the safe from the Loew's movie theater four blocks away and tried to hide it in his basement. And he could always get you a good price on anything you wanted. He took orders! Then he'd go out and get whatever you wanted somewhere.

When I first started talking to him, after I had gone back with David, he had just gotten out of the State Correctional Institution at Elmira, New York. He had been sent there after throwing the principal of Bryant High School over a railing. Louie wasn't a violent person, he never tried to hurt people. But he was wild, he just didn't care. He did exactly what he wanted to do when he wanted to do it. He was his own man, completely. Right from the very beginning.

He was six months older than I was and skinny. Skinny! He was 19 years old, six feet three inches tall and weighed 170 pounds. He got better-looking later, as he got older, but at this point he was homely. Big, skinny and homely, but always smiling and laughing. Always, when anybody thinks about Louie Mileto, they think of him smiling and laughing.

He was a bricklayer by trade, because all of his cousins owned construction companies, and when he would come out on parole or probation they would give him a job. But he never had any intention of holding down a steady job. He'd stay on the construction job maybe three days, then he'd cut his hand or bruise his leg. That was it, he started screaming bloody murder! He was a hypochondriac and as soon as he saw blood he'd drop his tools and rush to the doctor. Then he would want to sue his cousin's construction company. That was Louie, always figuring the angles.

He was driving a big limousine for some of the neighborhood gangsters when we first got friendly. He was supposed to drive them from one game to another, but he only did that when he felt like it. The guys would tell him, "Listen, Louie, sit here and we'll be out in three hours." He'd take the car and be gone for three days. He got away with it only because his father was so well respected.

At that point, between driving and hustling he was making at least $200 a night. He didn't know too many facts, and his language wasn't good because he was thrown out of school, but he loved to read newspapers and had a very quick mind. Particularly when it came to making a dollar. Once he needed money fast, so he went into Manhattan and bought 25 watches on 42nd Street for $6.99 apiece. Then he came back to the neighborhood and started showing them around. "Dese are the real ting," he'd swear in a whispered, New York City accent. "Real good buys, ya know."

"How much, Louie?"

"I'll give it to ya for fifty bucks, but only 'cause you're my friend." People were chasing him around the streets for watches; they figured if Louie was selling them they must be a bargain. They wanted to buy two or three, but Louie wouldn't let anybody have more than one. He was always willing to cheat his friends, but he didn't want to rob them.

After David, Louie was incredible. We didn't have a sex relationship, but we spent time together. We never made any plans—you couldn't plan anything with Louie, he just lived from minute to minute—but since he was staying with my friends Steve and Joanne we would constantly be seeing each other.

He was wonderful. He made me laugh, and there hadn't been too much laughter in my life before he came along. I missed him every time he was sent back to prison, and for years he was in and out, in and out, always for small things like parole violation or petty larceny. But he would never get down about it. He would just go and do his time and then get out and go right back to whatever illegal thing he was into.

I stayed with David. Somehow we muddled along. I kept seeing other men on the side and he kept getting me pregnant. I hated it, but I just didn't know any better. Abortions hadn't become popular, or easy to get. Our third daughter, Gay, was born when I was 21, and two years later, in 1963, Susan, our fifth child and fourth daughter was born.

We had managed to settle into some sort of relationship. David took charge of almost everything, and that was fine with me. He did all the shopping, he made sure there was gas in the car, he paid all the bills. I wasn't interested and I didn't care. I had never had any responsibilities in my life beyond cooking and cleaning, and I didn't want any. My life was simple, I had my children and my pills and my boyfriends, and I was at least content if not happy. David and I stayed together 11 years, and we might still be together today if Louie Mileto hadn't gotten paroled.

He came out of prison and moved in with Steve and Joanne Marchant. I immediately started finding excuses to spend time over there. Joanne encouraged me because she liked Louie and knew how unhappy I was with David. Finally, one day Louie asked me if I wanted to go out with him.

I'd been waiting seven years for him to ask me for a date. I jumped at the invitation.

Our date was set up for a Monday night. I still had to sneak around, so supposedly I was going out to play bingo. Over the phone I told Louie where I would meet him. Driving over, I was more excited than I had been at any time since I was a 13-year-old going out with the leader of the hot rod gang.

Louie had rented a car, which he always did because he usually could figure a way to beat the bill, and he was waiting for me. I parked my car and got into his rental. I smiled. "Hi, where we going?"

"It's a surprise," he said. He was always full of surprises, always playing little games with everybody around him, always playing.

It really was a surprise. He pulled into a motel parking lot. "Hold it, Louie," I said. "This is a little quick."

"Whattya worried about?" It never occurred to me that we were going there for dinner.

My education about Louie Mileto started that night. He had absolutely no manners. He ate his entire dinner with his salad fork lying in his plate. He picked up his meat with his hands. He just kept shoveling his food in and talked with his mouth stuffed. This was Louie, he just didn't care what other people thought. He did whatever he wanted to do and never seemed to care about the consequences. If he felt like picking his nose, that's exactly what he would do.

I was very impressed.

I had never met anybody like him. No matter what he did, people were attracted to him. He just had a special personality. After our first date we spent a lot of time talking on the telephone. He used the telephone more than anyone I've ever known. He had a way of getting right to the core, and I told him everything about my marriage. He and David knew each other from the old neighborhood, although they were never friendly. Louie understood how unhappy I was.

It took him one more date to decide he wanted me and he wanted my kids. We were going to be the big, loving family he'd never had. He had inherited the traditional Italian love for a big family, but he just didn't have the time to spend fathering his own. Mine came ready-made. So even though he'd never spent any time at all with my kids, he already decided they were going to be his. All we had to do was get away from David. "I'll just pack up one day and leave him," I said. He didn't want me to do it that way, he didn't want to sneak around.

He planned the whole scene. One night he just opened the front door and walked in. "Get your stuff," he said to me, "you're leaving now!"

For a minute David was too overwhelmed to say anything. He must have been at least a little intimidated by the fact that Louie towered nine inches over him. He recovered quick enough and asked if we could talk about it. Like three very well-mannered people we sat down at the kitchen table and talked the whole thing through. "It's over," I finally said flatly, "I'm leaving with Louie."

David very calmly got up from the kitchen table and went down into the basement. When he came back he was carrying a rifle. He put it right to my head and said to Louie, "Get outta my house or I'm gonna blow her brains out."

Louie just looked at him and didn't say anything. He was on parole at the time, as usual, but carrying a pistol. But he wasn't going to force a confrontation. Without saying a word he walked out of the house, got in his car and drove away. David followed him right to the door. Then he stuck his head, and the rifle, out the window and started screaming at him. He was swearing that if Louie didn't get out of there he was going to start shooting. To kill.

I was scared to death. So, while David was making sure that Louie drove away, I called the police.

David didn't seem to care. After Louie pulled away he turned around and he had this very satisfied smile on his face. He thought he had won.

He hadn't. Louie might not have won every time, but he never completely lost. He drove his car around the block and pulled into Steve and Joanne's driveway. Then he stashed his gun and identification and walked back into the house.

David was dumfounded. He couldn't believe anyone would come back and face a gun. He just didn't know Louie.

Louie didn't want to talk about it. "Listen, do what you want, call the cops, shoot the gun, whatever you want. But she's going." He looked at me. "Go pack some stuff."

I went to pack some stuff for myself and the children. Louie went to the refrigerator and opened a bottle of soda. Then he sat down and waited for me to get ready.

The police arrived before I was finished packing. First David started screaming at them, then I started screaming at them. Louie never said a word. Finally they shut us both up and asked me to tell them the story. I told them that David beat me and I wanted to leave him, that Louie was my boyfriend and he was going to take me away.

The cops told me to go finish packing. "Get your kids and go ahead." David was enraged. His whole face just turned red, but there was nothing he could do. The police held him there until Louie, me and the five kids were packed in the car and on our way.

I had no idea where we were going or what we were going to do. I was depending completely on Louie. All I knew was that I was finally free.

Louie had four dollars in his pocket, and six people to provide for. He was completely confident. All he ever needed to get by was his brain.

We were still on the Long Island Expressway when David caught up with us. He pulled up to Louie's car, a few inches away, and started honking his horn.

Louie just pressed down on the accelerator. David stayed inches behind. If we had to stop or slow down he was going to go right into us. The kids were in the back crying, David was sitting on his horn and I was petrified. I looked at Louie and thought he was ready to explode, but he didn't say anything, he just kept going faster and faster.

David smacked into us for the first time, just sort of nudged our bumper, just to let us know he was there. We were going over 80 miles an hour and I was scared. Louie was trying to pull away, but the car was so loaded down he just couldn't get any speed up. David stayed with us.

He bumped us again, a second time, a little harder. I had seen him when he lost his temper and I knew he could get really crazy, capable of anything. I didn't know how far he was going to go, and I was very scared.

Louie just kept driving, trying to get more speed out of the car. Finally we caught up to a few other cars and Louie managed to slip into the lane to the left, then back into the right. He was moving back and forth and David was having trouble following him. Little by little Louie managed to pull away. He was using the other cars as blockers. I looked back at David and saw him get trapped behind two slower cars. There was nothing he could do but watch us move away from him.

I glanced at Louie. He had a half smile on his face. That was the first time I realized he was enjoying the whole chase scene. From the beginning he knew he was going to win, he knew it, and everything that happened in between was part of the game.

I was pretty naive then and I never stopped to really think about what I was doing. I was escaping from David and that was all that mattered. It never even entered my mind that Louie was jumping parole. I never wondered how much money he had or where it came from. It never occurred to me that I didn't even really know Louie. I was free of David and that was what really mattered.

— 2 —

We were going to New Haven. My Aunt Margaret lived there and I knew I could depend on her for help. She welcomed us and took the kids for the night. Louie and I checked into a Holiday Inn.

We made love for the first time that night. With David and with everyone else it had been sex for the good feelings. With Louie it was love. He was so different from any other man I had ever been with. His years in prison had taught him how to control his sex desires, so he just lay back on the bed and let me be the aggressor. He let *me* make love to him. I had never done that before, I was always the object, but I wanted to do it with him. I wanted to bring him pleasure, I wanted to make him happy.

We just made love and held each other all night. Being with Louie was the best thing that ever happened to me.

I waited until morning to start asking him any serious questions, like where were we going. California, he said. He had friends out there who could put him on to some things.

"What kind of things?" I asked.

He didn't answer.

I decided to lay down the law. "Louie, I love you," I told him, "but I'm only going to go with you to California on one conditon. You have to go straight."

"Ceil, I'm——" he started.

I interrupted him. I was firm on the subject. "I'm sorry Louie, but I just don't know how to live your kind of life. You can do what you want when you're on your own, but if you want me and the kids, then it's got to be the straight way. You have to promise me that."

He looked directly at me. "I promise honey, straight."

Then he paid the bill with a stolen credit card. He also neglected to tell me he became a fugitive from justice the moment we crossed the New York State border into Connecticut.

I believed every word he told me.

We all piled into the small sedan and headed west. The trip was a dream come true, every day was Christmas. Louie would constantly be buying clothes for me and the kids. We'd stop at the best hotels. Eat at the best restaurants. One week earlier I'd been trying to talk David into buying meat for dinner, now we were all eating the best thing on the menu every night. I had no idea where the money was coming from. I didn't care. I just assumed he had it.

Actually, he wasn't paying for very much. He did his best to beat every bill. Those bills he couldn't beat he paid with a stolen credit card. And those places he couldn't use credit cards, he cashed bad traveler's checks.

He was an expert at beating bills. In restaurants we would all eat dinner, then get up to leave. Louie would go to the men's room and tell me to take the kids and go to the car. After we were outside he'd order a coke or something else cheap and get a separate check. When he stopped at the cash register on the way out, he'd just pay the smaller bill. But he always left a good tip for the waiter or waitress. No one could call Louie Mileto cheap.

Hotel and motels were even easier to beat. He'd just give the bellboy a good tip and we'd pack the luggage in the car and drive away. Louie didn't care if they charged the bill to our credit card, it was stolen anyway.

He really knew how to use stolen credit cards. Everyday he'd check with a friend in New York to find out when the cards hit the hot sheet and were no good to use. And he had a set of identification for every credit card. He kept four sets of license plates in the trunk of the car and every few days, usually just before we'd stop for gas, he'd change the plates. I didn't know what he was doing, and I didn't ask.

The real good cash came from the traveler's checks. He started out with $400 worth of checks. I don't know where he got them, but he didn't pay for them. Louie never paid for anything. We'd go from one state to another and he would stop at the traveler's check office and say he lost all his checks. "I think I left them in the restaurant we stopped at last night," he'd tell them. He would even go so far as to call the restaurant. The company would reimburse him for the checks. As soon as we got to the next state, before the check numbers would hit the warning list, Louie would cash the old ones, giving him another $400 in cash. Then he'd take the $800 and buy new traveler's checks, using a different name and identification. He just kept doubling his money.

I was so dumb, I didn't know any of this was going on. He would just disappear for a few hours and then come back. That wasn't unusual, that was Louie, in-and-out Louie, you never knew where he was. Besides, I was having too wonderful a vacation to be bothered with problems. He kept buying us gifts and making us laugh the entire trip. The kids fell in love with him and it was mutual. He was crazy about them.

The more time I spent with Louie the more he dazzled me. Nothing fazed him. Nothing bothered him. He had an answer for everyone, a solution for everything. In Ohio, for example, we were speeding and a cop pulled us over. This was really dangerous for Louie. He was in violation of parole by being out of state, plus he was driving an overdue rented car, for which he had no registration. I don't know any of this, of course. "Smack the baby," he said to me.

I looked at him like he was crazy. "What am I going to smack the baby for?"

"We got to make her cry, Ceil," he told me like it was the most obvious thing in the world. "She's got a high fever and I'm speeding 'cause we're rushing to a hospital."

"I'm not gonna hit my baby, Louie." I didn't understand his motives at all.

The cop was walking up to the car. Louie looked in his mirror, then he looked at me. "Okay, all right. Just hold her like you're really concerned."

I took Susan in my arms and held her tight. I wasn't going to hit my baby, but I didn't see anything wrong with holding her. So Louie gave the cop the story and the cop ended up escorting us right to the hospital. Louie never had to show the registration or his license or produce any evidence.

Later during the trip the kids came down with measles. It was so funny. The five kids, Louie and me, all crammed into this car, screaming, laughing, dropping food all over each other, trying to find places to keep all the clothes and gifts Louie was buying, and then the red spots started showing up. We really did have to stop at a hospital and we all got shots.

All except Louie, the hypochondriac. Louie was petrified of getting a needle and talked the nurse out of giving it to him. "I already had them," he swore, and then just about ran out of the room.

The kids were covered with spots, but even that didn't slow Louie down. He acted like there was nothing wrong. "We can't take these kids into public places, Louie," I pleaded with him, "measles are infectious. It isn't right."

He didn't care. When he got hungry he just marched us into a restaurant and watched the place clear out. "It's a free country, Ceil," he told me, "and we can eat anywhere we want."

He completely spoiled the kids. He acted more like a friend than their new father. He just immersed himself in their world. Once he told me that he had had a very lonely childhood, and it was obvious he was making up for it now. Paige, Nancy and Louie would play for hours. All of them hopping and skipping, jumping rope, playing hopscotch.

Louie was so proud of them. Right from the very beginning he wanted people to think they were his own kids. He didn't want to hear about any "first marriage." He was their father and that was the end of the argument, period. And he would brag about the kids to anyone who would listen. One afternoon we stopped at a Howard Johnson's and Philip started playing with another little boy. His parents complimented Louie on his beautiful family. "Thank you," he said, smiling, "we've never had too much trouble from them."

He was such a liar! Even I didn't know when he was telling the truth. At one point he got a discussion with a stranger. Just general talk. Louie gave him a phony name. "What business you in, Mr. Coyne?" the stranger asked.

"I own a recording company," Louie told him.

"Oh? What company is that?"

"Hoist records," he answered very honestly. An answer for every question. I remember sitting with him, listening to this conversation, knowing he was lying with every answer, and *still* thinking to myself, well, maybe he does own a recording company. It was possible. With Louie, anything was possible. A fact was never exactly a fact, things were never precisely what they seemed to be.

The trip took almost three weeks, and we arrived in Panorama City, California, in the summer of 1966. By that time Louie had turned his initial traveler's check stake into a roll big enough to buy a little car and rent a two bedroom, kitchenette apartment. He parked the rental in a vacant lot across the street and called the police to scream that somebody had abandoned a car in the lot and he wanted it out because it was messing up his neighborhood. We were just moved in, already it was his neighborhood. It was also his rental! He called every few days, until somebody came by to pick it up.

He always made me laugh.

At the beginning he tried to keep his promise about going

straight. He got a job driving a truck for a laundry service. He promised me he wouldn't steal. Life was wonderful. He was coming home for lunch every day. When he came home at night we'd all go swimming, and once a week the seven of us would go out for a nice dinner. We didn't have too much money, but we were happy.

At least I was happy. Louie never really was happy unless he had something going. After working for the linen service for a few weeks, he started coming home with sheets. He was stealing sheets! Soon we had sheets piled up in every closet. We had more sheets than a small hotel. I didn't even bother washing them, when they got dirty I just threw them out. I didn't like stealing, but sheets seemed so trivial I didn't say much.

Then he graduated. One afternoon, after he came home from work, he called me to come into the bedroom. "Com'ere and look, I wanna show you." I walked in and his eyes were like slits, just really tight. Laying on the bed were two rifles and about a dozen checks. He was smiling like a proud child.

"You promised me you weren't going to steal," I told him coldly.

He hung his head slightly. "I couldn't help it. I went to deliver sheets to this house and the front door was open and there was nobody home. What did you want me to do?"

He said it like there was absolutely no other answer. He interpreted an open door as an invitation. I didn't say anything.

"I need you to help me, Ceil. All you got to do is go to the motor vehicle and get a learner's permit and we can get rid of these checks right away."

He wanted me to get the permit in the same name as was printed on the checks. "Louis, I don't want to. I was never arrested in my life."

"We need the money, Ceil," he told me matter-of-factly. "Just think, we cash these checks, we'll buy some furniture, some clothes, maybe we'll go to Vegas for the weekend . . ." He just went on and on, building a gigantic bubble. Two months earlier I'd been virtually trapped in a small house in New York. Now Louie was offering me the world, dreams to come true, and all I had to do was sign some checks. "There's no risk, Ceil, I took 'em from the back of the guy's book. He won't even know they're missing."

I signed the checks. With that I signed away any right to object to Louie's stealing. In my own small way, I was now involved.

I wasn't the only one Louie involved. Soon after we got to California he looked up Billy and Frankie D'Angelo. They were the two sons of a man Louie had done time with in prison. At one time their father had owned a very successful construction company. But one afternoon he came home and found his wife in bed with another man. He took a shotgun, put it up inside of her and blew her away. "He was really a terrific old guy," Louie told me. "Even the guy she was in bed wit' went to court and testified in his behalf. And you know what? He beat the rap. He only did seventeen years!"

In Louie's mind 17 years was beating the rap. The old man did his time and came out on the streets and died. But Louie felt close to him, and knew his sons and wanted to do something for them. The first thing he did for them was help them rob their cousin's house. The cousin owned a big business and lived in a mansion, and Louie explained to the boys how they could clean it out. I heard him discussing it with them and I interrupted, "Louie, you can't do that. You can't rob houses!"

He waved me away. "He's got too much money. And he's insured, don't worry about it. The only one who's gonna lose anything is the insurance company, and they're a bunch of thieves anyway." They never did the job, though.

Billy and Frankie were just overwhelmed by Louie. They couldn't do enough for him. They drove him everywhere, they ran errands for him, Billy robbed with him. Louie was only six years older, but they treated him like he was their father.

Louie left the linen company after seven weeks. He left by robbing the company office. He took a big check ledger, identification so he could cash the checks and the stamping machine that the company used to certify them. "They're gonna find you now, Louie, they know who you are."

"Do I look that stupid?" he laughed. "When I took the job I gave them a bad name and address. Just in case the job didn't work out."

We started fighting over his stealing. I reminded him that he promised he would go straight. "You gave me your word, Louie," I'd scream at him. "What about me? What about the kids?"

"I'm doing it for them," he'd shout right back. "They're gonna have the best of everything I can buy. And you too!" End of argument.

I was angry and confused. I knew right from wrong, and I knew what he was doing was wrong. But I also knew that I liked the money. And I liked the new life he was showing me. "Get some clothes together," he'd say Friday afternoon. "We're going to Las Vegas for the weekend."

"I can't go to Las Vegas, Louie. Who's going to watch the kids?"

"The babysitter," he laughed. The babysitter was Billy D'Angelo. The brothers had become almost inseparable with Louie, and Billy became our babysitter. Louie even used to introduce him to other people as "the babysitter," which Billy hated, and even the kids began calling him Mama Rosa because he stayed with them so much.

Vegas was like Oz. We checked into the Sands Hotel under the name of Kelly, so we could use a bad credit card. And Louie showed me that town—on other people's money, of course. We went to all the best shows, ate at the finest restaurants and gambled the whole weekend. I loved it. I absolutely loved it.

Because I did, it was getting more difficult for me to try to uphold morality in front of him. I liked the life as much as he did. So we compromised, I stopped complaining and he stopped telling me what he was doing. I was happier, again.

That shaky peace lasted about a month. We moved out of the small apartment into a three-bedroom place, and we needed furniture to fill it up. Louie found an ad in the *Los Angeles Times;* somebody had to sell an almost-new bedroom set. "Must sell," the ad read. Louie called.

The add had been placed by a recently married young woman. Her husband was a soldier stationed in Europe, and she was selling their furniture and going to meet him over there. Louie grabbed a bad check and went over to see the bedroom set. He bought it with a bad check, and made arrangements for Billy and Frankie to pick it up that evening.

But he wasn't through. She made the mistake of telling him she was also selling her car. "I'd like to try it out," he told her, "but I've got to get home. How about tomorrow?"

She agreed. The next morning Louie took Paige with him and met this woman at her office. She gave him the keys to the car. He drove it directly from her office to a used car lot and sold it, using a phony name and registration. Then he took the apartment keys she had left on her key ring and went back to her apartment and cleaned her out. He took her jewelry, her albums, clothes, whatever wasn't nailed down.

He thought the whole thing was so funny he couldn't resist telling me about it. I didn't think it was quite as funny as he did. "How can you do this to people, Louie? I don't understand you." I really felt sorry for this poor girl. He took her for everything, her car, her bedroom set and everything in the house. She was going to have nothing when she got to Europe. I had reached the point where I didn't care about him stealing from the rich. I excused it by thinking they were insured, they could afford it. But this young girl was different. "And what'd you do with the baby while you were cleaning out the apartment?"

"Oh, she waited in the car. She was watching the car for me." He made a joke out of it.

That was it for me. I just couldn't take it anymore. I loved Louie, but I couldn't stay with him. As much as the kids adored him, he had to be a bad influence on them. He taught them to do almost anything they wanted to. I decided to go back to David.

I really felt I had no choice. I had nowhere else to go. Even though David is a rotten father, I said to myself, he still is their father. I'll stay with him until they grow up and then I'll leave and make my own life. So I waited until Louie was gone the next afternoon, packed up the kids, took a handful of bad checks and went to the airport to fly to New York.

Louie was there before the plane took off. I don't remember what name I was using that time—we were always using phony names—but the stewardess came up to me and said quietly, "Mrs. so-and-so, all your luggage has been taken off the plane by your husband. I'm afraid you'll have no clothes when you reach New York." He was hoping he could get me off the plane, too. But I was disgusted. I was determined to go back to David. I was going to forget Louie. It was over, I convinced myself. I'd given him four months and he had no intention of going straight. It had been fun, for a while.

I started missing Louie even before the plane reached the end of the runway.

−3−

David made it very easy for me to come home. "I'm glad you're back," he said quietly. There was no yelling, no swearing, no I-told-you-so scenes. Instead we sat down at the kitchen table and talked everything out. He realized he hadn't been a good husband, but he was going to try to change. There was no reason for him to be jealous, he said, because I had always been a good mother to the children. He made the whole thing sound like it was his fault and I wasn't to blame. I made it that way, too.

I didn't have any high expectations that my life was going to improve. I really couldn't believe he could change drastically after 11 years, but I was resigned to staying with him and making the best of our bad marriage. For the kids. Only for the kids. I had had my fling. I had lived my dream. For four months it had been like being the grand winner on a television quiz show. Now it was over. Now I was back in the house to stay. I owed that to my children. I loved them.

The first two days I was home David did try to change. I could see him working at it. Maybe, I began to hope, maybe it really will be different. On the third afternoon I started out the front door to visit a girl friend.

Louie was waiting on the sidewalk. "Let's go," he said.

I laughed. "Louie, I can't go with you. I can't do it again."

He looked me right in the eyes, his personal version of an honest look. "I'll try to go straight this time. I'll really try. It's not so easy breakin' long-time habits, ya know."

"But Louie . . ."

"We'll make it another vacation," he said in an excited voice. "We'll stop in every town, buy all new clothes, big dinners, the whole deal." He talked on and on, painting his pretty dream pictures again. And I listened and I believed again. I never even bothered to think about David. We waited until the oldest kids came home from school and took off cross-country again. This time Louie didn't rent a car, he sort of borrowed one.

From the time he was 15 years old Louie had been transporting other people's cars around the country. He loved the freedom of being behind the wheel of a car, any car. So he used to answer ads in newspapers asking for somebody to drive a car to another destination. He used phony identification and always managed to keep the car much longer than he was supposed to. Every car he drove either "got busted" or "got lost" during the trip, giving him extra time to use it. Once, he told me, he really struck it lucky. A famous bandleader hired him to drive his car from New York to Palm Springs. The bandleader made the mistake of leaving the keys to his house in Palm Springs on the car key chain. Louie drove directly there and cleaned out the place, using the bandleader's own car for transportation of everything he stole. Then he called the bandleader and told him the car was broken down in Los Angeles.

This time he was driving a brand new, air-conditioned, big yellow station wagon. He packed it with pillows and blankets and toys for all the children. We were on our way before David got home later that afternoon.

I once believed that if you really wished hard for something, really hard, your wish would come true. I was wishing as hard as I could that Louie would go straight. But I knew it would never come true. He just didn't know anything else except hustling. It was his life, it was what he did best, it was his occupation. The first place we stopped at on the trip was a Stuckey's. That's a chain of general-type stores. We went in and Louie bought something for everybody. After we drove away he started laughing. "What's so funny?" I asked him.

He gave me a big smile. "We sure stuck Stuckeys!" He had paid with a bad credit card.

That was the way the entire trip went. Every place we'd stop he'd turn around and ask, "What do you want, kids? Sit in the car and tell me your sizes." And bring more junk into the car.

The kids were overwhelmed. "Please," Paige told him. "I don't want to try on any more shoes."

"But these are moccasins," Louie explained. "We didn't get you any moccasins yet."

He wanted to buy gifts for my mother. "No, Louie," I tried to say to him, "you know my mother, you can't send her any stolen stuff."

It was funny. We just laughed from state to state. And again I was telling myself stories, trying to convince myself that everything was going to be different once we reached California. That Louie really was going to go straight. Meanwhile we were sticking Stuckeys from state to state.

We moved into another new apartment. This time I decided I was going to set an example for Louie. I was going to show him how to earn an honest living. So I took a job in a beer bar. It was the very first job I ever had, and I was pretty excited about it. The place was big and alive, and the customers were friendly and the pay was good. I had to wear a bikini bathing-suit costume while I worked, but that didn't bother me. I knew I had a good figure and enjoyed showing it off.

The job lasted almost four hours. I was working behind the bar and I looked up and saw Louie sitting down at one end. Louie was never a drinker or a smoker, so he just sat there watching me work. Finally he stood up and walked over to the manager. "She quits," he said. Then he turned to me. "Put your clothes on. We're leaving." I didn't argue with him. When he made up his mind about something he was unchangeable, and I was a little worried about him creating a big scene.

I tried to talk to him about it while we drove home. He listened to every word I said, to all my arguments, to my rationale, without saying one word. When I was completely finished he said, without even looking at me, "You're not working anymore. You're staying home with the kids." End of argument. Again.

Louie was making money, but he refused to tell me what exactly he was doing. "I'm working with an old friend," he would say. His old friend was a private investigator in California, and I couldn't really believe Louie was working as a detective. Most of what I knew I found out from the babysitter, Billy D'Angelo.

Louie was working with both Billy and Frankie, but not together. The boys didn't get along with each other very well, they were competing with each other for Louie's approval. "Louie likes me better than you," Billy would tell Frankie, and Frankie would scream right back, "Yeah? Then how come he told me you were a big jerk?" It finally reached the point where Louie had to separate them and work with them one at a time.

Louie really did like both of them, but he wasn't really interested in teaching them how to earn quick money on their own. He used them, like he used almost everybody he came into contact with. They would drive his car so he would have somebody to talk to. They would help cash the bad checks, do the hard jobs, carry the bundles and jump when he told them to jump.

I liked both kids, too, but I got to know Billy much better because he was the babysitter. He loved to gossip as much as any woman, and we'd sit at the kitchen table and he would tell me exactly what Louie was doing. "We were in the supermarket cashing a check," he'd say, "and Louie had a basket full of soap. This woman tried to cut him off. He started screaming at her, 'You old bag, get in the back of the line where you belong!'" I'd listen like an eavesdropper, and I both enjoyed hearing and hated hearing about Louie. Billy told me the little bits and pieces of Louie's life I didn't know about, what he did during the day, who he saw, where he went, what he did for money. Knowing his secrets was fun, but I hated knowing them, because I had to face the fact that Louie was as bad as ever. He wasn't going to change. He couldn't change. After one month together, I decided to leave him again.

He was making me a wreck. He'd come home from a day of cashing bad checks at every supermarket in Ventura with bags full of things we didn't need, but he had to buy something in order to cash the checks. We had 40 cans of Maxwell House Coffee, 30 boxes of soap powder, 200 sponges. As a shopper, he didn't have much imagination. I'd ask him where I was supposed to put everything. "In with the dishes," he'd tell me, like that was an answer.

I couldn't stand his pace. He was just like a flash. Here. Gone. Here. Everything was always happening so quick. Never any time to think. I didn't see enough of him, but when we were together I got mad at him for making me a hypocrite. I knew he was robbing, I knew he was cashing bad checks, and I couldn't bring myself to say anything to him because then I'd be accepting his behavior. So I pretended everything was fine. Inside, I was dying.

I left the same way, packed up the kids, cashed a bad check at the airport and flew home. This time David wasn't so willing to take me back. Who could blame him? He had found himself a new girl friend, and she was getting ready to move in with him. I sold him on the fact that he already had five children and was responsible for them. He bought it. We compromised: He would cut his girl friend loose if I cut Louie loose. We never really talked about his new girl friend, her baby or our relationship. We didn't have time to, I didn't stay long enough.

Louie showed up two days later. As long as he wasn't around I could be strong, I could convince myself I wasn't going back with him. "Not this time," I told him. "I'm not going back with you. There's absolutely no way in the world you can convince me. This time I'm staying and I mean it!"

David was out working when we left for California. But before we took off we went through my house, room by room, and cleaned the place out. We took anything of value we could carry. I wasn't really robbing David, Louie explained, because we weren't going to hit him for any child support. We were just taking what was mine.

This time I did one more rotten thing. I let Louie talk me into temporarily leaving the kids with David, in order to give us a chance to really get to know one another. It was a bad mistake.

We drove back to California in a small Ford Maverick that belonged to some gay musician. The trip was the first time we really spent any time alone together. Although I was unhappy, missing my kids, he still kept me laughing the whole trip. We'd stop at motels and not only would he beat the bill, he'd rob the room. He would unscrew the pay-box for the television and the vibrating bed, take the paintings off the wall, steal the blankets and pillows and shower curtains, anything he could get loose. I would scream at him, warning him that I was going to call the police.

So he'd rip the telephone out of the wall and put it in the trunk.

I just couldn't stay mad at him. He had a story for every state we were in. "One time I was friends with Rick Elgar and we stole this Corvette and I convinced him to let me sell it. So I took it to California and I got four thousand bucks for it. That's two thousand for me and two thousand for Rick. But, unfortunately, on the way home I stopped in Vegas and started playing the dice. I lost two thousand, so I said to myself, 'Well, now that I lost all Rick's money for him, what should I do?' I decided to be fair about it and bet my own money. I lost that too.

"Rick don't understand how fair I was either. He still thought I owed him money. That was almost the end of our friendship."

By the time we reached Los Angeles I missed the kids desperately. It was so lonesome without them. I'd call them all the time and the phone conversations would be crazy. "When are you coming to get us, Ma?" Nancy would ask. "I wanna come to California," Philip would scream. The little ones would be yelling that they wanted to speak to Mommy. My mother-in-law would grab the phone and start yelling at me, "You're no good, ya bum." Philip would grab it from her and warn her, "Don't you call my mother a bum. You're a bum!" They weren't conversations, they were circuses.

We were living in a motel and Louie kept promising me we'd go get them as soon as he got a job or made a big score. One month passed. I wanted them. Louie and I argued about it all the time. Finally, just like my mother, I got violent. I smacked him in the face. "I want my kids!" I yelled, "I wanna go get my kids." Louie finally realized I was right, and I flew back to get them. David didn't object to me taking them.

Now, for the third time, we tried to settle down as a family. Sometimes it worked; sometimes it didn't. Louie and I kept fighting and I kept falling more in love with him. He was just as much my sixth child as my lover. The kids treated him as an equal. And he was making more and more money.

At first, like before, I didn't know what he was doing. He'd get up late in the morning or early in the afternoon, play with the kids and then disappear for a few hours. While he was gone he would call at least once an hour to make sure everybody was all right, to remind me to do something or just to say hello. Nobody ever used the telephone as much as Louie. And when he was in Los Angeles, he would come home every night. Every night. He never missed one.

He started making short trips. I didn't know where he was going or how long he would be gone. He'd just tell me he had to travel for a few days and then leave. But he would always call. And he would always tell me he loved me.

Billy D'Angelo was the one who told me the details of Louie's house robbing. Billy would sit like a little washerwoman and drink coffee and laugh about Louie's latest caper. "When we robbed this one house," he would say, "Louie got hungry and went into the refrigerator and got some cookies and milk. 'Louie,' I kept saying to him, 'the people are gonna come home soon and . . .' And he said to me to sit down and relax because he had to go to the bathroom. 'Make yourself at home,' Louie said, 'I'll be out in a while.'

"And then when we robbed this other place he actually heated up the baby's bottle and gave it to the baby so he wouldn't cry and wake up the parents." And on and on and on. I would listen, and laugh, and feel like giving Louie a spanking. It was much easier to think of him as a naughty kid than a professional burglar, because that's the way he acted.

But he was a real professional. I knew he was crazy, but I also knew he was very good at what he did. Once, after we had been together about three months this third time, he started becoming very interested in coins. He told me he was going to become a coin collector. He didn't have to tell me he was going to collect other people's. He brought home books and studied them, and then started bringing home coins. "Look at this, Ceil," he'd be all excited, "I got a nineteen-fifty four goody thing over here and it's worth . . ." As soon as he found out how much rare coins were worth, he became an avid coin thief. That led to one of our last real fights.

Louie had become friends with a nice old coin dealer who was teaching him everything about coins. Then Louie found out this nice old man had a nice old coin collection of his own and decided to rob it.

He set the man's house up, but Billy had to actually go in and take the stuff because the old man knew Louie and might recognize him. Louie waited outside in a rented car. In the middle of the robbery the dealer came home and Billy panicked and jumped out of the window empty-handed. He hit the air conditioner on the way down and tore open a huge gash in his chin. Louie picked him up and threw him in the car.

The kid was hot, so Louie parked him in a hotel. Louie's got nothing to do with it. He's innocent, he certainly doesn't want to be connected with Billy. But Billy kept calling all night. I couldn't hear what he was saying, but Louie kept telling him, "Put a Band-Aid on it." He'd call back 20 minutes later: "Put another Band-Aid on it," Louie said. Finally Louie got up, got dressed and left. I found out later that he took the kid to a hospital to get stitched up.

When I heard the whole story I really became angry. Robbing is one thing, but taking advantage of Billy like that was something completely different. "How can you be like that, Louie?" I asked him. "How could you do that to a nice kid?"

"How come he told you about the job?" he asked mildly.

"What difference does it make, Louie, that's not the point. The point is——"

He interrupted me. "Look. The kid's a jerk, that's all. He's a jinx and he's stupid and he don't listen to me when I tell him something." As far as Louie was concerned the conversation was over.

As far as I was concerned our living together was over. I was going to leave him again. This time, I tried to tell myself, this time it really is for good. I couldn't believe he could treat the kid so badly. And I had to wonder what he would do to me or one of the children if we made a stupid mistake.

We left while he was still sleeping. I went in his wallet and took every cent he had, $700, and his car keys, and we drove to a helicopter port. We flew directly to Los Angeles International Airport, and less than an hour later we were all sitting on a jet getting ready to take off for New York.

The kids were in the seats in front of me and I was sitting next to an elderly lady doing a needlepoint of a tiger's head. We had just started talking about raising children when I heard this booming voice coming from the front of the plane. Louie was screaming at the stewardess, "Wait a minute, just wait a minute. What's your hurry, New York is gonna be there if you're five minutes late. I've got to get my wife and kids. They're on the wrong plane."

I hunched down in my seat. "That's my husband," I said. "I don't want him to find me."

Louie appeared a moment later. He came striding down the aisle wearing plaid Bermuda shorts, a white T-shirt and sandals. The little old lady next to me smiled and said, "You have a nice-looking husband."

I was hoping he wouldn't find me. "Hi, Daddy," Susan laughed.

He kissed her. Then he saw me. "C'mon Ceil, get off this plane."

I couldn't understand how he had managed to get to the airport as quickly as he did. He had no car and he was fast asleep. But here he was. "I'm not coming back, Louie. You promised me you'd go straight, but you're just doing the same things all over again."

He leaned over the little old lady. She kept working on her needlepoint. "I don't know nothin' else, Ceil. That's me, that's what I am."

"You're a crook, Louie. A crook! How can I live with you? How can I let the kids live with you?"

A few of the other passengers began listening to the conversation. The little old lady pretended absolutely nothing was going on. "Look, let's really be straight, Ceil. You like the money as much as I do, right?"

"I'm not—"

"Who you kidding? You like the clothes, the hotels, you like going to Vegas."

'I do, but that doesn't mean—"

Louie was really at his convincing best. "And you know the kids are happier than they've ever been before in their lives. What about you? You never laughed so much ever. C'mon, get off the plane."

I just looked right at him. "Can you at least think about getting a job? Just try it again."

He gave me a look of disgust. "I'm not gonna work straight Ceil, we both know that. Let's not kid ourselves around, okay? I know what I know, and I know it good."

He was right. I did like the lifestyle. I liked the nice clothes, the big apartment, the expensive furniture. I liked going to fancy restaurants and weekends in Las Vegas. I liked the kids having somebody they loved to be with and play with. And I really loved Louie.

I knew he was crazy, and I knew that the life he had to offer me was crazy. But it was California and money and I was going back to Queens and tight budgets. "I just don't know, Louie."

" 'Course you know. You know you love me and—"

The stewardess interrupted him. "I'm sorry, sir, but we're about to take off. I'll have to ask you to get off the plane now."

"Go ahead, kidnap me to New York," he told her without turning around. "I'm not going without my wife."

The little old lady continued weaving her needle in and out.

There was really only one decision for me. I gathered up my belongings and stood up. "C'mon kids, let's get off the plane."

Louie stepped back to give me room to get out. He had a very satisfied look on his face.

The little old lady lifted her head for the first time, as I stepped over her. "It was very nice meeting you," she smiled, and went back to her needlepoint.

"I guess I love you, Louie," I said.

"Yeah," he agreed.

− 4 −

Once I accepted the fact that Louie was never going legitimate, our life together became better than ever. There were no secrets between us, no hidden bad feelings, no resentments. We were together, in everything.

I didn't like Louie's work, but I accepted it. David was a mechanic, Louie robbed houses. That was their occupations. And Louie was as much a professional in his line of work as David was in his. He used to tell me how glad he was when people left their lights on while they were away, because then he could see what he was doing. He hated working with flashlights.

He knew exactly what he was doing, and he did his best to prepare for every job. He'd pick out a house and watch it for a week or two weeks, and write down the family schedule, and check it, before planning the job. Once he had a job in the Trousdale Estates and every day for two weeks he'd take Gay with him and sit across the street from the house, in a children's playground, watching the family routine through a pair of binoculars.

And after a job he'd come home and spread out the take on our bed and tell me to take my pick of whatever I wanted. I was like a millionaire at Tiffany's. "I'll take this pin, and this necklace, and this——"

"Nah, ya can't have that necklace 'cause it's too outstanding."

At one point I had a bigger jewelry collection than Hollywood stars like Polly Bergen. In fact, at one point, my jewelry collection had once been Polly Bergen's. Louie knocked her house over.

He got other things besides jewelry. When he took checks I'd sign some of them for him. Some pieces of art stayed in our apartment, and I kept a few of the less spectacular coats.

He did a little more than one house a month. When he wasn't working we'd party, go to every movie in town, go to Palm Springs for the weekend, or just lie on the beach. He'd never talk about money, but every once in a while he'd say something like, "We're down to our last four thousand. Next week I'm gonna have to go back to work."

I don't think I'd ever seen Louie quite as happy as he was during this house-robbing period. "This is what I really do best," he explained to me. "Ceil, I enjoy this so much. This is my high, this is what I really get off on."

Billy told me that Louie would actually get a white foam coming out of his mouth during the robberies. "You should see him," he told me. "It's like flying on drugs. He can go through a whole house in thirty, forty minutes, room after room, and find everything worth anything. He's a tremendous man."

Once Billy told me Louie ripped up a wall-to-wall carpeting during a robbery. "Louis," I pleaded with him. "Why can't you just go in and steal nicely? Just leave things as you found it. Why do you have to wreck the whole place?" It never occurred to me that I was just as crazy as he was, asking him to rob with good manners.

Of course he had an answer. "Ceil, you'd be surprised where people hide money. I've found more stuff in the linings of drapes, under carpeting, inside zipped-up cushions and under mattresses than you could believe."

I believed. I believed everything he told me. Even when he decided we were going to get married. I knew I was already married. I knew I wasn't divorced. I knew you weren't allowed to be married to two people at the same time. But when Louie said it was all right, I knew it was all right.

It happened about two months after he took me off the plane for the last time. We had been together, on and off, for about eight months. One morning he woke up and said, "We're going to get married today."

I laughed. "How? I'm already married. Don't I need divorce papers and things like that?"

"Don't worry about it. Just follow my lead. Talk when I tell you to."

That was easy for me to do. I was the perfect woman for Louie. I never had the slightest responsibility in my life. All I had ever done was produce babies and cook food. I never paid a single bill. I hadn't even learned to do the food shopping by myself. That was the way David had wanted it, and that was what Louie wanted. It made my life easy.

We went to a place in Vegas named The Wishing Well and filled out all the necessary papers. I wrote down my name as Cecile Hartman, and when the clerk asked, "Are you married?" Louie said, "She's not," I said "No," and there were no problems.

This wedding was much classier than my first one. I wore a beige suit, Louie bought me a bouquet and we had real organ music. The whole ceremony cost Louie about $60.

We spent that weekend at the Hacienda Hotel. Normally we stayed at the plush Sands, but because we were getting married under our own names Louie had to stay legitimate. No credit cards, no checks. That's when Louie got cheap.

I was happy, I was thrilled but I was confused. I didn't understand how come all of a sudden Louie had decided to get married. He seemed very happy just living together. That night, as we were lying in bed, I asked him, "What's with this marriage? I didn't feel we ever needed——"

He stopped me. This was one of the few times I remember

him being completely serious. "As far as I'm concerned, we don't," he said. "It's a piece of paper. If I ever wanted to get a divorce, I'd tear up the paper and that would be it. But Ceil, you know I love you and everything, but see, someday I'm gonna have to go back to prison and——"

"Not if we're careful and we do——" I had become convinced that Louie was invulnerable. It was impossible for me to imagine a totally free spirit like Louie locked behind bars. It couldn't happen. I refused to believe it.

He was more practical. "It's gonna happen eventually. I'm gonna have to do my time and when I do I want you to be able to come and see me without having no hassles. Now that you're my wife they gotta let you in!"

I just lay back and went to sleep. Louie was not going to jail. I refused to even think about it.

He was such a smooth operator it didn't seem possible he could ever get caught. He worked so hard, he planned every job carefully. He'd sit and read every local newspaper from cover to cover. He never read books or magazines, but he never missed a newspaper. "It's where I get all my important information," he told me. Who was in town, who was leaving town, who died, what families were having funerals, who won or inherited money, who owned valuable jewelry, where the rich people lived, when the big parties were being held. He was a true professional, and it paid off. Our standard of living kept getting better and better.

We moved out of the apartment into a town house. We, actually Louie, furnished the place quickly. We walked into a store and Louie stood in the middle of the showroom and pointed out the things he wanted. "Gimme that, gimme this one, and that one . . ." Then he paid for everything, in cash, on the spot. He was a saleman's dream come true, but it was his way of insuring that we would get good service. We always got good service.

The kids were too young to know exactly what he was doing. They knew he was rich and when the older ones asked, "What does Daddy do for a job?" I'd tell them he owned a record company. I'd tell the neighbors the same thing. I was becoming just as good a liar as he was. "The company's in New York," I'd tell them. Once I got the hang of lying, and with his prompting, it was easy.

We had really just gotten settled into the town house when Mark Moffett arrived in Los Angeles. Mark and Louie had done time together and become very close friends. They had a lot in common; both were very bright, both were very crazy. After getting out of prison Mark had established himself in Brooklyn, but he got involved in a felony and had to run. He was a fugitive like Louie.

They loved each other but they always had to be proving themselves. They were the most competitive two men I've ever seen. They would bet big sums on almost anything. They played children's games, adult games, mind games, guessing games, fun games, stupid games, they were always playing, always for fun, but always for real too.

Louie took me to meet Mark for the first time at a topless bar named The Pink Pussy Cat. Mark was a little smaller than Louie, a little darker and maybe a little better-looking, but I was a lot more interested in the place than I was in him. I had never been to a topless bar before and it really turned me on. They had this one big fat girl dancing there, she must have weighed 250 pounds, and she had flags attached to both of her huge breasts. Somehow she managed to twirl them in opposite directions. I was hypnotized. That was one of the funniest acts I'd ever seen in my life.

Louie and Mark didn't pay too much attention to the acts, they were discussing business. Mark had made some connections in California and he was going into the marijuana supply business. He wanted Louie to work with him.

It couldn't have been an easy decision for Louie to make. He was doing good at houses, and he hated drugs as much as he loved money. Louie was always straight: He didn't smoke, he didn't drink and he never, never used drugs. He didn't discuss his decision with me, but I guess he finally decided running pot was safer than robbing houses, and he agreed to go into business with Mark. I really didn't pay too much attention to their first conversation, I was too busy watching this fat girl twirl her breasts. *That* was talent!

From that first night on Mark Moffett and his girl friend Mikey became our best friends. Either they were always over our house, or we went to their house, a beautiful place Mark had won in a poker game. Louie and Mark started doing a few small things together, but mostly they were just getting organized. I found myself spending a lot of time with Mikey.

When I first met her I didn't like her very much. Louie and I went to their house for dinner one night, and she had this I-don't-care attitude and seemed very uppity. She was also just as crazy as Mark. There were two real swords hanging over the fireplace and she took them down and made Mark duel with her. Right in the living room! She climbed up on the couch, ran behind a chair, she just kept running and laughing hysterically. This broad is crazy, I thought to myself, and Mark is crazier than she is to duel with her.

I didn't even realize she was stoned. She was always stoned on pot. Since Mark had been running marijuana she had an endless supply, and took advantage of it. She was the most in-credible pothead.

But once I got to know her, I really liked her. We got along well and she became my first girl friend in years. We talked about Mark and Louie and sex and children and television shows and, finally, about drugs. It was Mikey who got me stoned for the first time in my life.

It happened at the Manhattan Beach Hotel in New York City. Even though Mark and Louie were working in California, Mark still had good connections in New York. About three weeks after that night in The Pink Pussy Cat, he was offered a setup, an already planned and prepared jewelry robbery, in New York. He convinced Louie that the four of us should go together and make it working vacation.

So when Mark and Louie were working in the street, Mikey and I had to stay in the hotel. The first afternoon we were there we were talking about her relationship with Mark. It wasn't good. She said he would lock her in her room for days. "If I didn't have my pot," she said, "I don't know what I'd do." As we sat there she rolled a perfect marijuana cigarette, a joint, with her hands.

I'd smoked once before in my life. When I was 15 a group of eight of us had shared one joint. We all puffed on it and none of us got high. We thought, this stuff isn't any good, and went back to our beer.

Mikey never actually asked me if I wanted to share her joint. She just took a good drag and passed it to me. Not wanting to seem ignorant, or prudish, I took it and inhaled. "Hold it in," she told me. I did, and I started to get high on drugs for the first time in my life.

It was really wonderful. I just felt completely relaxed. I laid back on the bed and closed my eyes and entered a brand new world. It was warm and comfortable and easy. Mikey and I talked about all different things, but somehow none of the things we mentioned seemed very important.

We stayed in New York four days. Every day Louie and Mark would go out and Mikey and I would turn on. They pulled the job the fourth day and came back early. When Louie found me stoned he could hardly talk. He just looked at me with an incredibly angry glare and stalked out of the room.

Mark had an easier way of handling Mikey. He just slapped her.

The job had been successful and we flew home to California. But from that point on things started changing for me. I had discovered the wonderful world of marijuana.

The summer of 1967 started out wonderfully well. I was very happy, Louie seemed very happy and the kids were very happy. Louie was a wonderful husband, but an even better father. Sometimes he'd come home from wherever he'd been in the middle of the afternoon and decide, "It's too hot for the kids to be in school today." Then he'd go and get them out and take them to Disneyland or for ice cream or to a park to play. Or I'd be upstairs and I'd think everybody was downstairs and the phone would ring and one of the kids would be calling. "Guess where we are, Ma?" As long as they were with Louie I could never guess. He was capable of doing anything with them.

Susan was still too young to go along with them, but Louie made up for that. As far as he was concerned, she was his baby. He diapered her, toilet-trained her, took her off the bottle, did everything for her. The two of them would sit on the floor for hours and play baby games.

Louie still had Billy hanging around to run errands, and he was spending a lot of time with Mark, but the kids were really his best friends. "I just was lonely when I was a kid," he told me. "I never had a real childhood."

The kids were also beginning to pick up some of Louie's habits. For example, Louie also had a telephone company credit card number—not *his* number—and he'd make long distance calls all the time. I remember I once saw him leaning up against a phone booth with a pad and pencil in his hand, listening. "Let's go, Louie," I asked.

"In a minute, Ceil, soon as I get this number."

The kids were starting to do the same thing. They'd pick up the phone and invent a number, or they'd listen to Louie and use the same number he was using. They were also beginning to understand that Louie didn't really own a record company. Very often we would have to use different last names to match whatever credit card Louie had, and they had been taught not to ask or answer any questions unless Louie gave them a lead. They were better at playing his make-up games than I was. That came in handy the first time Louie was arrested.

We had been married about three months and Louie decided we needed another color television set. We had two, but Louie decided we needed three. It made no sense, but not a lot of what Louie did made sense. So we packed the kids into the car and went shopping. The moment we pulled into the department store parking lot police cars came at us from every side. It was just like in the movies, first nothing, then sirens and cars and doors flying open. In one split second Louie had his hand in his pocket and slipped me about five credit cards and $1100 in cash. "Get rid of these," he said quickly. The kids just sat quietly.

I was wearing a green dress that had two round pockets in front, and I had no choice but to put everything in the right-hand pocket.

The cops were all over the place. They kept their hands on their holstered guns. "Get out," one of them ordered.

Louie raised one hand. "Take it easy, take it easy," he told them, "these are my kids." He climbed out and they began frisking him.

A tall, blond policeman walked over to the car and leaned in. "That your father?" he asked Philip pleasantly.

"Yep," Philip answered proudly.

"What's you father's name?" he asked with a broad smile.

Philip smiled right back. "Well, you better ask my father."

They really didn't have to, they knew who he was. Louie was arrested for passing bad checks and using stolen credit cards. They didn't have anything on me, but they arrested me for consorting with a known criminal. Louie.

I was too dazed to feel anything. One second I was thinking color television, the next police were running all over and Louie was thrusting his bad cards at me. I had never been arrested before. I had never broken any laws before. I kept saying over and over, "There's been a mistake. I'm a mother. These are my children."

Once the initial shock wore away panic set in. I was sitting in a police car, on my way to jail, with a pocket stuffed with stolen credit cards, stolen airline tickets and $1100 in cash. "They're watching me," I kept saying to myself, "What am I going to do with these cards?" I knew it was only a matter of time before they found them and arrested me for possession of stolen merchandise. But I had no way of getting rid of them. I was trapped. Those damn police, those damn police, I kept thinking. It never occurred to me to blame Louie. It was the cops' fault for catching us, not Louie's fault for planting them on me.

I walked right in and out of jail with my pockets full. When the matron patted me down she completely missed everything in the pocket. It wasn't possible, but it happened. I didn't say a word.

Mark came down and bailed us out in two hours. On the way home Louie told us what to do. "In a few hours my fingerprints are going to bounce back from New York and the cops are gonna be swarming all over the house. Ceil, I want you to go back to the house and when they come in, just tell them I packed a bag and left you."

"What are you going to do?" I didn't cry. I just wanted to be told what to do. I didn't want to have to make any decisions myself.

"We're moving. Billy'll come by to get you tomorrow."

"Where are we moving to, Louie?"

He shrugged his shoulders. "I don't know yet," he said seriously. Then he smiled. "But Mark and Mikey'll come with us, we'll bring Billy and with the kids, we'll make a vacation out of it."

− 5 −

The police came in from the front and back. I had slept on the couch, because I didn't want them in the house without my knowing it, and they woke me as they came in. "Where is he?" one of them asked abruptly.

I was more asleep than awake. "Who?"

"Mileto."

"He's gone," I smiled. "He packed and left last night."

This cop kept asking me questions while five others searched the whole place. I had been so upset the night before I hadn't bothered to put the cash away. The cop picked it up. "What'd ya do, turn a trick?"

"What?"

"You know what I mean, you're a hooker. Where else would you get so much money?"

"I don't know what you mean." I honestly didn't know what the word meant. I sat there as they went through the house until they had satisfied themselves Louie was gone. They took the cash, as "evidence," and left. I sat there, almost motionless, waiting for something to happen, for the phone to ring, for Billy to show up, for somebody to tell me what to do.

Billy D'Angelo showed up just after the police left. He must have been watching them search the house. He packed the six of us into his car and, very carefully, making sure the police weren't trailing him, he drove us up to Big Bear, a California resort area. Then Billy went back and packed all our belongings into a van and parked the van in his own garage.

Louie had rented a nice bungalow in Big Bear for $50 a day. He was waiting for us, along with our family addition, a big German shepherd. "It's important for a married man to have a dog," he explained seriously. "That way you don't beat your wife. You take out all your anxieties on the dog." Of course, he never touched the dog. Louie was totally nonviolent. At least he was then.

Just like he promised, he turned Big Bear into a vacation. There was our family, Mark and Mikey, Billy, one of my cousins from New York came to stay with us, and Mark's dog, also a shepherd. I'd get up early every morning and take the kids to the beach. We'd all be back by lunchtime and Louie would be just getting up. Most of the time he went off for the afternoon with Mark—the pot operation was getting going now—but he'd usually be back by dusk. We'd all take long walks into the sunset. It was quiet and beautiful. Louie would just talk softly about being free. I don't know anyone who ever appreciated freedom more than he did.

At night we had the most fun. The kids would be asleep and Mark and Louie would start playing their games. They would sit in the middle of the floor and play pick-up sticks for $1000 a game. And they would scream and fight, "You moved the blue one!" "No, I didn't!" "I'll bet you another hundred you moved it." "That's a bet."

They spent a lot of time playing Frustration. That's a game with two parallel steel rods and a steel ball. The object was to get the steel ball to roll up the two rods. The higher the ball rolled, the more points scored. They would play for ownership of the car! They would play for $100 a point! I'd come to realize that Louie was an unusual person, but Mark was completely crazy. Once Louie and I gave Mark and Mikey an "M" branding iron as a joke present. Mark put the iron in his fireplace and branded every piece of furniture in the place, and the only reason he didn't brand Mikey was because he couldn't catch her. She locked herself in the bathroom! So he ended up branding the bathroom door.

But Mark's real insanity was long hair. Because he'd spent so much time in prison, without women, he just went crazy over long hair. If I was wearing a long fall and he was gambling with Louie, he'd talk Louie into playing for the hair. And if he won I had to take it off and give it to Mikey. He didn't care what a woman looked like, as long as she had long hair. Once, I remember, Mark, Louie and I were sitting in the Orchid Room at the Manhattan Beach Hotel. Mark had locked Mikey in her room for the night. There was this girl sitting there that Mark knew, but this night she was wearing a long fall. This girl was a beast. Louie and I were nudging each other, and laughing. She was a dog! But Mark gave her $500, he just peeled off the bills, to spend the rest of the night with him. Just because of the long hair.

The money had no meaning. Louie played Nancy in Frustration. When she won he handed her the stakes, $800, for keeps. Between Mark and Louie they were making enough to pay all the bills, buy whatever we saw, go wherever we wanted and have enough left over to use as play money. We went water skiing, we had maids come in every day to clean up, we went horseback riding, to beautiful restaurants, we bought more new clothes than we could wear. I began to think we would live this way forever.

We stayed in the woods three weeks and, although I didn't fully realize it then, some very serious things started happening. Whenever Louie and Mark left, Mikey would pull out her pot—we had Maxwell House two-pound cans filled with cleaned grass—and we would just get wrecked. We got blasted out of our minds every single day. The more we did, the more we en-joyed it.

Then Louie sent me to New York for the first time. "Just go," he told me, "and visit your mother. There'll be a guy meet you at the airport. Give him your luggage tickets." I didn't think anything of it. I flew into Kennedy Airport and this big, smiling baldheaded guy met me and took the luggage tickets. I didn't understand it, but if Louie said it was all right, then I knew it was all right.

It wasn't.

After I had made about four of these trips into New York, Billy finally told me what was going on. I was transporting suit-cases packed with marijuana. Hundreds of pounds. I couldn't believe Louie would use me like that. "Yeah, you're bringing pot in," he admitted, "but it's no big deal. You're covered from one coast to another, from bail bondsman to lawyer."

"But why me, Louie. I'm your wife. How can you use me?"

He was always honest. "Because you're completely legitimate. You got no record, they can't hold you for anything, and you're smart." Louie made sure my one arrest had been wiped clean. He even made me go to court to get the $1100 back.

I didn't like it one bit. "Louie, I don't want to do it anymore. I don't want to go to jail, and that's what's going to happen."

He didn't say anything for a little while. Then he made a motion with his hand sweeping the whole room. "You like this place?"

"Of course."

"You like the way we live? The clothes? The dinners? The jewelry?"

He knew I did. I loved it.

"Where do you think the money comes from? It don't grow on trees. It comes from the marijuana. I wouldn't let you do any-thing that I didn't think was safe. Now, you gotta decide what you want. You don't wanna go no more, that's okay. But just remember that when there isn't so much money floating around here."

He was right. I really liked the way we were living. I liked having more money than I could spend. I liked being able to go into a store knowing I could afford absolutely anything I wanted. And he told me I was safe and I had confidence in him. He was the professional, not me. "Okay, Louie, you're right," I told him. I kept making the trips. Our marriage really was a partnership.

Louie was so different than David. When I was married to David I never knew what was wrong and what was right. Not with Louie. Louie had specific rules for me. The kitchen was my place. Louie couldn't boil water. The only time he ever cooked in his life was in prison when he cooked the steaks he would steal between bars of the radiator. Louie wouldn't put sugar in his coffee. He wouldn't butter his toast. He wouldn't salt and pepper his egg. Nothing. When he sat down at the table he expected to be able to pick up his knife and fork and eat. His meat had to be cut for him, his potato buttered. Everything. That's the way his mother treated his father, and that's the way he expected to be treated.

I loved it. I knew where I was at with him. This was the first time in my life I'd ever had any real direction. I knew my place and I didn't step out of it. If we went out with friends of his I didn't talk too much because he told me right out to shut up. That never bothered me, because I was too busy laughing at his conversations.

When Paige and Nancy got a little older, they cut his meat.

When Philip got a little older, he expected his meat to be cut.

All Louie did we take the garbage out. That was the man's job.

We were on an up escalator.

When Louie felt things had cooled off enough he decided to find another place to live. He rented this beautiful 11-room house up in the hills in Ventura. We all loved the house, but Louie was particularly proud of it. It was his status symbol. "We're living right up on the mountaintop with the straights," he would laugh. It was true. One neighbor was a successful television producer, another was one of the heads of the state welfare department and another owned a really swank restaurant in Beverly Hills. "These are the people I used to rob," he liked to joke, "now I gotta worry about somebody robbing me. I guess that's the price of success!"

The pot business caused Louie to do a little more traveling than I liked, and sometimes he was gone for days at a time, but our marriage was strong. All the things I never had in my first marriage I had with this one. There was almost no jealousy whatsoever. If anything, I was the one who was jealous. I was afraid he was running around. Finally we reached an understanding that he could see other women as long as he didn't do it in front of me, and as long as it didn't take anything from our relationship or his relationship with the children. I was allowed to do the same thing, of course, but he knew I didn't want to. I was just too happy. I didn't believe he'd see anyone else, either.

Besides, when he wasn't there I had my pot. I was really getting into it every day now, even without Mikey. I'd wake up in the morning and pop a joint into my mouth. This is just something I enjoy, I told myself, I'm not at all addicted.

What I really wasn't was bright. I'd been taking pills since I was 18 years old. They made me feel better. Neither David nor Louie knew about them. That was my secret. I never realized I was addicted to them either, I just thought I was keeping my weight at a certain level. But one day Mikey saw me pop three of them and said, "Hey, you're a pill head! Why didn't you tell me?" I didn't tell her because I didn't know what she was talking about. I wasn't any kind of head, I just took some pills because they kept my weight down and I happened to like the way they made me feel.

Besides, once I really got into grass I forgot all about my pills. I was even learning how to roll my own. They were pretty fat in the middle and the ends didn't exactly taper off so much as just end, but they smoked pretty well. Eventually we started using a water pipe when we were at home, so rolling was never a problem.

Louie hated it. Whenever I'd smoke I'd spray the house with an air freshener, but he would still manage to catch me from time to time. He'd start screaming and yelling, "Don't try to be slick, 'cause you're not. Don't try to be cool, 'cause you're not!"

He liked me exactly the way I was, and hated anything that changed me. I thought he was just being the same old straight, prudish Louie.

The kids started seeing me stoned too, but that didn't bother me. I figured, as long as I can do all the things I'm supposed to, then I'm still a good mother. And I was doing everything I was supposed to. Occasionally, when Mikey and I were getting stoned in the afternoon, the kids would come home from school and we'd give them a few drags. I didn't see anything harmful in that. I didn't feel I was addicting them to anything. I never forced them to do it. My children have always been free-thinking anyway, and I knew if they wanted to try grass they would do it. I figured, if I let them do it, at least I can maintain some control over other things they might want to try.

It all seemed so right, so simple, so well thought-out. And somewhere it all went so dreadfully wrong.

It just didn't seem possible. It was such a special time. A time for laughing and good living. Everything was so calm, so smooth. There was so much love in our home, and so much money. We even hired a maid, a nice black girl. Louie loved that. He hated "the coloreds." I never knew why, but he despised them, so he loved the idea of having one hanging around the house waiting on him. Mark didn't think it was such a good idea. "How can you have a nigger working in the house?" he asked Louie. "You know she's only gonna rob you."

Even though Louie was often gone for four and five days, he managed enough time for all six of us. Each of us was someone special to him. Paige was 11, Nancy was 10 and Philip was 7. Each had personalities of their own and he catered to them. Gay was only 5, and Susan just 3, so they were still the babies. There was no jealousy, only affection, fun and love. He kept me on a pedestal, a nice change from my first marriage when I was kept behind the eight ball. He treated me like a queen. And he kept telling me that our relationship was the best, most wonderful thing that had ever happened to him. My feelings were the same. I knew exactly what he was, but I never stopped loving him.

He kept all of us laughing. Once, just the two of us drove down to Mexico for a short vacation. As usual, Louie never paid a bill, we just beat motel after motel. But he made the unusual mistake of beating a Holiday Inn in one town and booking us into another one a few nights later. As soon as we checked in the manager called the room and said, "Mr. Greco," or whatever name we were using, "you'll have to come down and take care of your bill right now. It seems you left an outstanding bill at another Inn."

Louie didn't even hesitate to think up his lie. It just was right there, right on the tip of his tongue. "Oh. Well, you see, I'm a private investigator and I'm on a divorce case. The woman I'm with is my client and we're traveling under a fictitious name. What I normally do with that place is have them bill my office when I'm back in San Francisco. So you can see there's been some mistake. I'll be glad to come right down and settle this bill, of course."

Of course. We grabbed the linens and blankets and got in the car and took off.

He was such a good liar. He always told me, "Think up the most outlandish lies you can, and then stick to them. People believe ridiculous things."

"But Louie," I laughed, "would you at least tell me what lie you're using so that I can know."

"You have a good imagination. Just follow me."

"I can't Louie, I'm not used to lying like that."

He'd wave his hand at me. "Anybody can lie. All you need is a brain and a smile." And then he'd smile.

Like everything else, the pot business was booming. Mark and Louie were importers. They bought the uncleaned grass from a Mexico connection and sold it still in the cartons. Most of their transactions took place in restaurant parking lots. I never realized the size of their business until Louie let me ride along one Saturday afternoon. The Mexican connection showed up driving a truck with an enclosed wooden back about 14 feet long. "Is the pot in the back?" I asked Louie.

He showed me. The entire rear of the truck, back to front,

side to side, was stuffed with uncleaned grass. I couldn't estimate how many pounds. I stood there with my mouth open as
Louie reached in his pocket and pulled out a thick wad of bills.
He always kept his money very meticulously, all the ones together face up, then the fives face up, the tens, twenties, fifties
and hundreds. All together and all face up. He counted out
$17,000 in cash and handed it over. That was a lot of money.
Later, when he got into the heavy business, that would be everyday walking-around money.

The more business Louie transacted, the more pot I smoked.
After four months all the kids, except Susan who was only just
four, were smoking. Mikey and I would put some crème de
menthe in the water pipe and let the kids get high with us. I
figured, they were home, they were safe. We even thought it
was cute when six-year-old Gay asked, "Mommy, can I have a
toke on the water pipe before I go take my nap?"

There was so much grass around it would have been impossible to keep it away from the kids anyway. I had coffee cans
filled with really good, cleaned grass. Once, in fact, I had too
much.

I was never paranoid about the police. I had confidence that
Louie could always protect me. But one day he and Mark
climbed into his car, Philip followed on his mini-trail bike and
went up into the woods to shoot a custom-made machine gun
Mark owned. The police showed up because they were on private property and Louie whispered to Philip, "Get on your bike
and go home and tell Mommy to clean house."

Philip came running into the house like he was being chased
by the cavalry. "Mommy! Mommy!" he was screaming, "Daddy
said clean house." I knew that meant I was to hide everything.
I took all Louie's guns, cash, credit cards, checks and airline
tickets, put them in a suitcase and hid the suitcase in a neighbor's backyard where I could watch it from the kitchen window.
That left a coffee-tin and a half of grass that even Louie didn't
know about. "What are we gonna do with it?" I asked Mikey.
"We can't smoke it."

She had a wonderful idea. "Let's bake brownies!" So while we were expecting the police to show up any minute, we got stoned and poured all this grass into two big pots of cake mix and spent the afternoon baking Alice B. Toklas brownies.

The police never showed up, somehow Mark and Louie talked their way out of trouble. Mikey and I had five tins of stone-brownies, and absolutely no idea what to do with them. We shared one tin with the kids. Mikey took two home. One I put in my refrigerator to be eaten over the next few days, and the last one I wrapped up tightly and put in a cabinet above the refrigerator. I promptly forgot all about it.

Three days later Louie told me to pack because we had to make another trip to New York. That was nothing unusual, we were going back and forth about once every six weeks. Billy D'Angelo and his girl friend arrived to stay with the kids. Now, neither Billy D'Angelo nor his girl friend were heads, but they were hungry. They searched the whole house for food. The kids had cleaned out the refrigerator. There was nothing in the breadbox. Nothing in the freezer. And nothing in a can closet.

Then they discovered the fifth tin of chocolate brownies. Three days later they came down. "They were good," Joey said, "but they tasted funny."

Even old straight Louie had to laugh when he heard the story.

We were settled down enough even to invite relatives out to stay with us. Louie would call my aunt in New Haven and order her to "pack your bags and get out here. Your tickets are waiting." He'd call friends, cousins, cousins of friends. He wasn't paying for the tickets, he didn't care who used them. Everybody loved him, but I don't really think they trusted him. My mother was typical. She was the straightest woman in the world. If my stepfather had dared to bring something into the house that he hadn't paid for, she might have even called the police on him! She was that honest. And she was a wonderful lady. "I really like Louie," she would tell me, "but I just have the feeling he's doing something wrong. I don't know what he's putting in my basement. Probably something stolen and I'll get arrested."

"Don't worry about it," he'd say reassuringly. "If you get arrested I'll get you the best lawyer around. And if they send you up the river, we'll come and visit you and bring big cakes. 'Cause nothin's too good for my mother-in-law!"

My mother took him seriously. "What river? What's he talking about, sending who up the river? Oh my God, oh my God, I know I'm gonna get arrested." But she couldn't help liking him.

Everybody liked him, he was so very easy to enjoy. He was always polite, well-dressed, personable and as he got a little older and picked up some weight, he had gotten better-looking. He hated violence and never hurt anyone. That was Louie, in-and-out Louie, easy-to-like Louie, the good bad-guy, the man I loved.

I really believed our life together would never end. Days of getting stoned, nights of partying. He loved the nightclubs, the big spenders, the celebrities. He lived his life quickly, knowing he didn't have enough time to do everything he wanted to do. I lived slower because I had seen my wildest dreams come true, and I just wanted to enjoy every single minute of this life. There isn't any reason this should end, I thought, no reason at all. This is going to go on forever.

And I really believed that, too.

– 6 –

Mark called from New York to tell us about our next adventure. "I got something good for the two of you," he said. That meant he had some sort of setup that both Louie and I had to work on. "What I want you to do is go to my house and get fifteen hundred cash from Mikey. Then go out and buy complete new wardrobes, from luggage up, just like you was newlyweds. Ceil, I want you to get yourself some good falls, too. Make sure the hair is different colors and different lengths."

"What's the job?" I asked him.

He laughed. "We're gonna have breakfast at Tiffany's."

It wasn't exactly that, but the job was a big jewelry heist scheduled to take place in Philadelphia. Louie was supposed to be a young, rich, fast-rising business executive and I was supposed to be his sexy fiancée. Our cover story was that we just got engaged and wanted a beautiful diamond ring. Mark told us not to bother with any diamonds less than five carats. Nothing under five carats, no matter how pretty. We were given sets of business cards, identification and $15,000 cash. I have no idea who set the job up or sponsored it or even how much Louie was paid, but I feel it was probably an organized crime family. It was just too well set up.

We started shopping Monday afternoon. We went from jewelry store to jewelry store, picking up beautiful diamonds and leaving deposits of $200, $500, whatever they asked for. We didn't dicker about price. We made arrangements to have each stone picked up the following Saturday afternoon.

The job was really fun. First of all, what woman wouldn't want to spend a week picking out beautiful diamonds? And being with Louie made it that much more fun. He would tell the store owners the most ridiculous lies; make up college names, degrees, businesses, friends' names, where his money came from and even what his family did and no one in almost 50 stores challenged him once. They'd all just smile and nod their heads. "Assinine University? Of course I've heard of it. Great place to go to school."

"Yeah, I was on the football team," Louie would explain. "Broke my carburetor."

"That's lovely," the jewelers would agree as we put deposit after deposit down. It was amazing. We went to almost 50 stores and each one had "the perfect diamond" for me. We bought every one of them. Some we even had inscribed with whatever initials we were using.

After the stores closed for the night we'd quick drive to New York and party for a few hours. It was one of these nights that I met Danny Orini. Danny Orini was a local hustler who was supplying all the checks for the operation. He had a machine that printed certified bank checks, and he was printing them up in a basement somewhere. But one night he got drunk and he started complaining about Mark to me. "Who does that guy think he is?" he said in a nasty voice.

I told him straight out. "Mark thinks he's the boss and he *is* the boss. And I wouldn't mess with him."

He challenged me. "Whattya mean, 'I wouldn't mess with him'?"

I didn't want to argue with him. "Well, I don't know too much," I said, "but Mark will hurt you. He's really tough. I'd behave if I were you."

He laughed quietly in a sort of smug way. "Listen, I got a few things to tell him, you know. He may think I'm a flunky, but I ain't. I'm a killer." He paused and waited for my reaction. I didn't know whether he was a killer or not, Louie's friends were always bragging about one thing or another. So I just stared at him. I didn't react at all. "Whattya think about that?" he asked.

I shrugged my shoulders. I'd met people who said things like that before. I just stayed clear.

Danny couldn't take my shrug for an answer. He moved closer to me and whipered, "A few months ago I hijacked this truck and I killed the guard."

"I have to go get high," I explained, excusing myself to go into the ladies' room and puff on a joint. I didn't really believe he was a killer, but I knew that his shooting his mouth off could put everyone involved in the jewelry job in danger, I knew that much. So that night, on the drive back to Philadelphia, I told the whole story. "He's really got a big mouth," I said. Mark didn't say a word.

"The kid's no killer" was all Louie said.

We spent the next day being engaged eight different times, and buying a ring to mark each engagement. Louie would write the size, price, amount of deposit and description of the stone on the back of the jewelry shop's card. The stack of cards was getting thick.

We stayed overnight in New York Thursday and Louie disappeared for a few hours Friday morning. When he came back to our suite in the Americana he looked like all his blood had drained out. He was absolutely white. "Louie, what's the matter? Are you all right?"

He sat down in a thick chair. "Ceil, I never seen anything like I just saw. Mark and Georgie . . ." he started to say, but he didn't finish. He ran into the bathroom and started throwing up. I didn't know what to do. I had no idea what he was talking about, but I knew it couldn't be good. Georgie Farber was a fence, a jewelry dealer who handled stolen goods, and he really prided himself on being tough. He was the man who'd met me at the airport when I was bringing the cases of marijuana in.

Little by little the story came out. Mark and Georgie had decided that Danny had to be taught to shut up. They grabbed him and took him to a warehouse in Brooklyn. They chained his leg to a pipe and began working him over. "I never seen anything like this. They *beat* this guy, they beat him with their pistols. I heard his arm snap. His nose was just squashed all over his face, and he was just bleeding all over and screaming . . ."

I looked at Louie with real disbelief. I was responsible for that beating. Louie knew that. "How could you let them do that, Louie?" I asked in a rising voice. "He's got a pregnant wife and you let them beat him like that? Are you some kind of animal? I mean—I just—I don't understand what you were doing." I was screaming at him.

He didn't even look at me. "I watched it for a little while, then I had to walk away. I just couldn't watch it anymore." He shook his head from side to side. "I just couldn't watch it anymore."

"Where is he now?" I asked him.

"I walked out. I guess he's still chained to the pipe. They can't let him go, he's still gotta do some more checks."

I didn't like Danny, but I hated what they did to him. Business, I was beginning to understand, is always business. Personal feelings just don't matter. Except for Louie, I thought to myself, except for Louie. He was different, he was the exception. I had to believe that.

Louie managed to put Danny out of his mind and we were back in Philadelphia, buying rings, having them engraved, working the stores, by three o'clock that afternoon. But the fun was completely gone. Now it was just a day's work.

On Saturday morning the collection began. Both Louie and Mark got on the phones and started calling every jewelry store. "This is Mr. whatever-name," they both said. "My messenger will be by shortly with a certified bank check for the full amount of the ring. Please give it to him."

The deliveries to our hotel room started about two hours later.

We used every messenger service in Philadelphia. The pile of diamonds on the bed got bigger and bigger, the value kept increasing. I had no idea how much the whole haul was, but there were approximately fifty pear-shaped rings above five carats. As the deliveries were being made, Louie and Mark and Georgie wiped the entire suite for fingerprints, from the floorboards to as high as Louie could reach on the wall. They covered every square foot of the apartment, and then they went back and wiped it a second time.

Then we checked out, charging our bill to Mr. Tompkins's stolen credit card.

The diamonds went directly to another fence in the jewelry district of Manhattan. He disposed of the settings and sold the diamonds. We all flew back to California to celebrate. We bought the Philadelphia papers for two weeks after that, but there was never a word about the robberies printed.

Louie never told me what we were paid for our week's work, but he decided to invest part of it. "Silver bars," he said like he really knew what he was talking about. "That's the thing to get into." So he went out and bought $8000 worth of silver bars. "There's gonna be a big inflation in silver and those bars are just gonna get more and more valuable."

What they did mostly was take up space and collect dust. Louie's safe deposit box was his shoe, he just didn't believe in giving his money to a bank. "Banks are where you get money, not where you put it!" he said. So he wrapped these silver bars in his underwear and put them in his dresser drawer.

Then the four of us went to Palm Springs to relax and really have a good time. It was pleasure as usual for us. Mikey and I brought enough grass to keep us high, Louie and Mark brought their games, and Louie brought the credit cards and checks. It started out as a very normal trip.

Louie never really believed in luck. "There's no such thing as luck," he used to tell me. "It's what you do to take advantage of a situation. It's how you get ready." I felt differently. I knew we had been very lucky. We'd been traveling cross-country, renting cars, flying, staying at good hotels, eating at fine restaurants for almost two years, all of it on bad checks and credit cards. Louie had been doing houses, transporting drugs, passing bad checks and credit cards from coast to coast and he had had almost no trouble. We were lucky. I didn't realize it in Palm Springs, but our luck was starting to change. The good days were about to end.

We had been in the hotel four days when Mark noticed the manager getting very interested in the car we were driving. There was a phony sticker on it, or it had bad license plates, I don't remember, but both Louie and Mark decided to pack and leave immediately. But they were packing their own special way, which involved stealing everything that wasn't nailed down. They were just getting ready to unscrew the paintings on the wall when two police cars pulled up. Mark didn't even stop to put a jacket on. "C'mon Louie, let's get outta here." They took off through the back door.

I didn't know what to do. I'd always had Louie to tell me how to act, what to say, when to scream bloody murder. But he had taken off like a shot, he was gone. Mikey took charge. "Okay," she explained to me, "we're gonna have to make believe like we're hookers."

I'd learned what the word meant. "I don't know, Mikey. I——"

"I know. Just don't say anything. I'll do the talking."

She did. The cops started asking us what we did for our living.

"We're here with Harvey Bristol. We're friends of his," she said calmly. Harvey Bristol was a code name the four of us used when we wanted to make contact with either Mark or Louie, like having them paged at the airport. We picked that name because Mark always drank Harvey's Bristol Cream.

I agreed with Mikey. "Yes, officer, we came here with Mr. Bristol." Inside we were laughing hysterically. Outside we were trying to play it straight.

The cops knew the game. "Where'd you meet this Bristol?"

"Oh. Well, he and his friend picked us up on the corner the other night and we're gonna make a few dollars," Mikey told him.

I shifted my hip hard to the side, trying to look hookerish.

The cop had his pad out and was writing all this down. He asked us where Harvey Bristol was and we told him we didn't know. "He and his friend walked out a little while ago. They said they were going for a quart of milk," Mikey added.

The cop smiled. "How come you ladies aren't registered in the hotel under Bristol's name?"

We returned his smile. I was starting to enjoy this. Louie was right, once you really got into it, lying was a lot of fun. "Oh, I don't know," Mikey said in a deep voice, "do you suppose they're married?"

I spoke up. "We just met them in Los Angeles and came down to party, that's all. We're just two nice girls trying to have a good time. Did those guys do something wrong?"

He avoided the question. We never did find out how they got on to us. "Well, ladies, I'm afraid the management would like you to leave."

"We didn't mean to hurt anybody," Mikey told him.

"I know," he agreed. "Hearts of gold."

That was it. The police made us pay the entire hotel bill in cash, and, indignantly, Mikey and I checked out. "Remind me never to come back to this hole," she said in a loud voice as we walked through the crowded lobby for the last time.

"Okay," I reminded her, "don't come back to this dump."

The whole scene was a joke. We didn't worry about it, we laughed. It had no meaning. It was just a touch of bad luck. But it was the first bad luck we'd had after a long string of very good luck. And it marked the change.

Our luck stayed bad. The little things that had always gone right started going wrong. My kids accidentally set Billy D'Angelo's garage on fire. A truckload of grass arrived with a short count. Louie tried to buy a bicycle for one of the girls with a bad credit card and was stopped. He had to make a desperate dash out of the department store, knocking over some women in the process, in order to get away. Mark was playing with his gun one afternoon and it accidentally went off, hitting a friend of ours in the foot.

Our life had been like a big pendulum, swinging only up and

up and up. Now, slowly, it was starting to swing in the opposite direction. The pot supply was scarce and there wasn't enough money coming in, so Mark called New York and a house job was set up for him and Louie in New Jersey. Mikey, who was a terrific makeup artist, did disguises for them from chin to hair. She colored their lips, dyed their hair and gave them glasses. They grew their own beards for the job. Louie filled the car with gas, washed it, did the grocery shopping, got the clothes out of the dry cleaners and gave me $500 in cash for emergencies. It was his usual way of making sure I'd be all right while he was gone.

The job started out easily. Mark and Louie got into the house with phony identification, handcuffed the wife and maid together in the middle of the floor and started going through the place. Everything was right, just as planned. But then Mark heard another voice from upstairs. For some reason one of the kids had stayed home from school and was on the telephone. Mark picked up the extension just in time to hear her pleading with the police for help. They ran out of the house empty-handed.

They were saved by their disguises. They ditched the rental car, stopped at a bargain store and bought new clothes and went into a men's room and changed and shaved. Then they beat it back to California. The job was a total loss.

Louie never changed. From his attitude you couldn't tell if he was on top of the world or in the sewer. He was still Laughing Louie. As long as he had his freedom, he could survive anything.

As long as I had my pills and my pot (which were becoming my freedom), I could survive too. I was so wrecked most of the time I didn't even realize things weren't going well. I wasn't interested in eating, or drinking, just getting high. I had gotten thin to the point where I had absolutely no breasts. Louie didn't care. He used to tease me, "Are you lying on your front or your back? I'm going to have to buy you an undershirt!"

Our relationship hadn't suffered. As long as I kept a clean house, made sure the kids were okay and cooked dinner, we had no problems. I loved him more than ever. I depended on him more than ever.

Mikey was usually higher than I was, so she didn't react to the problems either. Mark was the one beginning to feel the crunch. He was getting nervous and irritable. He always had a quick temper, but now he started losing it for almost no reason at all. He scared me.

We were at his house one afternoon and he was telling us how well trained *his* German shepherd was. He gave the dog a command. The dog sat and stared at him. He repeated the command. The dog didn't move. Finally he walked over and gave the dog a shove. The dog jumped for him and grabbed his arm. He didn't bite through the skin, he just held Mark's arm.

Mark tore it loose and kicked at the dog, missing him. He didn't say a word, he just walked back into the house and returned with his pistol. Still, without a word, he raised the gun and fired twice into the dog's head. Then he picked up the body and dropped it in the garbage pail. Mark scared me.

He was always playing with his guns. He had a whole collection, including machine guns, and he was always pulling them on people. We'd be sitting in his living room and all of a sudden he'd take a pistol out and start shooting at the bottles sitting on top of his bar. Right in his own house!

Louie would really get angry with him every time he played with the guns around the kids, but Mark kept telling him there was nothing to worry about, he was too careful for any accidents. He kept telling him that until one afteroon, in his own living room, he shot this one guy, Tony, right in the foot while showing off his fast draw.

The games of California were different than they'd been back in Queens.

We weren't poor, we certainly weren't starving, but the money wasn't rolling in as easily as it had. Louie was having to hustle a little more, taking smaller, less lucrative jobs, passing more bad checks, using bad cards. He went back to doing houses for a time, and even went so far as to deliver subpoenas for his friend the private investigator. "You never know what's gonna turn up," he explained. I knew too well to even think he might be going legal.

It wasn't that we didn't have money, there was always a few

thousand lying around the house, but our standard of living was so high that we required a constant flow. The grass had been paying our way for months, and when that slowed down, Louie had to pick up the slack.

He tried. He worked very hard. And no one else realized we were having problems. Christmas, 1967, was unbelievable. Louie loved holidays in general and Christmas in particular, because it was a kids' holiday. He told me to make a turkey with all the stuffing, and cranberry sauce. Then he wanted lasagna. And antipasto. And whitefish. And potatoes, and vegetables. I cooked all day December 24th, and all night I wrapped presents. He never knew when to stop. There wasn't a single thing the kids asked for that they didn't get; jewelry, clothing, toys, electronic equipment, records, games, candy. I must have had 30 gifts of my own. He bought two more television sets; we had seven in the house. He bought a stereo. Pots, pans, rings, necklaces, dresses. We opened presents all morning. When you run in the circles Louie ran in, everybody you know has a line of something. Louie bought one of everything. He spent thousands of dollars. He didn't worry about paying January's rent, that would come from somewhere, he worried about giving us enough for Christmas.

It was a wonderful Christmas. I bought him a pretty watch. The kids got him small things. We couldn't afford anything else, he had all the money. One of my favorite memories of Louie is him sitting in his big easy chair, a huge smile on his face, watching as his kids opened their Christmas presents.

It was the end of a wonderful time.

– 7 –

One day early in March Louie washed the car, filled the gas tank and picked up the dry cleaning. He was going to New York. But this time, because he needed cash for some reason, he took his silver bars out of his underwear drawer and hocked them. Without thinking, he used the identification Mark had taken off Danny Orini when he beat him up. It was the kind of stupid thing Louie never did. Except this one time.

I didn't want him to go. I didn't know what he was going for, he normally never told me until after he got back, but I just had a bad feeling. I wanted him to stay home. We had a big fight over it. I was screaming at him and he wasn't paying the slightest bit of attention to me. He was just sitting at the kitchen table eating cookies and drinking milk. Finally I just got so upset, so mad, so jealous, I smacked him. The milk just went flying all over him and the glass smashed to the floor. "Don't go," I screamed at him, "I don't want you to go!"

"I gotta go," he said in an even tone. He wasn't really mad, he understood. He simply got up from the table and went into the bedroom to pack. I cleaned up the milk and broken glass.

Mikey had the same feeling. We all went to the airport together and just as we were saying goodbye, she said, "Louie, don't go. Wait a couple of days. Please, just don't go." It was the first time she'd ever said anything like that.

But Louie wasn't going to listen. Not Louie Mileto. He made up his mind and that was it! He didn't change his mind for anyone. He kissed me goodbye, climbed on his plane and took off for New York.

I went home and blasted some pot. I was wrecked before his plane was halfway cross-country.

He called me that evening. "How are you, hon? Kids okay? What's the weather like?"

He called me late that night. "Everything good? Watch Johnny Carson tonight. He's really funny. Kiss the kids."

He called me the next morning. "I love you. I'm having dinner with Steve and Joanne tonight. Don't forget to feed the dog."

He called me in the afternoon. "Kids home from school yet? Tell them I love them. Everything's going good here. I'll call you tonight."

He never called that night. Joanne did. Louie had been picked up by the police. "It was all a mistake," Joanne kept saying over and over again. "They thought he was somebody else. It was a mistake." I tried to make some sense out of what she was saying. It was just the final stroke of bad luck.

Louie had been wrong. Danny Orini was a killer. Just as Danny told me, he had hijacked a truck and killed the guard. Hijacking is a federal offense and the FBI had put out a nationwide alarm for him. The pawnbroker contacted the police as soon as Louie used Danny's identification.

I never found out how they tracked him to Steven and Joanne's. Louie was a compulsive phone user and had probably given a dozen people Steven and Joanne's phone number, and told them he could get messages there. He had just as likely told the pawnbroker he could be reached at Steve and Joanne's apartment.

"We were eating dinner," Joanne tried to explain, "when they knocked on the door. I asked them who it was and they said 'FBI.'

" 'Louie,' I told him, 'it's the FBI.' He got up and took all his identification out and sticks it under one of the cushions . . ."

I knew it, I kept repeating over and over silently, he shouldn't have gone. I just knew it. I knew it.

"He climbed right out of the window, Ceil, right onto the fire escape and starts going to the roof. The next thing I know I open the door and there's Louie with his hands against the wall being frisked. They had a guy with a shotgun up there waiting for him."

"But how could they know it was him?" I asked. I was starting to go into mild shock. "How'd they know Louie was there?"

"They didn't," she said, "they didn't. They asked him for his ID and instead of telling them he didn't have any, or giving them his own, he goes to the cushion and hands them Danny Orini's."

"Oh, my God," I cried, "they arrested the wrong guy."

"Right! Right! Ceil, they thought he was Danny Orini."

None of it made any sense. "Joanne, how could they think that? He don't even look like him."

She was frightened and confused. "I mean, they knew that. But when they asked him who he was, he gave them some name he made up. Some crazy name."

It was all so silly. They thought Danny Orini was in that apartment, so they made their raid. They knew Louie wasn't Orini, but they figured he had to be somebody to be using false identification. They arrested him. "Listen Joanne," I said as calmly as I could. I didn't have the slightest idea what to do, but I knew I had to stay calm. "Where is Louie now?"

"He's arrested," she repeated, like I was an idiot. "I told you."

"No. Not that. I mean, where did they take him?"

She didn't know. I was really remarkably calm, for me. I started thinking of what to do. I surprised myself. "Joanne, I want you to get on the phone and start calling around. Try to find out where they took him. Find out where he is." I knew instinctively that everything would be okay if we got him out before they put a good make on him. But once they got his identification, Louie was going to be in real trouble. We all were.

I called Mark. I called his father in New York. I called some of our mutual friends. "Get him out," I told them. Mikey came over to stay with the kids and I got the late flight to New York City. I landed there at 6:30 in the morning, with $3000 in my purse.

Louie's father knew the right people. We got the lawyer Louie would want. We had the bail bondsman all set. All we needed was Louie, and we couldn't find him. We went from precinct to precinct, but he was nowhere. The police were moving him around, keeping him hidden, until his prints came back. He wasn't booked, arraigned, arrested, nothing. He was hidden. We couldn't find him for two days.

I didn't take a puff of grass the whole time. My whole mind was on Louie. I was desperate for him. I didn't dare let myself think about how I would survive without him. I wasn't sure I could.

By the time the police let us find him he had been identified through his fingerprints and booked for violation of probation, seven counts of forgery on bad checks, and illegal possession of a draft card and identification. There was no bail.

They had him in Kew Gardens, Queens. When I went to see him I was nervous, it was the first time I'd ever visited anybody in prison, and I didn't know exactly how to act. So I smiled at him. He smiled at me. I didn't know how he was going to act. Neither of us said anything, we just stared at each other. Then he laughed. "For once I shoulda listened to you. I shouldn'a come." I laughed too.

We spent the time going over business. Louie told me that it wasn't as bad as it looked. He knew he was going to have to do the last six months of his previous sentence. He figured he could beat most of the bad check charges. "It's really tough to prove, and most places would rather have their money back than see me go to jail." And he figured at most he'd get a fine and maybe ninety days on the identity possession. Then he told me what to pay the lawyer. "And if he don't get me what I want, don't pay him no more, cause I'm gonna give him a smack." He smiled when he said that to me. Even in jail he was laughing.

"And one more thing," he told me. "I want the kids here for my trials."

I just sat there looking at him. "Louie," I said in a surprised voice, "what do you want the kids for? This will really hurt them. You can't do this to them."

He wasn't going to listen to me. "I want them here, Ceil." It was his order, not a request. We really argued over that. I'd never known him to actually use the kids for his own advantage, and I couldn't believe he would do that. But I also couldn't think of any other reason he would want them in court. "And make sure that youse all look really unhappy when you're sittin' there."

"Okay, Louie, we'll do it your way," I finally agreed. "I'll bring them for the trial." I walked out of that jail with a million thoughts running through my mind. I really didn't know what to do. I didn't know how we were going to live. There were no bank accounts, no savings. Our savings had always been what Louie had in his pocket, and now there was no Louie. I couldn't turn to David for help. Not now, not anymore. He had divorced me officially, I got the paper. I knew Mark would help for a while, but his financial situation wasn't good enough to take care of two families.

I had to think about being on my own for the first time in my life. Really alone. I'd moved from my parents' houses to David's house to Louie's house. In each of those places there was somebody to make the decisions, to tell me what to do, to do the things that had to be done. I was really afraid. And I was really excited.

There was another part of it. This was an opportunity for me to find out if I could take care of myself and my family. I gave Louie's attorney $2500 as a retainer and flew back to California to try to put things together.

The first thing I did when I walked into the house was kiss

the kids and roll myself a joint. I hadn't smoked in the nine days I was in New York and I needed to relax. Grass relaxed me. Slowly, I started getting organized.

At first Mark helped a lot. He was paying my rent and my bills, about $1000 a month, Louie's lawyers, his own rent which was high because the house he'd won in a card game carried a huge mortgage, plus the cost of all the cross-country flights Louie was telling me to make. Mark really was doing his best to help, but after Louie had been in jail for three months, all of a sudden he was hard to find.

And sometimes when I did find him, he gave me a really hard time. I'd trace him to his favorite hangout and he'd make every-body leave, including the bartender, lock the place up, roll a few joints and then chase me around the place. I told Louie, "What's with your friend? You're away a few months and now to get any money out of him he thinks I'm supposed to go to bed with him. What's his story?"

Louie wrote him a long letter demanding that he show some respect for me. We're good friends, he wrote, and I expect you to take care of Ceil the way I'd take care of your wife. It wasn't nasty, it was just friend to friend, but Mark didn't miss the point. He did his best to help us out, and I couldn't get mad at him, he just wasn't earning enough to run two families.

I told my landlord Louie had been in a terrible car accident in New York City and was on the critical list in a hospital. For three months. He was understanding and didn't push for the rent. He let us stay there, temporarily at least, for free. But I knew it was only a matter of time until we had to move.

The older children seemed to understand what was going on and didn't show any problem signs. Susan was different. She was old enough to miss Louie, but too young to understand what happened. She was so used to getting up in the morning and climbing into bed with him, taking a shower with him, eating breakfast with him, getting dressed with him and going off for the day with him that she stopped functioning. Now all she did was pull his silk pajamas out of his drawer and walk around holding them against her cheek and moaning. I didn't know what to do. I thought maybe the kid was having a nervous breakdown. She wouldn't listen to me. All she would do is hold his pajamas and moan.

I was so busy running back and forth cross country and lying to people I owed money to that I didn't have time to think about myself. I forced myself to pretend that Louie was just way on one of his jobs, and everything would be all right as soon as he got back. In six months, I told myself, he'll be out of prison and everything will be wonderful again.

I wasn't interested in dating anyone else. I sincerely loved my husband. Whenever I got too lonely, all I had to do was roll some heavy joints and I was gone into my own safe, happy, stoned world.

Louie was very confident the whole time. "Six months," he told me, "maybe seven. But it's nothin'." Even from prison he ran the whole show. The lawyer didn't tell Louie what to do, Louie told the lawyer. He told him how to plead, what to say, when to say it. He really thought he knew more about the system than the lawyers.

Like he ordered, I brought the kids in for his first forgery trial. I didn't have to tell them to look sad. When Louie walked into the courtroom, looking skinny and pale, his hands handcuffed behind his back, the kids became hysterical. They were crying "Daddy, Daddy, Daddy." Louie was crying. I was crying. It was no act.

He beat the charge. He beat all the forgery charges. Some of the forgeries were covered by his family and the rest he beat. That left violation of parole and use of a phony draft card. Louie figured he was home free.

Four months from the day he was arrested in New York we went on welfare. It was almost funny. We were living in this beautiful 11-room house, our neighbor was the director of welfare, we were wearing beautiful clothes, and we were collecting welfare. I had absolutely no idea how to handle money. I had never kept a budget in my life. We were broke, for example, but I still had the maid coming in. It was silly. It was stupid. It was funny. I just didn't know any better.

I knew we couldn't hold out in California too much longer. But I had to know how long he would be behind bars before I made any decisions. I was getting good at putting off things.

"Ceil," he told me on the phone before his last trial started, "I'm gonna plead guilty to the federal charge." That was illegal possession. "I want you to bring the kids here for my sentencing."

I hesitated. I didn't want to bring the kids into court again. "I can't afford it, Louie," I said. "We haven't got the money."

He didn't want to hear that. "Whattya mean you can't afford it? Hock some of that jewelry. Cash a check. Just make sure you get the kids in that courtroom."

"I can't, Louie. I can't. I just can't put the children through that again. You don't know what's it like——"

"LOOK!" He screamed at me. "I'm not askin' ya, I'm tellin' ya. You be here with those kids." He started yelling at me and calling me ungrateful and irresponsible and uncaring.

I was crying hysterically. I didn't know what to do. I just didn't want the children in that situation again. I was really upset with him, thinking only of himself. I didn't even have the guts to tell him about Susan. Finally I decided that I had to think about the kids. "We're not coming, Louie," I said. I don't know where I got the nerve from.

"Ceil——" he started in an angry voice.

I cut him off. "We can't Louie. It's just too much for the kids. It tears them apart to see you in chains. They're kids, Louie, little kids. They don't understand the whole thing. They're kids."

He hung up.

We didn't go in for the trial. Louie waived his rights and pleaded guilty, expecting to receive a light sentence. I spent the day of his court appearance at Mark and Mikey's, waiting for his call. Our own telephone had been shut off because I couldn't afford to pay the bills.

"Ceil," he started to say. I could tell from his tone of voice that things hadn't gone good.

"How bad?"

"They gave me a class A sentence," he said. It sounded like he didn't believe it himself. "One day to four years."

"Four years! My God, Louie, four years, what am I gonna do?" I was hysterical right away.

"Just calm down, just relax. It's not as bad as it sounds. There's no way I'm gonna do the whole time. That's the max. I got good lawyers, no way I'm gonna do it all."

I believed him, I really believed him. "How long do you think?"

There was a pause in the conversation. "A year, maybe," he said finally. "Maybe a little more. I can do it easy."

I wasn't worried about him. I was worried about myself, and my children. We talked for a little while longer. He was still angry that I didn't bring the kids, but at least he seemed to understand my reasons. I felt bad about that, it was the one thing he ever really asked of me, and I let him down. But I knew I was right.

"Don't worry about it," he finished our call, "I'm not gonna do the whole time. But maybe it would be a good thing if you were in New York. Think about moving here, okay?"

"I love you, Louie," I finished.

"I love you too, Ceil."

I went home by myself and got really wrecked on grass that night. Up until that point I had managed to convince myself that everything was going to be all right, that my problems were temporary, that Louie would be coming home soon and he would make everything right.

Only Louie wasn't coming home soon. A year in jail might not be much to him, but to me it was forever. Each day was a year. Every single bill was overdue. All our credit accounts had been closed. The lighting and heating hadn't been paid. The welfare department was pushing me to get out of the house. The kids needed clothes for the summer. The car was breaking down. All we had was money for food and the cash Mark could spare. It wasn't enough.

And we had dope. Lots and lots of dope. Not truckloads, but enough to stay high for a long time. I got high as often as possible. I had nothing else to do and it helped me forget. The kids were starting to get high a little more often too. But I let them. I felt they were entitled.

I knew I had to do something, make a move, get a job, borrow some money, something, anything to move off square one. But I had never done anything for myself in my entire life. I needed someone to give me a push, to tell me what to do. And finally Mark gave me that push.

He had been ducking in and out of New York to try to help Louie, and his business had gone to pot. Ha! Big joke! He decided that being in California while Louie was in New York wasn't helping anyone, so we should all move back to New York. He told me: "I think we should all go back together. I can't pay for the moving, but I'll get you an apartment back there, and I'll help you out as much as I can." I didn't really care what his decision was, as long as it was a decision. Somebody was finally telling me what to do. I didn't decide Mark was wrong or Mark was right. I didn't think about it, I just did what I was told. It felt very comfortable.

My mother agreed to pay for the move. "Just pack up everything and call in the movers. Have everything shipped to New York and put in a warehouse, then tell them to send me the bill."

She never even said I told you so.

The move was toughest on the children. They had to leave all their friends, their house, their whole life of the last two years. They were unhappy and confused. I couldn't straighten them out, I was pretty confused myself.

The kids had really grown up in California. Paige had become a pretty little girl, although she still sucked her thumb, which worried me. Nancy was the vivacious one, always bubbling over, always laughing. Philip was eight but already a miniature Louie. He'd strut around the house just like Louie did, and demand he be treated as the man of the house. Louie had certain rules for men and women, I always had to cut his meat for him, for example, even when we were out in a restaurant. Philip wanted to be treated just like Louie, because

Louie told him to be the man of the house until he came home. Gay and Susan were Louie's babies and God, how they missed him. The only memories they had at all were of the last two years with Louie. He was their whole life.

He had become my whole life too. My years with him were the wonderful years. He'd taken me from desperation and given me a real fun-filled dream life in California. We had money, clothes, big cars, we traveled, we gambled, went to shows and we loved. He gave me all of it.

Then he left me with nothing.

PART
II

Louie had his own definition for life: Beat the suckers and have a good time. That's exactly the way we lived.

But then he went to jail, and I found out without him there were no good times, and I was everybody's sucker.

I never could figure out what my own definition of life was. So I had to wait for Louie to come home and tell me. And while I was waiting I started sticking needles in my arm.

– 8 –

We moved from California to Brooklyn. It was a change.

Mikey was very friendly with a little old Jewish lady who immediately fell in love with my children. She had a fag son named Francis, who owned two apartments, one in Manhattan and one in Brooklyn, and she offered us the Brooklyn apartment rent free. It was a great deal.

Almost. We had to share the place with three fag friends of Francis's. The apartment was incredible. It was just off MacDonald Avenue in Bensonhurst, right under the el. The outside of the building was old and crummy-looking. The interior smelled funny and the halls were wall-to-wall cockroaches. But the apartment was immaculate.

It was a fag's dream come true. It had beds on the floor with tasseled canopies, stained-glass windows, delicate antique lamps, beautiful framed erotic etchings on the wall, and a wonderful stereo sound system and a complete record collection.

Our three roommates were hairdressers who worked in the same shop. I liked them immediately. They made a big fuss over me and wanted to "do" me up. They were always coming to me for fashion advice: Did their hair look right, were their clothes laying properly on their bodies, what sort of makeup should they wear. And they always wanted me to go out with them. "Oh, come on Ceily," they would plead. "Come and go dancing with us." I never did, I wasn't interested in being their fag hag, but we got along well and I thought the whole setup was sort of fun.

The kids didn't know what to make of our roommates. They were having enough trouble adjusting to living in a new, small place. In California everyone had their own room. Now we were squeezed into a bedroom and a living room. "What are they?" the older girls asked. "Are they boys or girls?" I did my best to explain to them that fags were boys who acted like girls, or girls who acted like boys. I wasn't worried about the girls being harmed, I knew the fags weren't going to bother them, but I was concerned about Philip.

He hated them, really hated them. He had just turned nine and, in the absence of his "father," tried to be the man of the house. He was really rude to them. He said, "You're either a man or a woman, you can't be both." He used to call them "the fags" right to their faces. And when they wanted to cut his hair, he started screaming. He didn't even want to talk to them, he certainly wasn't going to let them touch him.

I was embarrassed about the way he was acting, yet I felt he was entitled to his opinion. If that's the way he thinks, there wasn't much I could say. A lot of Louie had rubbed off on him.

Things got considerably easier in summer. The fags had a place in Cherry Grove on Fire Island, and they spent most of their time out there. We had the apartment to ourselves.

I was trying to get organized. I got onto welfare. I tried to keep the kids busy at Manhattan Beach, or the aquarium, or just window shopping in Manhattan. And every afternoon we went to visit Louie in prison. He had been transferred from Kew Gardens, where the kids weren't allowed, to the Men's House of Detention on West Street.

Those were our happiest moments. We would all dress up as best we could and take the subway to Manhattan. The kids lived for those visits. They absolutely idolized him. I never had any real discipline problems with them after he went away because all I had to say was, "I'm going to tell your father," and they would hop to. They knew, not that he was going to spank them, or take away their allowance, or keep them in the house, just that he wouldn't be pleased with what they were doing. That was enough. They loved him enough to do what I told them.

Louie was always in great spirits. "I'll bet you never thought you'd see me in one spot so long," he joked. He was right. I hadn't seen him so often since the first day we were together. No more in-and-out Louie, just in.

He was always figuring how to beat the four years. Every time I saw him he'd tell me what he had decided the day before. "Go and see Judge so-and-so," he'd tell me, "and explain to him. Tell him that we got five children and that I've been working." Then he'd tell me where to tell the judge he'd been working. I had to take notes. "Maybe he can get me a better sentence."

The lies were bigger and more believable than ever. I saw every judge he told me to see, and none of them wanted to do anything. "Mrs. Mileto," one of them said as politely as he could, "your husband is an incorrigible. With his record, I'm surprised he got such a light sentence to begin with!"

Light sentence! Four years! Who was this judge trying to kid? I couldn't believe he meant what he was saying. I wasn't sure I could survive another six months, and he thought Louie's four-year sentence was too light?

I was dong my best to put up a good front for Louie and the kids, but it was getting tougher and tougher. The worst thing was that, besides getting high every day, I had no outlets, no one I could talk to. Mikey was usually stoned out and I didn't trust Mark anymore. My other friends weren't around often enough. Too often I ended up crying to Louie. "What do you expect me to do for fours years, Louie? What am I going to do? I've never worked. Mark can't support me the whole time.

What am I supposed to do?" I don't know what I expected from him, but he had always had the answers before.

He tried. "Get a little apartment away from the fags. Put our furniture in there, and then wait. In a few weeks I'm gonna give ya some money to buy yourself a little car. Mark is gonna keep helpin' ya. My father's gonna help. Get yourself on welfare. And just put the kids in school and keep visitin' me."

I did just what he said. I got another apartment in Bensonhurst, put the kids in school there, got the furniture out of storage and waited. Three weeks later, at the end of my visit, he gave me an envelope. "Here's a check for five hundred dollars for you. Take it and buy yourself a car."

I couldn't believe he'd manage to scrape up five hundred bucks while he was behind bars. He was amazing. "Where'd this come from, Louie? Where'd you get it?"

He didn't want to answer. "Don't worry about it. I got it. That's all."

I was worried about it. I didn't believe he could get it legally, and I wouldn't have been able to take it if he had gotten additional time. "C'mon Louie, where?" I kept nagging and hacking at him, and finally he admitted that an ex-girlfriend had sent it to him.

"I told her I was in jail and needed it for bail. So she sent it."

I laughed out loud. "You're a character, Louie, you really are." He pulled this trick six or seven times, always five hundred or a thousand dollars, and always different girls as I later learned. He was making more money in prison that I could make on the outside.

But between Louie, his father, Mark and welfare, it still wasn't enough. I couldn't manage money when Louie was making a thousand, two thousand a week, how could I all of a sudden manage with less?

At the end of the summer of 1968 Louie was transferred to the federal prison in Lewisburg, Pennsylvania, almost a four-hour drive from New York. He was there at the same time as Jimmy Hoffa, and I met Jimmy and his wife quite a few times. His wife always seemed to have dozens of papers spread out all over the table, and he would be dictating notes to her. It looked like he was running a little office from his cell. I didn't know who he was, I never read the papers, but I knew he was somebody important because, on his birthday, a small plane flew over the prison trailing a banner which read "Happy Birthday, Jimmy Hoffa." Louie ran down his whole story for me, but the only reason I was really impressed was because Louie was impressed.

He was one of the few prison friends of Louie's that I met. When I went up to visit I always used to wear low-cut dresses because Louie liked to see my body. Jimmy Hoffa used to sit and stare at me when I was up there, and Louie loved that because it made him feel more important. The few times we talked Mr. Hoffa seemed like a very nice man.

I was allowed one visit a month and I looked forward to that visit every waking moment of every day. Louie would tell me what to do, how to get money, where to shop; basically, how to survive until another month passed.

The day before I was supposed to drive up for one of these monthly visits I loaned the car to Mikey. She didn't bring it back that night. First I got real angry, then I started worrying. She didn't have a driver's license and I was thinking that maybe she got picked up and they took my car. I called her hotel all day. Nothing.

Finally, after midnight, my phone rang. "It's me," Mikey said.

I started screaming at her. "Goddamn it Mikey, what the hell is the matter with you, keeping my car like that? You know I got to see Louie and . . ."

She waited until I was finished yelling, then said in an even voice, "You got some nerve yelling at me like that. Didn't you see the paper today?"

"No. Whattya talking about?"

She started crying. "They got Mark for murdering a cop."

My heart sank. Mark wasn't dependable, sometimes he wasn't around, but he was a close friend. With Louie gone, I needed him. "What?" I asked in a weak voice. I couldn't believe it was true. I knew it was absolutely true.

"They got him for murdering a cop." She became hysterical.

"It's just so terrible." She told me the story and it was terrible. It was just a case of more bad luck. Mark was with a crazy young kid named Jimmy Cacavo. They were on their way to a discothèque when an off-duty cop spotted Mark. He knew Mark was wanted, so he jumped in a cab and chased him. Mark didn't even know he was being followed.

When he got to the discothèque he started getting out of the car and this cop grabs him and starts hitting him. So crazy Jimmy grabbed Mark's gun from between the seats and starts shooting. He put two or three bullets into the cop. Mark just took off running, but they caught him. They got Jimmy too.

We didn't even have enough money to hire an attorney for Mark. We had to search around for a good lawyer who was willing to accept my washer, dryer and some furniture I'd left in storage as a deposit. It was a long trip from the thousand-dollar pick-up sticks games.

There wasn't too much he could do. Mark was being held without bail and the only witness who saw the kid do the shooting, the discothèque doorman, had disappeared. "Forget it, Mark is gone," Louie said disgustedly when I told him about it, "he's gone. They're gonna throw away the key."

"But what about the doorman?" I asked. "He saw the whole thing."

Louie laughed. "Yeah? Go ahead and try to find him. The cops probably got him on ice somewhere and he ain't never gonna be produced." Then he paused and thought. "Shit!" he blurted out. Mark was one of Louie's hopes for keeping things together.

Once Mark was gone Mikey disappeared. She just left. He wasn't even convicted yet and she was out of town. We had been very close friends and she left without even calling. A year later I heard she married an airline pilot who didn't want her associating with her old friends. I never heard from her again.

Now I was really alone. The only people I saw were my mother, my stepsister, who lived with her seven kids up in the Bronx, and a few old friends. I spent most of my time sitting around the apartment getting stoned and writing to Louie. By this time I really had a bad pot habit. I was getting high early in the day and trying to stay high every waking hour. It made me happy. It made me forget some of my problems. I also tried cocaine. I was at Steve and Joanne's one evening and Steve went into his pocket and pulled out a dollar bill with a white powdery substance wrapped inside. He started snorting it up his nose, then he offered me a taste. I tried to snort it up just like he had. All it did was make my throat numb. I wasn't crazy about it. "That's a rich man head," Steve joked.

"I wouldn't know about that," I told him. I'd started selling the furniture to survive. Somehow I'd stuffed 11 rooms of furniture into our four-room apartment. The refrigerator went first. Then the extra beds. After that everything started going, week by week.

I didn't tell Louie about my house guest. Her name was Rhonda Hinton and she was the 16-year-old daughter of a friend of Louie's from Queens. She showed up on my doorstep hysterical one morning. She had run away from home and somehow found me in Brooklyn. "They're going to come looking for me," she pleaded. "You've got to hide me."

I asked her why she'd run away. She had a nice story. It seems her father, Louie's friend, had been sexually molesting her since she was nine years old. At night he would come into her room and give her head and climb on top of her. I decided to hide her.

Even though she was only 16, she became my best girl friend. She was somebody to get stoned with. Somebody to talk to. What I didn't know was that she was a drug addict.

My kids didn't like her. Paige and Nancy were both jealous because I spent so much time with her. Philip was madly in love with her and was very hostile and angry because she didn't love him back. But I figured they would eventually accept her.

Her father showed up about six weeks after she arrived. I hid her out on the roof of the building next door and told him that she was staying with me, but he wasn't getting her back.

I told him that he was a disgusting pervert and his wife was digusting for allowing it to happen. There was a lot of screaming and yelling and threatening, but eventually he left. I thought he was gone for good.

A week later her mother called me and said that Louie had phoned and wanted me to be in Lewisburg the next day for a visit. A call like that wasn't too unusual, I'd often get calls from people who heard from Louie. So I packed up and went, never thinking that this woman was setting me up. This is how naive and mixed-up I was.

When I visited Louie in Pennsylvania I'd have to leave about 2:00 A.M. to make sure I was there at 7:00 A.M. when visiting hours started. I'd drive all night to see him.

Rhonda's mother had spoken to Louie. The minute I walked into the visitor's room he exploded, "What the hell are you hiding that kid for?" He screamed, "Are you nuts? That's none of your business."

I started crying. "I know it's not my business, I know she's not my kid, but I think of her as a daughter. I think, well, suppose it was you and Paige, or you and Nancy. Think how I'd feel." I really resented his shouting. For once I was trying to do the right thing, I was trying to help this child, and everybody was coming down on me.

"Listen to me for once, huh! Listen to me, Ceil. Mind your own business. Go home and get that kid out of the house." Our visit went downhill from there.

I knew Louie was wrong but I decided to do like he told me and tell Rhonda she had to leave. It proved unnecessary. When I got home my apartment was locked and dark. My kids were gone. There was no note anywhere and I couldn't even get in because I gave my key to Rhonda. My kids were gone! I didn't know what to do. I didn't know where to turn. It was late. They should have been home. Where were they? I had one dime in my pocket and I called Joanne. "I have the kids," she said quickly, "don't worry, everything's okay."

She explained that Rhonda's mother had showed up with the police that morning. She took her daughter and left. The police wanted to put my kids in a shelter because there was no one home to watch them, but Nancy called Joanne and she came to the house and took them.

I couldn't believe things had gotten so bad so quick. I was 28 years old, living alone with five kids, without a dime. I tried to figure things out but everthing ran together. I always thought I was doing the right thing. At least I never hurt anybody. And now the police wanted to put my kids in a shelter.

I thought, they'll never get my kids away from me. I was positive of that. Then I thought, well, maybe, on a temporary basis, it might be better to put them in good homes. They were changing quickly and I was losing control of them. Paige had started shoplifting. She'd go into Manhattan and come back with a new jacket, new shoes, whatever she could pick up. She had started smoking cigarettes, as had Nancy. Both of them were making long-distance telephone calls to their friends in California and charging them to phony credit cards. Philip had become a real problem. On one trip up to see Louie in prison I caught him trying to rip the vibrator coin box off the bed. "There's quarters in there, Ma," he said, not thinking for one minute he was doing something wrong. Another time he and Gay, who was eight, had kicked in a soda machine to get at the change. So, maybe, I thought, they'd be better off without me.

Maybe I should see about finding them a good place to live. Maybe. And, maybe, if I did, Louie would kill me. They were his kids and nobody else was going to take care of them. That would be a rough blow to his ego. All he had asked from me was to keep them together. I had to try, for him. I started disciplining them as best I could. Sometimes it worked, sometimes not. They had always been very independent kids.

My visits to Louie got worse. I needed to smoke a joint before I saw him, to help me relax, and that infuriated him. "Don't come in here stoned," he threatened me, "I can't stand it. If you got to smoke, don't come. I don't want to know you like that." And he simply couldn't relate to what was happening on the outside. His whole life was centered around prison. I'd go up there and he'd give me a long list of people to call and messages to deliver. He treated me more like a secretary than a wife. Our visits were like business conferencs. "I don't want to do these things, Louie," I'd tell him, and he'd yell at me.

"Whattya mean you don't want to do it? How do you think you get messages from me? Somebody's wife calls ya, that's how. Now you call these people."

We were drifting away from each other. I loved him, and I know he loved me, but the strain was causing us both to change. Louie seemed to be getting harder, tougher. He didn't make his little jokes anymore. He didn't tell me anything about his life, about what was going on in prison, about his friends.

I began to dread the trips to Lewisburg. It was a long drive and I hated it. Even the kids hated it, as much as they adored Louie. Finally I began looking for excuses not to go up. "The car broke down and I had no money for the bus," I'd lie to him. Or I'd tell him, "Gay was sick and I was afraid to leave her." Little excuses, but reasons for not going. After all this time I was finally getting to be as a good a liar as Louie. And it was Louie I was lying to.

− 9 −

I moved again, this time up to the Bronx. I wanted to be closer to my one friend, my stepsister, and I thought a change of neighborhoods would be good for the kids. I also managed to find a four-bedroom apartment on Billingsly Terrace for $35 less than I was paying in Bensonhurst.

It wasn't the best neighborhood in the world, and it certainly wasn't Ventura—there were a lot of junkies on the street—but it wasn't as bad as most outsiders believed. My cousins came down from New Haven and brought me a shotgun as a housewarming present. "You don't have to be a good shot or anything," they explained. "That's the beauty of a shotgun. Just point it and fire."

"That's wonderful," I said as happily as I could. I didn't like guns, big or small, in the house. I didn't like them when Louie had them, and I didn't like them when Louie wasn't there. But I did feel the need for some protection. On their advice I had a friend of my stepsister's cut down the barrel, making it a sawed-off shotgun. Then I loaded it, put the safety on and hid it under my mattress.

My stepsister also fixed me up with my first date since Louie was put away. I really didn't want to see anybody else, but I hadn't had sex in over a year and I was getting very uptight about it. The guy was a salesman in a shoe store and we saw each other from time to time. It had no meaning, it was just for sex.

Time was passing. Slowly, but passing. Louie had done almost eighteen months and I had managed to hold the five kids together. We weren't living in luxury, but we were together. I had my pot, Steve supplied me with all I needed, and we got by. I wasn't really living, but I was alive.

Then Rhonda came back. And she changed everything.

Like before, she just showed up one afternoon. She'd run away from home again, and found me again, and wanted me to hide her. I was glad to have her back so I'd have somebody to get stoned with.

She was crazy. She'd take my car and put dents in it, use my clothes, run up high phone bills and invite her boyfriends over at all hours of the night. But still I liked her. I guess I was even a little jealous of her. She was young, and beautiful, and free. When I was her age I was married with children and already desperate. I was subconsciously living my life through her.

But she was way ahead of me. She had been locked in the bathroom one afternoon for about an hour and I got worried. I knocked and she let me in. She had a needle in her hand. "Wanna try?" she asked.

"What's that?" I had a pretty good idea.

"Heroin. Want some?"

I'd been using pills for a long time, I was heavy into grass and I'd tried coke once. Heroin was something else entirely. I was afraid and I was fascinated. And I was bored. "Sure," I said. "Why not?"

I didn't have the slightest idea how you took heroin. I'd never been around it or anyone who used it. I watched her carefully, I was really interested, and she explained what she was doing as she went along. She didn't have the right equipment—"works," she said. All she had was a "spike," a needle, and a plunger that she normally used to insert some sort of birth control salve. She washed the plunger out very carefully. I sat on the edge of the bathtub, fascinated. She was like a teen-age chemist at work.

She had the heroin in a little plastic stamp bag. She poured a little out into a bottle cap. Then she added water and heated the mixture with a match. Finally she dipped a piece of cotton in and took up the amount she thought I could handle. "Take your belt off," she told me.

I didn't expect that. "Why?"

She laughed. "Come on, silly, just take it off." I did. She tied it tightly around my arm until my veins popped up. "Are you ready?" she asked like an excited schoolgirl. I nodded yes.

She carefully inserted the needle into my arm and pulled the blood back into it. I felt a slight pain from the needle, then I waited. She pushed the needle down.

A new world opened. I fell right back into the tub. It was incredible. I got the most unbelievable rush. She pulled the needle out of my arm and skin popped me with the rest of it. "Wow," was the best I could say. It was wonderful.

I was still coherent. I'm stoned and she's going to give me more. I remember thinking, this is the best.

As soon as I got my balance back I started scratching and vomiting. But I even liked that. I liked the scratching and the throwing up because the more I did it, the higher I got. And I was flying. I was stoned, whacked out, gone. I didn't think about anything. I just loved it. I could feel it moving in my body, and I just kept getting higher and higher. I wasn't worried about money, I wasn't worried about Louie, I wasn't worried about the kids eating that night, I was in my own wonderful world. I loved every minute of the high, from the blood rising in the needle to the final letdown. It was really love at first try.

When I finally came down all I wanted to do was get up again. "Let's get high again," I said, really excited. "Right now. Can you get some more?"

"You got two dollars?"

"What's two dollars gonna get us?" I was really that ignorant.

"Well, that'll get us a two-dollar bag. We'll both get high on that."

I gave her the two dollars. She was right, a little two-dollar bag of heroin was enough for both of us to get stoned on.

We got high every single day. As soon as the kids were out of the house we'd run into the bathroom and shoot up. But sometimes we wouldn't be down by the time they got home, and they started worrying. "What's the matter? You sick?"

"I just don't feel good." I was ashamed. I hated the thought of really using hard drugs. It just loved the damn drugs.

My life changed completely in one week. I tried snorting heroin. That was terrific too. I stopped writing Louie letters completely. And I was so busy getting high, and staying high, that I completely forgot to feel sorry for myself.

It took me six weeks to become an addict. By then I'd made my own connection and was shooting two two-dollar bags with or without Rhonda. I missed my buy one day because my welfare check was late and I didn't have the four dollars. I got through the day, proving to myself I wasn't addicted. But I didn't sleep that night, I just tossed and turned. And the next morning I could hardly get out of bed. I had terrible pains in my legs. My back hurt. My arms felt heavy and sore. I started punching at them to make the pain go away. I rubbed Ben Gay in. I took aspirin. There was nothing I could do to satisfy the pain. It kept getting worse.

My God, I thought, I've got polio.

It never occurred to me that these pains were withdrawal symptoms. I got so scared I called an ambulance and they took me to the hospital. The doctor took one look at me and asked, "Do you use drugs, Mrs. Mileto?"

I told him no.

He laughed at me. "Well, you're addicted to heroin. It must

have gotten into your system somehow." He explained exactly what heroin was, how it worked and what it eventually did to your body. It was all new to me. I thought he was just trying to scare me. Then he tried to convince me to sign myself into a clinic.

Instead I signed myself out of the hospital. Rhonda was waiting in the apartment with two four-dollar bags. As soon as I got it into me I felt good again. The pains just drifted away. I was high. I was happy. I knew the doctor was wrong. I knew I had what the regular addicts called "a small chippy," but I knew I wasn't an addict. I knew it!

I felt so good that I even looked forward to visiting Louie. It wasn't a good visit. At Lewisburg visitors are allowed to sit at tables with prisoners. Louie took one look at my arms and knew exactly what I was doing. "What are those black and blues on your arm?" he challenged me.

I made up some excuse.

"Where's Rhonda at?"

I made up some excuse.

"How come you didn't bring the kids?"

I made up some excuse. By now they knew about my habit. I didn't want them telling Louie.

"Who's watching them?"

I told him Joanne. It was another lie. I just told him one lie after another. I thought I was fooling him. I thought I was too clever for him.

He just sat there shaking his head. "You think I'm that stupid?" he said finally. "Ceil, I grew up with these people on the streets. I been in and out of jails since I was a kid. You ain't foolin' me. I know what you're doing. I know you're shooting junk."

"I'm not!" I said angrily. "I'm not shooting junk."

He didn't even get angry about it. He just tried to reason with me. "I know what that stuff does to ya, Ceil. I seen it too many times. It'll kill ya, plus it'll kill me, being in here and worrying about you out on the streets."

"Louie, I'm not taking——"

"Oh, shit, Ceil, don't lie to me. You can't lie to me. You're gonna get a habit, if you don't already got one."

"I don't have a habit," I said quietly. "I just do it because it feels good."

"Where you gettin' the money?"

"The welfare."

He started telling me the same stories the doctor tried to tell. "You're gonna end up in a gutter somewhere, Ceil, and there ain't gonna be nobody around to help ya." Louie had been brought up to hate drugs. His family had strong feelings about them. Almost everything else you did was all right, as long as you honored your parents, took care of your wife and children and didn't touch drugs. Finally, just before our visit ended, when he saw I wasn't listening to his warnings, he told me, "Ceil, I want you to give the kids up."

I couldn't believe he was saying that.

"You're not a mother anymore. You can't possibly be a mother to those kids and be shooting junk." And then, for the only time in the years we were together, Louie cried.

Even that didn't make me want to stop. I felt he didn't understand at all. I needed the drugs so I could stay faithful to him. With my heroin I didn't need sex, I didn't need food, I didn't need friends.

And how did he know about what was best for the kids? They had begun to like the neighborhood. They had become self-sufficient. Paige and Nancy took care of Susan and Gay. Philip tried to be the man of the household. They were having fun. They loved taking showers under fire hydrants, sliding down the street on shower curtains, playing games in the abandoned buildings.

I decided it would be best not to see Louie too often anymore. It would be for his own good. I was making him too unhappy, and I was too happy to be brought down by his head.

I *was* really happy, happier than I had been at any time since the good days in Big Bear and Ventura. Drugs were terrific. I felt they weren't hurting me and they made me feel good. How could they be bad? So I just kept getting more and more involved.

Four days after my visit to Louie I tried psychedelics for the first time. This friend of Rhonda's was going into the army and we played up to him. We both put our arms around him and pushed ourselves against his body and suggested, "Since you're going in the service, let's go out and celebrate. You want to be seen with two nice-looking girls, right?"

He most certainly did.

"Well," I told him, "if you want to take both of us out, you've got to get us high."

He shrugged his shoulders. "Wanna trip?"

Rhonda said yeah; I didn't know exactly what he meant. I just went along. Rhonda hadn't put me on to a bad head yet, I figured. "All right," she said, "let's have a real party." So we rounded up some of her friends—by this time they were my friends too, I was finally getting to live my teen-age years I'd never had—and bought some Tuinals, some grass, some heroin, some wine, and some Yellow-Orange Sunshine, a type of LSD in clear tab form. Rhonda and I smoked some grass and shot some smack, then we drank a little wine and went dancing in the East Village. Some of the others did grass and downs and wine, and we all had big heads on. Finally Rhonda decided that we should do the acid. It was fine with me. Anything was fine with me.

She prepared me for the experience by telling me exactly what might happen. "We got to go back to the apartment and take baths," she said seriously, "because sometimes it gives you a feeling of being dirty and if you're not really clean you'll start picking at your face and see things that aren't there." Then we split the small chemical tab in half and swallowed it.

By the time it hit us we were all back in my living room. I had no idea where the kids were. We laid on the floor and watched the lights on the ceiling and listened to music. It was really a nice high. It made me feel happy and warm and in-vulnerable. I felt like I wasn't in control of my mind. Rhonda and I got involved in strange conversations and thoughts and just drifted together. For the first time, I really understood our relationship. She was the leader and I was the follower. I was trying to live her life. And she had taken the place of my parents and David and Louie. She was about 17 years old and telling me what to do.

Rhonda's army friend didn't trip. He just sat in a corner smoking pot and drinking wine. Rhonda noticed him and rolled over toward me and said, "Let's hold this guy up. He's got almost three thousand bucks in his pocket."

I agreed. I was game for anything at this point. I lifted up my mattress and pulled out my sawed-off shotgun. We're laughing the whole time. We were going to hold him up. It was really funny. "All right buster," she said. "Drop your pants and keep stepping. We know your money's in there."

He turned white. Every bit of color just drained right out of his face. He started unbuckling his belt. He really didn't know if we were serious or not, but he wasn't about to take any chances with two stoned-out girls holding a sawed-off shotgun on him.

"Give me the gun, Ceil," Rhonda said. "Let's shoot him." She kept laughing.

He dropped his pants to the floor and stepped out of them. Rhonda walked over and grabbed his wallet. There was a thick wad of bills inside.

"Get outta here," I told him, with a big smile. The poor guy ran out of the apartment in his underwear. We were laughing so hard we fell onto the floor. It was all a big joke, everything was a big joke. I really liked that acid.

Rhonda handed me a few hundred dollars. "We'll put this much away for the electric bill and the telephone bill and the rent," she said. "I'm gonna go cop some more dope with the rest of it."

I waited for her to come back for two days. She never showed up. I was beginning to learn the junkie rules. By then I had come down pretty hard, the acid was eating up the heroin and I was feeling very bad. I needed some money and I needed some dope. And I needed Rhonda for both. I couldn't find her. I walked the streets for another day just looking for her. She had disappeared. Nobody had seen her.

Of course the police finally showed up at my apartment.

There were two of them, a big tall one and a short one. "We have to arrest you for armed robbery," the tall one said.

"Are you crazy? Armed robbery? I've never been arrested before in my life."

"Where's the other girl?" the short one asked.

"What other girl? There is no other girl." Lying had become second nature to me. I knew Louie would have been proud of me. The cops took me to the station house and arraigned me. Then they put me in a detention cell overnight.

That night, for the first time in months, I really started thinking about the kids. I knew there was enough food in the house for them to eat, and I knew my stepsister would watch them, but I worried that the courts were going to take them away from me. They might decide, with good reason, that I was unfit to be a mother and put my children somewhere. It scared me.

Louie had already decided I was unfit. I would get letters from him every day, one day he would demand that I get up to see him, the next day he would apologize, asking me to forgive him for putting me in a position I couldn't handle. But he also said he had been writing to my aunt and my cousins up in New Haven. "It might be better for everyone," he wrote, "if maybe the kids stayed with them for a while. That way you wouldn't have to worry about them so much and I wouldn't have to worry about all of you so much."

In the jail cell I began to understand what he was talking about. It would be easier for me without the kids. I wouldn't have all the expenses. I wouldn't have so many worries. I could learn to live by myself. It would be best for everyone, like Louie wrote. Besides, if the court took them away, who knows where they might put them. This way they'd be with relatives, and we could get them back as soon as Louie came home.

The next day I was released without bail. I contacted my aunt and she came right down. She agreed to take the kids until I got myself cleaned up. We went to a lawyer and for $50, her $50, we had temporary custody papers drawn up.

I was almost proud. I lied to myself that I was thinking of

my children first. The truth was that with them out of the house I had no responsibilities and no guilt feelings.

The night they left I stayed almost straight and cried. Louie had been right, I wasn't a mother anymore.

I missed them. It didn't take me long to discover I needed them much more than they had needed me. They had survived without any help from me, but I desperately needed their company, I needed the noise they made around the house, I needed even that slight feeling of being needed that they gave me. I needed the voices of other human beings.

I'd lost everything, my family, my house, my money, my own self-respect. I stopped fooling myself, I knew exactly what I was—a cheap junkie. I had an important choice to make: I could either clean myself up or continue going into the gutter with drugs. It was not an easy decision. I knew what was right, and I knew what I wanted. They were direct opposites. I thought of Louie. I thought of my children. I thought of my own life. I loved my drugs, but I understood what they were doing to me. I stayed as drug free as possible for a full day, trying to make my decision.

Finally I reached the inevitable conclusion. I would continue to shoot drugs until Louie came home.

– IO –

It took me another seven months to become a complete street junkie, living from bag to bag. I was always strung out, but I was enjoying what I was doing. I liked hurting myself. My veins were starting to collapse and my habit was getting more expensive every day. Piece by piece I sold off all my furniture and jewelry. I was selling it for nothing, for two bags of dope. "Here, you like this diamond ring? Take it. It's yours. Four bags." The last thing to go was Philip's mini-bike. I really wanted to keep that for him. It's his, I kept telling myself, you have no right to sell it.

It went for thirty-five dollars.

Rhonda was gone. The police took her in, then released her to her father. Later I found out he wasn't as sick as I thought. She was as crazy as he was. She used to arrange it so they would be alone in the house, then parade around half-undressed in front of him. About the nicest thing I could say about her is that before she left she put me on to her drug connection, two Puerto Rican brothers who lived up on Burnside Avenue.

I completely stopped writing or visiting Louie, although we managed to keep in contact through my mother. He'd write to her, and whenever I needed money I'd show up at her house for a loan, or to steal something I could sell on the streets, and she'd give me his letters.

My mother was getting old very quickly. She was only in her early fifties and still looked very good, but her mind was aging much faster than her body. She acted just like a little old lady. She was afraid of everything. The house was completely sealed up, every window and every door had a lock on it. No salesman or delivery people were allowed in the front door. But the person she was most afraid of was me.

She couldn't understand how I had became such a mess, but in a real way she blamed herself for it. My mother had never really recovered from my sister's suicide. She felt very guilty about it and believed that it was her fault because of the way she treated us. Now that I was killing myself, only slowly, all her guilt feelings came back, so she really tried to help me. My stepfather had done well in business, so she had plenty of money, and usually gave me whatever I asked for. And whenever I needed a place to lie down, she let me stay home and didn't bother me. It was sad; she was trying to do her duty as a mother, and it was too late.

Seeing her suffering made me feel bad, so I stayed away as much as possible. Eventually my money ran out and, like every other street junkie, I drifted into crime.

I did the normal shoplifting, passing bad checks and using stolen credit cards, but the first time I got caught it was for something I didn't even do. I went to a connection's apartment, looking for some free dope. I was going to tell him I was sick and I'd pay him later. But I got lucky. When I walked into his hallway I saw a set of keys hanging out of a mailbox. I checked the number of the apartment and grabbed the keys. This was a dopie's gold mine.

I dangled the keys in front of my connection. "They're the

keys to apartment 3F. Why don't you go get somebody to rip the place off?" He traded me two bags of dope for the keys.

He didn't bother getting anyone else to do the work, he robbed the apartment himself. Unfortunately he got caught carrying a color television set upstairs to his own place. Instead of taking all the heat himself, he told the police where he got the keys. He also rode in the patrol car with them and pointed me out. I was arrested on a burglary charge and sent to the Woman's House of Detention in Greenwich Village. For the first time in my life, I saw a prison from the inside.

I was really afraid. The jail, the so-called House of Detention, was a big, ugly brick building. It was the first time I'd been inside a woman's prison and I didn't know how to act. I learned very quickly.

They put me in a cell on the drug floor. They had this ten-day detox plan, after which you were supposedly drug free. It was disgusting. This girl two cells over from mine died, and they just left her lying in her own vomit. Everybody was screaming and yelling and crying and throwing up that green bile that comes when a person is kicking. The place smelled disgusting because everybody had the runs. One girl wanted to get out of there so badly she tried to hang herself. She did manage to get out. They put her in a straitjacket and checked her into the Bellevue mental hospital.

The detox was a waste of time anyway. After I got into the general population I did whatever I could to get high. I smoked ground-up aspirin, palm leaves, even eggshells. None of them really worked, all I ever got was headaches, but after a while I began to believe that whatever I was doing was making me high. In that way it was successful. The majority of the inmates were either addicts or ex-addicts, and I learned more about drugs inside than I'd learned in a year out on the streets.

The first week I was there the lesbians checked me out to find out what my way of thinking was. Once I told them I didn't fool around with women, they left me alone.

In fact, because I didn't figure to be there too long, I stayed pretty much to myself. The girls that were in for a long stretch, or figured to be back in soon, really made the place their home. They decorated their cells like little apartments. They hung curtains on the outside bars, pictures on the walls and used whatever else they could find to make their "homes" more cheerful. One Cuban girl, I remember, took the gauze out of some Kotex and tied bows up and down her bars, about fifteen bows to each bar. That night one of the matrons, a big fat bull dagger, came walking by and saw the decoration. She panicked. "Get 'em off there, get 'em off there," she was really screaming, "get 'em off them bars." We thought she'd gone crazy. Finally we understood. "You ain't puttin' none of them spells or hexes or voodoos on me!"

Except for the lack of drugs, life inside wasn't too bad, but after a month I wanted to get out on the street and get high. At first I hadn't let anyone know I was inside. I finally got up enough courage to write Louie and ask him to send me some bail money. He wrote me back an angry letter telling me never to write him from one prison to another. He was completely disgusted with me, he wrote, and even though he wanted me out as soon as possible, he wouldn't help. "Maybe this will teach you something. I told you you weren't so smart. You didn't believe me. Look where you ended up." He signed it "Love, Louis."

Right, Louie. And look where *you* ended up.

I threw his letter in the garbage and wrote to my mother. She bailed me right out. Exactly two months from the day I was arrested I was back on the street, shooting heroin.

When you shoot enough heroin you reach a point where you aren't shooting it to get high, you're shooting just to take away the sickness. There is no high, but your body craves more and more and more. It's an endless roller coaster ride.

Finally I managed to get off. I almost died. It happened really quickly. I nodded myself to sleep one night and when I woke up the next morning my whole body hurt. I ached, I had fever, I had trouble walking.

I had hepatitis. My mother just about carried me to her family doctor and he made all types of tests. "Your liver is in very bad shape," he finally figured out. "If you don't stop shooting heroin, I think you'll be dead within six months." Boom. Just like that. Stop shooting or die. One or the other.

Suicide was one thing, that was my choice, but I didn't want the choice taken away from me. Death didn't have any great appeal to me, so I stayed home with my mother and tried to clean myself up. My mother played the suffering mother role very well. She took very good care of me, but did her best to make me feel guilty. "I'm not smoking any of your cigarettes," she'd warn me, "because who knows what you're smoking this week." Or, "I always knew you were taking some drug because your breath smelled sweet."

"Okay Ma," I told her, "no more smelling my breath."

I really decided I wanted to kick. On the suggestion of a doctor I went to Daytop, a drug rehabilitation program, on 14th Street. Daytop tries to teach addicts to deal with the problems that drove them to drugs in the first place. Instead of running to the cooker when things didn't go your way, you were taught to deal with them. Overall, they tell me it's a successful program.

I lasted five days. Then I grabbed as much of my personal belongings as I could and ran out the back door down Seventh Avenue.

Daytop isn't for me, I convinced myself. It's too harsh, too quick. I needed more of a physical withdrawal program rather than a psychological program. But in the meantime, I thought, until I find that program, I'll just do a little drugs to help me get by.

It all started again. Hanging out in the streets, hustling for dope, living for the next rush. I kept telling myself it was only temporary, until I found the right program. Somehow I couldn't seem to find the right program.

Finding drugs was no problem, but paying for them was. I had absolutely no income, so I got together with two male junkies and we started ripping people off. We bought a little toy gun and started holding up dealers outside our area. When that got too dangerous, we decided to take off some easy marks.

Our first target was an old man who worked as the superintendent in the building he lived in. He must have been close to 80, and his wife wasn't much younger. We heard that he collected all the rent money on the first day of the month and kept it in his mattress until the bank opened the next day. We decided to open his mattress. I put on boy's clothes—I had short hair and was very skinny then anyway, so I looked like a boy—and I pulled a longshoreman's cap over my head. The two guys I was with hid on either side of the super's door and I knocked. It took the old folks a few knocks before they heard me. "Who's there?" his wife asked.

"I wanna talk to you about an apartment," I yelled back.

She opened the door partway and my partners went bursting in. I was right behind. My job was to hold the man and woman away with the toy gun. The job looked very easy. "Where's the money?" my partner asked in as tough a voice as he could manage.

"There's no money here," she said. "Who told you we have money?"

The old man stepped forward. He wasn't the slightest bit afraid. "You young hoodlums," he started shouting. "If I was ten years younger I'd——"

"Stay back," I warned him, stepping back myself. All of a sudden this job was not going at all like we had planned it.

"What? What did you say?" He didn't hear too well.

I shouted at him, "You better stay back, or else I'm going to shoot you."

"Oh," he said. "Well, I'm going to call the police," he finally decided, "I'm going to phone."

"Don't do that," one of my partners screamed, "or she'll shoot you!"

That was all the old lady had to hear. She panicked. She picked up the long steel bar that they used to jam the door shut and started swinging it over her head. "Kill me! Kill me!" she starts screaming. "Don't kill him, please. Shoot me, I'm older!"

She was screaming and moving all over the apartment, swinging the bar over her head. We're ducking and looking for the money.

"I'm trying to call the police," the old man kept repeating.

"Please shoot me, don't shoot him!" Swish! Duck. The bar went whizzing overhead. "Kill me, kill me." Swish. Duck. "There's no money here, we don't have any money." Swish. Duck. "He's not calling the police." Swish. Swish.

By this time the old man had managed to get to the phone. "I'm calling the police, you hoodlums."

"You people are nuts," I screamed at them. They didn't listen. Swish. Duck. "Let's get outta here," I yelled, and we ran out the door and across the street into the projects. We split up, for safety, but our big robbery plan had been foiled by two nutty old people. They were too much for us.

I was never too successful as a criminal. The police kept catching me. I went back to the House of Detention. I did time on Riker's Island for possession of stolen property, a credit card. No matter what I did, it turned out wrong.

There were times when I honestly tried to clean myself up. I joined a private methadone maintenance program in Queens. The plan was to combine gradual drug withdrawal and group therapy. The director of the program was an ex-junkie and, after a few weeks, we started dating. He was the first male since Louie I'd taken an interest in, and the program seemed to be working. He convinced me that I had to learn to respect myself in order to kick drugs, and one way to do that was to be completely self-supporting. "Get a job," he told me.

I got a job as a waitress at Schrafft's on Second Avenue. I dropped a few trays and mixed up some orders, but for a newcomer I did well. I was making $25 a day, including tips. I was heroin free. I even went to Boston to see my children, but my aunt wouldn't let me get near them. She made me sit in the airport alone all night until I could get a plane back to New York.

Then Schrafft's hired a junkie busboy. He got me shooting again. Within a few days I forgot about working and was back on the streets again.

Whenever I was going through one of my clean periods I'd fix myself up as best I could and go to see Louie. "I'm clean now, Louie," I'd tell him, "and I'm finished shooting and can't

I please take the kids back now?" I knew I could just take them whenever I wanted, but I wouldn't do that without Louie's approval. He wouldn't give it to me. He'd scream and shout that I was a slut, that I was a junkie whore, a bitch, terrible names.

He just couldn't understand that I had built a closet to hide in for protection until he was free. I wasn't happy, but the drugs kept me alive and sane while I waited for him to get out.

The time somehow passed. In the fall of 1970, when Louie had six months to go on his sentence, he was transferred to the prison-farm at Allenwood. Allenwood is more of a community than a prison, it has no walls, and Louie took full advantage of that. He was calling me so often I thought he had a telephone right in his cell. Finally he called me and told me he had this plan. He wanted me to check into a certain motel near the prison and at midnight I was to walk along the road up this big, long hill, until I reached the stop sign at the top. At the stop sign I was supposed to slide down the gully and then crawl under a small fence and wait for him there.

I told him he was crazy.

He told me to be there.

I checked into the motel just like he told me to do. At quarter to midnight I started walking up the hill. I was wearing a long suede coat with snaps, and boots, and I had nothing on underneath because I knew what Louie wanted. The truck drivers were shining their lights on me and honking and even slowing down, but I kept walking. I was really scared, it was dark and I was alone and I was walking alongside the woods. When I reached the stop sign at the top of the hill, I just did like he told me, I slid down the gully. I walked a few feet and found the opening in the fence and crawled under that.

I didn't see Louie. "Louie," I whisper-shouted. There was no answer. It was all dark and I could just feel the bugs flying around. I was getting more and more scared. "Louie!" Still nothing.

Then I heard something moving in the woods. And all of a sudden Louie comes running right up to me. He was wearing his white prison suit, and he had a blanket in one hand and a stopwatch in the other. "Hi, Ceil," he said.

"Hi, Louie," I said. I took off my suede coat. He laid the blanket down on the ground. And then we made love for about three hours. It was wonderful, just being with him, feeling him, smelling him, being held by him. There were about one million stars out that night and when we were resting we watched them move across the sky.

After what seemed like no time at all Louie checked his stopwatch and said he had to get back for head count. I put on my coat and crawled back under the fence, climbed up the gully to the stop sign and walked down the hill. The next morning I put on my good clothes and went up to Allenwood for a regularly scheduled visit. We argued about my drugs and the kids. Louie never even mentioned our night in the woods.

I finished the last six months of Louie's sentence just as I'd passed most of his other time, getting high, cleaning up, getting high. Once I collapsed in the A&P of an overdose of pills as I was in the middle of writing a bad check. All the pills just hit me at once and I fell out. They rushed me to the hospital and pumped out my stomach. I woke up in a rage, I thought I was being arrested because of the bad check, and ran out of the hospital into a taxicab.

I took the cab to my connection's place and just left it sitting there waiting for me. I did that a lot. Sometimes I'd carry a bag of garbage with me when I had to take a cab. I'd go about a block away from my destination and tell the driver to wait for me. "I'm only gonna be a minute," I'd lie, "and I'll leave my bag here so you know I'll be back." They all agreed. I left cabs sitting with a bag of garbage in the back all over New York.

Sometimes the drivers tried to be sharper than I was. They took off as soon as I disappeared into a building. They figured they were beating me for a bag filled with groceries!

I didn't hear from Louie too often after my visit to Allenwood. There just didn't seem to be any reason to communicate. He knew what I was doing, and hated it, and I hated him for hating it. But one afternoon I called my mother for a small loan and she told me she'd gotten a letter from Louie. "He's being transferred to West Street to get ready for his release," she told me. "He wants you to come see him there."

All my hatred for him disappeared with those words. "When, Ma?"

"In two weeks." I went out and got high in celebration. Louie was coming home, everything was finally going to be all right again. It was all that simple.

Almost. I was on probation from a shoplifting charge at the time. When I stopped in to see my probation officer, she took one look at the new tracks on my arm and said, "You've violated, you're going back."

I couldn't believe she was putting me back in prison. It didn't seem possible. I was going to be in jail when Louie was released. That wasn't right, it wasn't fair. I'd waited too long for him. I wanted to be there to meet him. I started screaming and crying. "Put me in a program. Please, find me a program."

She gave me a wary look. She didn't trust me, for good reason, but she'd never seen me cry real tears before. "We'll see," she finally said.

I went back into jail and the Quakers came and picked me up. They operated a girls' live-in therapeutic community house in Greenwich Village. It was a combination home-school. They taught high-school equivalency courses as well as secretarial skills. Right from the beginning I thought it was a nutty program. At breakfast they started me off with 24, not 1 or 2 or 3, but 24 vitamins of every shape and color. As soon as breakfast was over, just when I'd finished swallowing the first 24, they hit me with a second barrage of vitamins. By the time I got to the classroom I was having hot flashes. I felt like I'd just shot some quinine. I spent the whole day going from vitamin pill to vitamin pill. I was so healthy I felt like I was going to die.

There was no way I could stay there. This was a voluntary program and if an individual wanted to leave, the Quakers had to let them go. I found one of the program heads and told her I wanted to leave. "Let's talk first," she said nicely.

"I don't wanna talk. Open the door."

"Just five minutes, Ceil, please."

"Open the door or I'm going out the window."

Some of the other girls in the program heard the argument

and came running. They tried to talk me out of leaving. "Ceil, you don't know what you're doing. Think of your children."

That line always made me laugh. I hadn't thought about them for 18 months, I'm going to start thinking about them now? "Just open the door." If I'd thought about my kids in the first place I wouldn't have become an addict. The one thing I'd learned, the only advice I'd ever give an addict, is that you can't stop doing drugs for your children or your husband or wife. You have to stop for yourself. You have to really want to stop, desperately want to stop. I hadn't reached that point yet.

"Now!" I demanded. "Lemme out!"

They opened the door and I walked out. It was the day Louie was being transferred back to New York City. I was ready to begin my life again.

PART
III

Louie came home from prison to give us a new life. He got himself a new job with a big salary, he got us Herbie and Josephine, our new best friends, and he moved us all into a big new house. With the old Louie it would have all been wonderful, but new Louie came home from prison. And he wasn't laughing so much at the world anymore.

I wanted to go home to California. I don't know exactly when I began to realize that California didn't exist anymore.

— I I —

March 1971.

I couldn't wait to see Louie.

I didn't want to see him at all.

I loved him; I hated him. I was excited; I was depressed. Every different emotion was running through my body. I knew exactly what I wanted; I was totally confused. I wanted to be straight when I saw him, but I didn't have the courage to see him without support from my drugs. I decided, instead of walking the 15 blocks from the Quaker house to West Street, I'd go up into the Bronx and get high first. Then I would be ready to see Louie again.

I took a cab to a friend-dealer named Darlene. We'd met while doing time together, and she told me to drop by whenever I needed a quick hit. It was really a coincidence because I'd been shooting dope with her 19-year-old son a year before I met Darlene. Later I also shot up with her husband, so I was almost part of the family.

It was her husband who opened the front door for me. "I need money for a cab," I told him.

"Beat the cab," he told me.

"Okay," I shrugged and stepped inside. As usual, the apartment was filthy. It looked a lot more like a crash pad than a family home. There were newspapers all over the floor, bits and pieces of clothing lying on chairs, overflowing ashtrays, discarded food wrappers and, inevitably, three sets of works sitting on top of the color television set. "Where's Darlene?" I asked.

"She's in the bedroom," he answered quietly, pointing with his thumb.

I started to walk in. I stopped exactly one step inside the room. Darlene was sprawled on her back, half on, half off a filthy bed. She was naked, her legs wide open, and her head was hanging over the side. A horrible deep-colored gook was dripping out of her mouth onto the floor. I stood transfixed. This was something I'd seen before. Darlene had overdosed.

Her son was sitting next to her on the bed with a tray of ice cubes, shoving them up inside of her. "Hi, Ceil," he said when he noticed me, but he didn't stop helping his mother. "She O.D.'ed," he continued. "Me and Dad are bringing her around."

I nodded. I couldn't say anything.

Her husband shouted in from the kitchen. "You want a cup of coffee, Ceil?"

They were acting like this was the most normal thing that ever happened. I couldn't believe it. I'd heard that ice cubes helped greatly, and I could even see her husband treating her. But her son? It really digusted me. If I didn't need drugs so badly I would have walked out.

A few hours passed. Little by little Darlene came around. First she started moaning, then crying, then speaking short sentences, then, finally, she became almost coherent. When she finally became straight enough to sit up in bed by herself, her son came out and shared a small bag with me. We both needed it to relax.

Then we did another. I decided not to see Louie that day. Or the next day. I decided to wait a little while, to try to sort out my feelings about him. I knew it had to be either Louie or the drugs. They weren't compatible, I could keep one, but then the other had to go. If I knew it was going to be just like California I would have stopped taking drugs instantly, but there were no guarantees. At least the drugs guaranteed I would get high. That was something.

I stayed as high as I could for a few days, then I woke up and decided to try to quit. The impact of his coming home hit me, and I knew I wanted him back more than anything. Much more than drugs. I went to the methadone clinic at Bronx State Hospital and enrolled.

He was emptying the garbage the first time I saw him. He'd called my mother and told her what time he wanted me outside the prison gate. I was there at exactly ten o'clock the next morning. I was straight. I was ready for him. He came out with a full pail of garbage and a guard. I stood back for a few seconds, just watching him. He looked terrific—tan and strong and handsome. He didn't see me at first. "Louie," I finally said softly.

He put down the garbage pail and looked at me. "Hi, Ceil," he answered.

"I'm here," I told him. Then just like in the movies, I ran up to him and threw my arms around him and started crying. He held me tightly. "I missed you, Louie, I missed you so bad. I need you, I can't live without you anymore." I cried on and on and he just kept holding me.

"It's gonna be okay," he assured me, "everything's gonna be good. We'll get a place, we'll get the kids back———"

"And I'll stay clean, Louie, I swear I'll stay clean."

"And you'll stay clean," he agreed. We only had a few minutes and he told me when he was getting out, when he wanted me to come back and who he wanted me to call. He just took over my life again, just like before he went to prison. It was just what I wanted him to do. "Now I got one more week in this place," he finished, using his hand to emphasize what he was saying, "and I want you to stay clean and stay outta trouble this week. Go stay at your mother's house . . ."

I just kept nodding my head in agreement. Anything he said

was fine with me. I did just as he said, I went home to my mother's house and I sat and I waited. I watched television, I read magazines, I went to Bronx State for my methadone. But I stayed clean and I stayed out of trouble.

He was scheduled to be released on a Wednesday. I put on my prettiest clothes, did the best I could with my hair and waited for his phone call. He called about 11 A.M. "I'm doing my paperwork now," he told me. "I'll be out soon."

I couldn't wait. "Louie, can I come and meet you? Can I pick you up?"

"Nah, don't bother," he answered casually. "I'm gonna get me a haircut and a shave and have my nails done and buy some clothes. I'll be over later to see you. I just gotta do this stuff, you understand, right?"

"Yeah, Louie," I said quietly, "I understand." I did too, he hadn't changed at all. Four years had passed and Louie was still the same Louie. I was really hurt, but I sat with my mother and waited for him. I'd been waiting four years, a few more hours couldn't do any more damage.

He showed up clean, shaved and smiling, like he had been gone four days rather than four years. We sat and we talked, just feeling each other out, trying to get reacquainted. "Mark is really in the hole," he told me.

"My aunt says the kids are fine and they miss you," I told him.

"Prison wasn't too bad. Nice people at Lewisburg."

"I'm still on probation for that silly robbery with the shotgun."

"They offered me parole twice, but then they told me you were a junkie and asked me if I was gonna steal to support your habit. I spit in their faces."

"Most of the furniture is gone. I sold it for drugs."

"Got a letter from Billy. He's got a gas station now. Everything is okay with him. The station's in the Bronx. On Fordham Road."

"I really missed you, Louie."

"There's a lot of homosexuals in prison, you know. I didn't let them mess with me."

"I know, the Woman's House of Detention is filled with bull daggers." Finally we had some common ground. We discussed every topic except the future, that was something neither of us wanted to get involved with yet. After maybe ninety minutes Louie stood up and stretched his long arms to the ceiling. He was skinny but tanned, and he looked wonderful.

"I'm going out for a while," he told me.

"But you just got home, Louie."

"I know, I know, but it's been a long time, honey. I got a lot of people to see. I got to start getting things organized." In-and-out Louie, home again.

He walked back in around midnight. We made love that night. It was sweet.

My mother let us stay at her house until we found a place of our own. She wasn't happy that I was staying there because I had robbed her so many times, but she offered anyway. She never really understood my problems, but that didn't stop her from trying to help me. Every time I pawned a piece of my jewelry she would go and buy it out. She'd bring it home and lock it in her cedar chest. And every time I needed money I'd break the lock with a screwdriver and sell my own jewelry all over again.

So I owed her a lot of money, which she never tried to collect. She wasn't happy that Louie was back, she figured he'd hit the streets and end up back in prison, and then she'd have to support me again. But she still invited us to stay with her. She was still feeling responsible for me.

We only stayed about four days, then we rented a studio apartment in the Elmhurst Towers in Queens. Louie was constantly running in and out of the place. "Where you going, Louie?"

"I'm working."

"Working? What are you doing?"

"I'm working, gotta go." Boom, gone.

I didn't know what he was doing, but I knew he was being successful at whatever it was. Every day he'd give me $300 or $500 cash and tell me to buy linen and dishes and furniture and clothes and food and appliances. I bought drugs. As soon as he left in the morning I'd go to my connection and spend about half of it copping, not only for myself, but for my friends. I tried not to buy hard stuff, I really wanted to kick heroin and never missed my methadone, but I was doing pills and pot. I'd get high, spend the day shopping and be reasonably straight by the time Louie got home.

I slipped a few times and Louie caught me high. He would blow his stack, screaming and yelling, threatening to throw me out of the house. "Gimme your driver's license," he'd yell, "gimme your credit cards. No junkie's gonna use my name." Eventually he made me produce receipts for everything I bought, so I had to cut back on my drug buying.

I didn't really care. I had my methadone, and Louie was filling the need I'd used drugs to fill while he was in prison. And we were quickly getting back into the big money again, although I still didn't know what he was doing. I wanted to know, but he wouldn't tell me.

"I'm working for Herbie." That was all he would say.

"Who's Herbie?" I asked. I'd never heard of any Herbie.

Louie was crazy about him. "He's the greatest guy in the world. Thanks to him I'll never go to jail again, because I'll be making so much money I can buy my way out of anything."

"Terrific, Louie, but what are you going to be doing for him?"

"I told you, Ceil, working for him. Wait until you meet him, you'll love him."

I could see I wasn't making much progress. "Okay, I'll love him. But who is he?"

"He's a really terrific guy. I met him in Lewisburg and we really hit it off. He's this little Jewish guy who speaks Italian. He's an ex-fighter, and he's been in prison most of his life. Really a terrific guy."

"What was he in for, Louie?"

"He was a dealer." I found out much later he had been arrested in 1959, when he was 20 years old, together with Vito Genovese and Joe Valachi.

I knew I had to like him, I had no choice. For days Herbie was all Louie could talk about. "He has this mother you wouldn't believe. She would probably even clean your gun if you asked her. Herbie can't do a thing for himself, his mother does everything. I wish my mother was like that."

"But Louie, what are you doing for him?" I asked over and over.

"Don't you listen to anything, Ceil? I told you, I'm working for him."

Eventually I stopped asking and started spending.

As soon as Louie had some real cash in his pocket, he wanted the kids back. "They're ours" he told me, "all we have to do is go pick them up."

It wasn't quite that easy. My aunt had kept the three oldest children, Paige, Nancy and Philip, in her house for 18 months, and put Gay and Susan with my first cousin. She had a really good deal going, she was getting welfare from the state, child support from David, and she had the kids keeping house. She didn't want to give them up. "That junkie's no mother," she told Louie, "and she'll destroy these kids. At least I'm giving them a home."

Louie didn't want to hear that. "I can give my own kids a home. We don't need you bad mouthing us."

"Well, you can't have them back," she said. "I've got legal custody. I've got papers!"

"Sure, okay," Louie agreed, "now lemme speak to Paige." Paige got on the phone and Louie told her, "Mummy and I want to see you and your sister. Can we meet someplace on Sunday?" Paige named a place. "Good. We'll be there in the afternoon. Don't tell your aunt we're comin' up. Okay?"

"Okay Daddy," she answered. "And we both love you very much."

We picked them up Sunday afternoon. The girls just climbed all over Louie, they couldn't get enough of him. They hugged and kissed him the whole trip back to New York. And Louie returned their love. Paige's fifteenth birthday and Nancy's fourteenth were only about a month away, and Louie spent the drive listing the things he was going to buy them. "You tell me what you want and that's what I'm going to get you. You just name it. All the bad things are over now. We're gonna get a nice house, nice clothes, anything you girls want you're gonna have."

I sat quietly in the back seat and listened. The girls had been polite toward me, but they really didn't know how to act. My aunt had spent the last 18 months convincing my children that I was a rotten junkie, that I was sleeping with blacks and that I was walking the streets and turning tricks. It would take some time for me to undo those bad impressions, particularly since a few of them were the truth. But with Louie's help, I knew I could win them back.

Louie stopped on the way home and called my aunt. "Listen," he told her, "we got the girls with us and we're bringing them home."

She was furious. "You can't do that," she screamed. "I've had them eighteen months and I've given them a good home."

"Well, their mother's had them fourteen years and I don't want to hear about your home."

"I'm gonna get a lawyer," she threatened, "because I've got papers!"

Louie told her what she could do with her papers. Then he hung up on her. "Your aunt sends her love," he told the girls.

Now that we had the older girls, Louie wanted Philip back. So he drove out to Long Island to make a deal with David. "Call the aunt," he offered, "and tell her you want your son back. You're his father so she's gotta give him to you. And then after that you don't have to pay any more support. Deal?"

Deal. It was a good one all around. We drove to the airport in the new car Louie had bought and paid for in cash. Whatever it was he was doing for Herbie, business kept getting better and better. We watched as Philip climbed off the plane and started walking toward us. He saw Louie first and started running toward him. Then he saw me and stopped. He stood motionless for one second, just staring at me, then he took off running in the opposite direction. I took off after him, screaming his name. Louie was behind me, then ahead of me.

Louie finally caught him, and Philip stopped and threw his arms around him and was crying hysterically. "Daddy, Daddy, I'm glad you're home. I missed you. I missed you."

I reached the two of them and started to touch Philip on the shoulder. He jumped away. "Don't let her near me, Dad, don't let her touch me." I could see he was really frightened. My aunt had done a good job on him.

"Don't say that, Philip," Louie told him firmly. "You don't mean that. That's your mother."

"That's not my mother," Philip cried, "she's a stupid drug addict."

I just stood there. There was nothing I could do. My son was paying me back. I knew I deserved every bit of his hatred.

Louie tried to help. "Listen to me, Philip. That's all over now. Mummy's fine and there aren't going to be no more drugs. We're gonna be a family again. Just you and me and Mummy and the girls."

Philip stared at him without saying anything. Hs tears just slid down his face onto the floor. Then he grabbed Louie around the neck as hard as he could and buried his head in Louie's shoulder. He wouldn't let go the entire ride to Elmhurst.

The studio apartment had filled up quickly, so we moved into a large one-bedroom in the same building. But that filled up just as quickly. Every day Louie would give me money and tell me what to get for the kids. Or he would take them all shopping. We ran out of closet space very quickly. Things were fantastic all over again. It was almost as if the last four years had never happened. Louie was back again.

The only people missing were Gay and Susan, and Louie wasn't about to let them stay in New Haven. Louie was putting *his* family back together again. My cousin was tougher than my aunt had been. "You're not taking them back to that junkie," he informed Louie. "The only way you'll ever get these kids back is through the courts."

Louie didn't care. "Get yourself a good lawyer," he warned him. Then he went out and hired an expensive lawyer to represent us. Papers were drawn up threatening my cousin that unless he returned the kids to us by a certain date, kidnapping charges would be filed against him. "You're gonna go to jail,"

Louie said easily when he called to inform him about the lawsuit.

My cousin had no choice. He had no legal right to the children. "You'll be sorry," he told Louie. "You'll see what the junkie's gonna do to them. You'll wish you let us keep them, see if you don't." Paige, Nancy and I flew up to bring them home. The six of us were finally together again. For good this time, I promised myself. Forever.

– I 2 –

I went from filthy streets to satin sheets in a month. The day Louie got out he took me shopping and bought me $200 worth of clothes, and that was only the beginning. He did his best to make up for four years of living in a cell in a few weeks, and we went on one continuous buying spree. We bought two of everything, except color televisions, and we bought three of those. Every afternoon he was coming home with boxes of clothes, underwear, stockings and socks, and jewelry. One night he came home with a box full of Ohrbach dresses, about 20 of them, all knits, all different colors, all for me. I didn't like them though, because they were the maxi length, so he told me to take them to the tailor and have them cut to the length I wanted. "But that'll cost a fortune, Louie," I told him.

"Whatta we care?" he asked. "We got all the money we need."

It didn't take him very long to outspend the space in our one-bedroom apartment, and he announced at dinner one night, "We're building a house."

I served him an extra portion of spaghetti. "A house?" I was thrilled. A few months earlier I'd passed out on the street and woke up naked in a strange man's apartment with a big German shepherd looking down at me. Now I was having my own house built. "Where are we building?"

"Out on Long Island," he told me, "near Herbie's place. It's gonna take awhile to get the place ready the way I want it, so I'm looking to rent a house meanwhile."

"Where's Herbie live exactly, Louie?"

"Bellmore. They call him the Baron of Bellmore. He's building this great place right on the canal they got out there. I'm looking for a place to build right near him. You're gonna love him, Ceil."

Herbie, Herbie, Herbie, that's all I was hearing from Louie. Herbie told him this, Herbie wanted that, Herbie gave him that, Herbie did this. For a man who'd been in prison at the same time with Louie, Herbie was doing okay. I was getting anxious to meet this Baron of Bellmore. I asked Louie when that was going to happen.

"When the time is right," he told me.

"When's that gonna be?" I wanted it to be soon. I was beginning to feel left out. I had fallen in love with Louie all over again and I was getting jealous because he wasn't spending too much time with me. I figured that once I met Herbie and his wife, we'd start socializing more. It would be just like in California with Herbie and his wife taking the place of Mark and Mikey.

But Louie wasn't ready. "When the time is right, Ceil. I don't know when that's gonna be. Soon, though."

The only times I saw Louie were in the morning and at night. In the morning he'd take a cab with me up to my methadone clinic, in the Bronx, and then spend a few hours at Billy D'Angelo's gas station while I was given my dose. He didn't want me going up there alone because he didn't trust me around junkies. Once I was standing and talking to the boy I'd gone out with while Louie was in jail, when I saw Louie's cab driving up. "Please go," I said to the kid, "that's my husband in the cab."

He was stoned, and he didn't care about my husband. When the cab stopped he leaned into the back seat and said to Louie in a slurred voice, "Listen, why can't I see your wife anymore? I wanna go out with her."

Louie just glared at him for a minute, then he pushed the door of the cab open and jumped out. He grabbed this kid by the throat and pushed him against the cab. "Listen. If I ever see you or any other drug addict near my wife, I'll blow their fucking heads off! You got it?"

The kid sort of nodded. Louie pushed him off to the side. "Get in the cab," he ordered me. On the drive home he laid it out quickly. "I don't want to see you near any of those people again, you understand? You get your methadone and you get home. You don't talk with them, you don't socialize with them, you don't do nuthin' with them." He didn't ask me if I understood, he knew I did.

When Louie wasn't with me he was doing whatever he was doing for Herbie and looking for a house. I was busy trying to reestablish some sort of relationship with the kids. They had changed in the 18 months. Paige and Nancy had become teen-agers; Philip was quieter, but somehow tougher, and the two little ones were more demanding.

Because I was afraid of what Louie might do if he saw me talking to any of my old friends, I quit the methadone clinic in the Bronx and joined a private program on 58th Street in Manhattan. I paid $59 a week and was given take-home doses, so I only had to go twice a week. The problem with the methadone was that until my body became really accustomed to it, I couldn't have orgasms, so I had no real sexual desire. Louie had never been a great lover, but he was a normal male. He liked sex and wanted sex. I wasn't enjoying it, so I didn't really want it. That did nothing to strengthen our relationship.

I could feel Louie growing away from me. We'd both waited so long to get back together, and built our hopes so high, and now we just didn't seem to be able to get along. Louie was sometimes edgy, he made me feel uncomfortable when I was with him. He started staying away from the apartment more than he ever did before prison. I knew I was losing him, and I didn't know how to get him back.

I started using my pills again, and a little coke when I could get some. Louie found out, but instead of screaming and making a big scene, he just packed his bags and said he was moving out. "I just can't take it anymore, Ceil," he said. "We're through." He left me a lot of money, but he left. I didn't hear from him for three days. Finally I decided to show him how much I loved him.

I found out what hotel he had checked into and went to see him. We talked for hours and I begged him to come home with me. "I'm gonna give you one last chance to come home with me," I threatened.

"I'm not coming, Ceil. It's over between us."

"Then I'm going to kill myself." He started laughing at me and kept laughing when I walked into the bathroom. Very easily, I opened up six one-hundred milligram bottles of methadone and swallowed down each one.

I could hear him laughing from the bed, "Go ahead, kill yourself, whatta I care?" When I walked out of the bathroom he said, "And how you gonna do it?"

I held my pocketbook upside down. The bottles fell onto the floor. "I just drank six hundred milligrams of methadone," I told him.

He stopped smiling and rushed me to the hospital. He stayed with me all night as they pumped my stomach and walked me around for hours. Then he told me how sorry he was, repacked his bags and came home. I promised him I was finished with drugs. We made a big effort to get close again, we both really tried. And we were making progress. He started looking for a house again.

It took him about a week to find the one he wanted. We rented a beautiful five-bedroom home in Bellmore, right across the canal from Herbie, for $430 a month. Louie furnished it just like he furnished our apartments in California. The builders were closing their model home, so Louie took a pocketful of cash and we went to see it. The model was furnished beautifully. We walked from room to room, looking at the furniture and telling this little guy with glasses, "We'll take everything in this room. How much?"

He sat down and started figuring. His tongue slipped out of his mouth and wiggled from side to side as he figured. He'd name the amount and Louie would just peel it off the bankroll. "Have it delivered," he'd say.

We bought so fast we couldn't even keep track of things we were purchasing. "We'll take that," Louie said about one long hall table.

The salesman looked down at his book and said, "Oh, I'm sorry, Mr. Mileto, but you've already bought that."

"Oh," Louie said. "Yeah, that's right. I forgot." We almost bought out the whole model. We bought three bedroom sets, the kitchen set, a few living and dining room pieces and even the model washing machine. As we were buying there was another couple behind us. And every time Louie would buy something, the man would say, "Oh, I wanted to buy that." Finally Louie got tired of hearing that, so he turned around and said, "Listen, you can't afford this stuff. Get outta here, you damn creep."

"You can't tell me——"

Louie took one step toward him. "Wanna bet." It was a real threat.

"Gentlemen, gentlemen, gentlemen," the salesman said, stepping in to break it up. "Let's not get excited, now, shall we?"

I just stood back and watched. I didn't say a word. But this was the first time since I'd known Louie that he'd been nasty to a complete stranger, and I'd never seen him threaten anyone with violence. Maybe prison had changed him a little more than I realized. That thought turned out to be wrong, it had changed him a *lot* more than I realized. But it would take me time to see the changes.

We couldn't move right away. With all the furniture to be moved in, and the house still to be repainted, we were told it would be almost another month. That seemed to bother Louie more than it did me. He was edgy and nervous, and that just wasn't Louie. He continually called the painters and builders, trying to rush them along. "How come you're in such a hurry, Louie?" I asked him.

He never answered me directly. "I need the space," he would say one day, and "I'm just ready to move" an another. It was obvious he had something on his mind, and it became more of a mystery one afternoon when he told me to take the kids and leave for a while. "Don't argue, okay? Just take the kids and go way for a while. I'm gonna have some people over and I don't want you here." He didn't look at me when he said it.

"What's this all about?" I wanted to know. "You never did this to me before. What kind of crap is that? Who do you think you are that you can just kick us out whenever you want to?" I decided I wasn't leaving.

He wasn't going to argue. "It's business. I got my reasons and I don't want you here." He handed me $100. "It's business, Ceil." I decided that maybe I would leave.

"All right, Louie," I finally said calmly. "We'll drive to the beach. The kid's like that."

He stopped me again. "You can't take the car," he said quietly.

I couldn't believe it. "What?"

"Take a cab. Don't go near the car. Okay? You understand? Just leave the car sit right where it is."

"Louie, what's this all about? I got a right to——"

He cut me off. He didn't want to hear about my rights. "Don't argue with me, just do what I tell you. This is business. This is what's paying for your new house. This is what's paying for that furniture. This is what's paying for that diamond ring you got on and the clothes the kids are wearing and the car and the dinners and the cab rides. You understand," he yelled, "business, Ceil, business." He was screeching when he finished.

"All right, Louie," I said calmly, "we'll leave." We piled into two cabs and took a $26-round-trip ride to Rockaway Beach for the rest of the day. And the next day. And the day after that. I kept trying to figure out what kind of business required Louie to have an empty apartment and an unused car sitting in a locked garage. But he didn't give me any hints and I was never too good at guessing games. Whatever it was, I knew it couldn't be legitimate.

He was making too much money for it to be legitimate. Nothing paid that well. Louie had only been out of prison six weeks and already he was earning more than he had ever made in his life. Every night he would sit down on the bed with Nancy, who was 14, and empty a big brown paper bag filled with cash out onto the spread. The bag was always filled with an enormous amount of singles and tens and twenties and hundreds, and he'd just dump them into a big pile right in the middle. "Okay kid," he'd tell Nancy, "put the singles face-up in this pile, the twenties in this pile and the fives here. We got to get this money counted." I'd be downstairs doing the dishes, the rest of the kids would be doing their homework and Louie and this 14-year-old kid would sit there counting and piling up twenty-five, thirty thousand dollars, every single night. When they finished, Nancy would neatly put the stacks of bills into shoe boxes and gift-wrap the boxes, complete with ribbons and bows. Louie would sit there there totaling the figures, then Nancy would check his addition and finally go off to do her own homework and "hit the sheets."

He didn't get to keep the money. After the counting was finished, he would call Herbie and make his nightly report. "I picked up twenty-five balloons," he would say. "Want me to bring it over now?" Or he'd ask, "How many shirts should I buy tomorrow?" They would use street talk that I didn't understand, but the message was clear. Louie was buying and collecting something for Herbie. Actually I didn't pay too much attention to their conversations because I wasn't that interested. I figured when Louie was ready to tell me what he was doing, he would tell me. He had to have his reasons for keeping it secret.

As it turned out, he had very good reasons. And he didn't have to tell me, I found out for myself. I accidentally stumbled onto evidence of his new job while I was packing up to move out of the once-beauitful Elmhurst Towers into our place in Bellmore. I found two unsealed, plain white envelopes tucked in with his underwear. I looked inside and my eyes just lit up. Both of them contained maybe two ounces of a white powdery substance. I wet the tip of my finger and gave it a little taste. A sometime dope addict like me didn't have any trouble recognizing pure cocaine. Pure, beautiful, happy-to-meet-you cocaine lying casually in Louie-who-hated-drugs' drawer. I knew he wasn't using, I'd have been able to recognize the effects on his body immediately. All of a sudden I realized that Louie had gone into the drug business.

I wasn't completely positive, a few ounces of coke didn't amount to very much proof. That came a few nights later. I was sitting alone in the apartment watching television when he called. "Listen," he started, "I'm down at the barbershop and I did a stupid thing and left some things I need home. I want you to go in the bottom of my closet and get my attaché case and bring it to me."

I didn't mind. It would give me something to do. "Where'd you leave the car keys?"

"No," he said quickly, "leave the car alone. Just go to the corner and grab a cab. And Ceil, be a little careful with the case. I've got some expensive equipment in there."

Now I was going to find out for sure. I dug the attaché case out of the closet and opened it. And I found a bag of milk sugar, a very large thermometer and some small cutting tools, equipment for cutting drugs.

Then I went down and searched the car. There was nothing inside, but when I looked in the trunk I found a bag full of money. I made a very rough estimate that there was $10,000 in cash there. The car was obviously a drop point for drug dealing. I stood in the garage and laughed out loud. Now, finally, I understood why he wouldn't tell me what he was doing. He didn't want his wife the addict to know he was in the drug trade.

I didn't know exactly what he was doing—buying, cutting,

dealing—and it didn't make an difference. He was still an incredible hypocrite. It was hard to believe, him criticizing me all the time, threatening to kill my friends who used if he ever saw them near the house, screaming about my drug use, refusing to see me while I was using, and he ends up making his living off people like me.

I decided not to confront Louie with the evidence. Instead I thought I'd just lie back and take full advantage of my discovery. So I just dropped the attaché case off at the barbershop and went back home.

From that night on I started tossing everything the moment Louie walked out of the house. I'd go through his drawers, his clothes, his closets, I looked under the mattress, behind the sofa, inside the television set, and finally searched the car. Usually I found something before I got to the television set. It was always cocaine, never heroin. And I'd never take enough that he would notice, usually just a few spoons. I had gotten myself a set of works again and I was shooting coke. It was nice and it was controllable. If I couldn't find it, I did without. Louie never realized I was shooting.

In fact, I wasn't even using all the coke myself. Paige and Nancy had started going out with two older boys from the neighborhood who were 19 and 17, and they confided in me that both boys were addicted to heroin. The girls hated drugs as much as I believed Louie had, and both were doing their best to help these boys break their habits. So, as my good deed as a mother, I shared the coke. The girls felt as long as the boys had coke to get high on, they wouldn't need heroin. They saw it as a slow remission. I was glad to help; besides, I started getting high with them.

Just before we moved out of the apartment I made the biggest score. Until then I'd be dipping into Louie's little leftovers, but one night I checked his clothes out while he was in the shower. And I found at least a kilo of coke wrapped up in his shirt. I stole about four full coke spoons (those are small spoons) and put it way for safekeeping. I decided to make half of it a going-away present to the boys.

I gave it to them the day we moved out of the apartment to Long Island. Paige and Nancy gave them keys to the empty apartment, so they would have a place to get high in. In fact, Louie had decided to keep paying the rent on the empty apartment, so he kept a set of keys, I kept a set of keys and the girls kept their keys. We all had plans for that apartment.

Unfortunately, some of our plans converged. The boys were getting high in the apartment on the coke I'd stolen from Louie when Louie walked in. Without saying a single word he beat up both boys and then threw them out the window. It wasn't a long drop—eight feet—but it was another indication that the new Louie could be vicious. He didn't scream at them or yell at them, he just beat into them.

I was safe, he had no idea where they got their coke. In fact, I probably could have gone on forever tasting and touching and stealing and Louie would have never known. But all that changed when I paid a visit to the apartment. I hadn't intended to go, but Louie made such a point of telling me not to go near the the place that I couldn't resist.

I gave the place a quick visual toss and found nothing. Then I began to dig a little deeper. I went through the cabinets, looked under the beds, picked up the mattresses and looked in the toilet bowl. I really gave the house a thorough going-over and I didn't find anything. I was going through a closet for the final time and I patted down one of Louie's old, torn suit bags. I felt a large bulge in the bottom of it. I smiled. I knew it wasn't dirty socks.

The bulge turned out to be a thick, clear plastic bag, about a foot long and eight inches wide. The whole bottom half was filled with a pale white, almost yellow, powder. It weighed easily over two pounds. I couldn't find any paper in the house so I tore some pages out of the phone book and put the bag on top of them. Then I took a bobby pin and tried to poke a hole in the bag. It wasn't easy, the plastic was thick and I couldn't push the bobby pin through. But I just kept pricking and poking until I managed to open a hole, then I sprinkled out a tiny amount onto the phone book pages.

I wet my finger and tasted it. I'd never tasted anything like it before.

I smelled it. No smell I could recognize.

I snorted it. Still nothing.

I was really disappointed. I thought I'd made a big discovery and it turns out to be some sort of cut, a diluent, that I wasn't familiar with. I put the plastic bag back into Louie's suit bag and locked the front door of the apartment on the way out. It had been a wasted visit.

"Were you in the apartment?" Louie asked me anxiously the next night.

"No," I lied.

"Ceil, this is really important. You gotta tell me if you were there. I'm gonna ask you again, were you?"

Since I hadn't discovered anything, I figured I might as well tell him the truth. "Yeah. I was there yesterday."

He started to get angry; "I thought I told you not to—" But then he stopped. He asked calmly, "Did you find the bag in my closet and poke a hole in it?"

I nodded. "What was in there anyway?"

"You don't know?" he asked almost unbelievingly. "You really don't know?"

"No, Louie, I don't know."

A big smile split his face. "Heroin, Ceil. Pure, uncut heroin."

It just hadn't occurred to me, with all my drug experience, that I'd never seen heroin in its raw state. I couldn't even estimate the street value of that plastic bag, but it had to be enormous. "Louie, that much heroin?"

"You're really lucky," he said in a nasty voice. "I ought to kick your ass for being so stupid. Suppose a drug bust had come down while you were in there?" He was swinging his arms around for emphasis. "Suppose some junkie had———"

Now it was my turn to interrupt him. "So you're in the drug business, Louie. You know that's really funny. Here you are hating junkies so much and you end up putting the stuff on the street that turns them into junkies. That's really very funny, you know."

We weren't even arguing, just discussing. "There's a lot of money in it, Ceil, quick money. I'm making it for all of us. We're gonna have everything that money can buy. And Ceil, that is everything."

Now that the subejct had finally come up, I wanted all the details. The car, as I suspected, was a pickup and delivery point. Different people had keys to the garage and they did their work in the privacy of a locked garage. Herbie ran the operation in partnership with a man named Benny Mallah. Louie cut the drugs for them, and for that he was being paid about $5000 a week, depending on how much work he did.

"Five thousand," I almost gasped. "That's incredible."

"That's nothing. You got no idea how much money there is in this business." Actually I had a lot of idea how much money there was in the business, although I was really surprised when he told me there had been $85,000 in the pickup bag I'd found in the trunk of the car.

"Eighty-five thousand," I said, not even believing what I was saying, "that's incredible!"

Louie took my hand and led me over to our bed. "Ceil," he said softly as we sat down next to each other, "this is the thing I've been looking for all my life. This is the jackpot. There's enough money to be made here so we can be happy for the rest of our lives. We can have everything you want and I want and the kids want. It's all here for the taking and I'm gonna take it, Ceil, I'm gonna grab ahold and take it. This is our chance. And there's nothing that can go wrong, Herbie's got the operation protected from one end to the other. Nothing."

"If you say so, Louie," I agreed softly. But I wasn't really concentrating on what he was telling me, I was thinking of the two pounds of heroin I held in my hands and let go. Two solid pounds of heroin. A lifetime.

Louie did seem to be right. Weeks passed and everything was better than perfect. We did have enough money for all of us to have our dreams come true, even if they did take different shapes. For Gay and Susan the money meant they could have all the shoes they wanted. They both loved shoes and every time Louie took them out they would drag him to a shoe store and he'd buy them whatever they wanted. Philip got his mini-bike back. Nancy got an expensive ring. Louie promised Paige a Corvette for her upcoming sixteenth birthday. And when the girls complained about having to do the dishes, he grabbed both of them by the hand, took them out and bought them a dishwasher. "No more complaints," he warned them. "This is your dishwasher. It's not your mother's, it's yours."

I had everything I wanted. I had my methadone, my bits and pieces of Louie's drugs he left lying around, all the money I could spend and my family. And, on July 4, 1971, I finally met the remarkable Herbie Sperling, his wife Josephine and his mother. They were living in a small apartment on Spring Street in Manhattan while their house in Bellmore was being built and we were going to meet them at the end of Spring Street to watch the fireworks.

Walking down Spring Street, on the way to meet the Sperlings, we bumped into Richie Maxton, who Louie later told me was a junk dealer for Herbie. I thought he was a little strange mainly because he had his hair cut really short while everybody in the country was wearing long hair, but Louie told me he had a beautiful girl friend, a redheaded model named Patsy Parks. I stood there for a minute listening while he talked to Louie about "this many balloons," or "getting that many shirts." Then Louie told me to walk away.

A little while later we met Herbie, Josephine and his mother. He didn't look anything like I'd imagined. From the way Louie talked about him, I expected Herbie to be tall, handsome and tough-looking. He wasn't. He had a nice face, but he was short and sort of dumpy. As I got to know him, I also realized he was one of the worst-dressed men I'd ever seen.

Herbie used to argue with Benny Mallah, who was supposedly his partner in the drug operation, about who was the better dresser. Benny would tell him that you were supposed to wear black socks with everything except white shoes, and with white shoes you didn't wear any socks at all. Herbie laughed at him because when he wore a green shirt he had on green socks, a green ring, a green watchband, everything green. One night I watched him walk out of his apartment wearing some terrible clothes. "Josephine," I asked, "how can you let him go out dressed like that?"

How she laughed! "If you think he looks bad now," she told me, "you should have seen him when he came home from prison with his pointy shoes and pegged pants!"

Their apartment on Spring Street was absolutely awful. Herbie and Josephine shared it with her mother and Josephine's two boys from her first marriage. I couldn't believe that with all the money Herbie was making they would stay there, even temporarily. It was small and dark and old. A railroad flat. It had a drop-down ceiling with plastic tiles, and I remember once we took down some tiles to try to clean them and the ceiling was filled with roaches. The place was beautifully furnished, but in the kitchen, over the refrigerator, they had a poster hanging that showed two prisoners in striped suits, wearing the small prisoner box hats, holding a birthday cake. "Fuck you, Warden," it read.

I liked Herbie right from the beginning, even though he was very bossy and enjoyed ordering Louie around. I loved Josephine and really got a kick out of Herbie's mother, who was even tougher than Herbie. Josephine was the same birth sign as me, Sagittarius, but she was much tougher than I was. While I listened to whatever Louie told me, she fought with Herbie over everything. She was just this little tiny woman, but she was a terrific yeller. She had a mouth on her that just didn't stop, and she could really dish it out. Herbie liked us spending time together because he thought I acted well and he wanted Josephine to pick up on it. "Ceil's got class," he'd tell her right in front of me, "you don't hear her arguing all the time. You don't hear her talking language like you use. Maybe some of her good habits should rub off on you!"

Of course, neither of them knew about my bad habits like pot, cocaine, methadone and heroin. I had a liver problem, we told them.

Louie and I started spending part of almost every day with

Herbie and Josephine. Every morning he would get up and drive into Manhattan to see Herbie and do his work. Sometimes I went with him, and then I'd spend the day with Josephine. If I didn't go in during the day, I'd usually go in at night. And whenever I wasn't with her, we were on the telephone. "What are you doing?" "What are the kids doing?" "Where are the boys?" Woman-talk.

When I went into Spring Street, I'd stop at this dirty little delicatessen across the street and either bring up some Italian heroes, filled with eggs and onions, or cannolis. We used to go through a dozen cannolis a day.

Josephine and I did the things that most wives, including gangsters' wives, do. We shopped and ate and talked about our children. We did most of our clothes shopping at an expensive store on 47th Street that had Herbie listed on the books as a salesman. That was his legitimate front. A lot of dope deals went on in that place too. I'd hear Louie talking to Herbie about how many dozen shirts he wanted. "Gimme twelve dozen shirts," he'd say, which I knew was dope. I didn't know how much it meant, but I knew they weren't talking about shirts.

I was really getting an education about the drug world. To me drugs were small bags and street-corner pushers, I never realized how many people and how much money was involved. Josephine and I would sit in the living room on Spring Street and a few feet away in the kitchen Herbie and Louie and Benny Mallah and Richie Maxton would be pouring out paper bags just overflowing with cash. Herbie'd be laughing, "We should get a haul like this every day," and the table would be completely covered with green bills of every denomination.

Josephine and I would pretend to be holding our own conversation, but we were really listening to what was going on inside. I know she was proud that her husband had put together an operation like this. I just kept wondering how much of it was Louie's.

There was so much money. "Here's seventy-five thousand," I heard Herbie tell Benny. "Is that enough or you need more?"

"Here's my collection for the day," Richie would tell them as he was emptying his bag on the table. "It's twenty-five."

Most of the people we saw during that time were drug people, people like Johnny "Hooks" Capra and Georgie Farber and a guy I only knew as Bozo and Alvin Gibbon. I never knew they were big-timers, I thought they were one step higher than my street-corner friends.

That Alvin Gibbons was something. Louie and I were driving along one afternoon in Manhattan and Louie starts blowing his horn at this sports car. I saw there was a Negro in it and I said to myself, why doesn't he leave the poor guy alone. Louie hated blacks, from prison. He thought they were animals. One thing he never, ever forgot was the time he was taken by a black man. He was standing outside the Barbury Barbershop where they all hung out when this black guy offered to sell him a supposedly hot diamond ring. Louie told the guy to wait and took it to a jeweler who told him it was genuine. Then he made a bargain with the guy, believing he was cheating him out of a good price.

The black stiffed Louie. Somehow he substituted a fake diamond for the original. When Louie had it appraised, the jeweler told him it was glass. Louie put it on his finger and never took it off. I couldn't understand why he was wearing a glass ring.

He told me. "If that guy ever comes back, he'll see I got the ring on and figure I never found out it was glass. He'll come close enough so I can kill him." I believe he probably would have too, but the black never came back.

Louie opened the window of the car, I figured he was going to yell at the black in the sports car.

He did. "Hey!" he hollered, "I was just going to meet you." I couldn't believe Louie was talking friendly with a colored man. "He's a different kind of nigger," Louie told me.

We followed him down to the diamond district and we all got out of the cars. Alvin was really outstanding-looking. He was enormous, and he had this shaved, shiny head and was wearing these beautiful clothes. He wasn't good-looking, but he was outstanding. Louie introduced him to me and then walked away. I was looking in the window of a jewelry store and Alvin said to me, "Pick one out, go ahead, we'll get you whatever you want." I was going to do it, too, but Louie came back and told me to sit in the car and wait. The two of them went upstairs over the jewelry shop. Louie told me Alvin was a very big customer of Herbie's from Jersey.

I met some of Louie's best customers too. He'd take me along on his drops and I'd sit in the car and watch. He was selling to one of the most famous football players in New York and we'd go by his apartment on the Upper East Side. He had a well-known comedian, he had the father of a famous girl singer, he had a UN ambassador.

I thought the whole operation was run by a French general, a man Louie kept calling the French connection. I didn't know who he was, all I knew was that Herbie called him in France a lot. We'd all pile into this little cigar store across the street from the Barbury Barbershop, and Herbie would make his overseas telephone call. He called from there, Louie told me, because he didn't want the phone number showing up on any bill, he didn't want anybody tracing that call. The whole thing became a big joke. Every time we went with Herbie, he'd stop the car and Louie would say, "He's gotta go call the general."

When Louie was in jail I'd learned about the street part of the drug business. Now I was seeing the real moneymakers in action.

Herbie and Josephine eventually became as close to us as Mark and Mikey had once been. We always seemed to be with them. Josephine and Louie were best friends. They talked more than Herbie and Louie talked, they even used to bet the horses together. And Herbie loved Louie and trusted him. I'm sure he liked me too, but we were never as close as Louie and Josephine. I always thought he was a little cold, a little too businesslike. When he called the house, he'd call me sweetheart and ask how I was, but I always knew he was just being polite. But I trusted him. I felt that if anything happened to Louie, like jail, I would be taken care of just like Louie was there, because Herbie would do right by me. I used to sit and listen when wives and girl friends of people he knew in prison called him for favors. He always helped them out. "C'mon over," he'd tell them. "I'll give ya a couplea hunded."

Josephine and I were the closest. In fact, the only time she ever got really mad at Louie was over me. In the winter of 1971 Herbie's stepson had his communion and Herbie threw a big party at a hotel in Manhattan. Everybody was invited, everybody. But Louie and I had a big fight, over drugs probably, and he told me he didn't want me to go. If he didn't want me to go, I wasn't going. I didn't argue with Louie.

But Josephine felt differently. "Screw him," she said and she told me to get dressed, and get the kids dressed, and come to the party. I told her I didn't even have the money to get there. "Take a cab," she told me. "I'll pay for it."

So we did. It was one of the few times I'd really crossed Louie, and I let Josephine talk me into doing it. He was furious when I walked into the ballroom. He was standing up at the bar drinking his Coke. Sonny Gold was there with his wife. Richie Maxton was there with his wife and kids. Jimmy Jones, Herbie's brother-in-law, was there with his wife and kids. Louie just tried to ignore me completely. I walked over to him. "Can we talk about it at least?"

He just stared at me. I think he was so angry he could hardly talk. Finally he said, "Whattya think you're doin' here? I'm the boss and I told you not to come. What makes you think you're a boss? You're not a boss. The only thing you're the boss of is the *bockows.*" The Italian slangword for bathroom. Then he walked away and ignored me for the rest of the night.

We had a huge fight about it at home. "I don't care what Josephine told you," he screamed at me, "I told you not to go." He smashed his foot down on top of mine. I thought he broke my toes. I couldn't understand why he was so angry, so upset. I was really beginning to see the second Louie, the Louie from prison, changed, tough Louie.

Josephine helped smooth everything over. She yelled at Louie and he listened to her. She talked to me. He got over it pretty quick.

Our kids were just as close friends as we were. Gay had decided that she was going to marry Josephine's 11-year-old "because he has money in the bank." Sure he had money in the bank, Herbie gave him a thousand dollars for his 11th birthday. Philip was best friends with their eldest son. They played football and hockey together and they bet together, just like their fathers. Herbie's son always won. Philip got so fed up he told me, "I'm not gonna bet against him anymore. I'm just gonna go with him and bet against my other friends." Philip used to sleep over at their house, even when they were on Spring Street, although I have no idea where they put him.

Josephine and I did everything together, including getting pregnant. I had secretly planned my pregnancy because I decided it was time for Louie and I to have a child of our own. We were both 30, we had a house, money and the time was right, meaning I was off drugs. My methadone clinic took a urine sample and told me I was pregnant. I told Josephine and Herbie, but not Louie. I knew he would be afraid the methadone was going to affect the baby and want me to have an abortion, so I decided to try and hide it until I was too far gone for one.

I managed to hide it for almost five months. But when Josephine told Herbie she was pregnant, I realized the time had come to tell Louie. We were sitting in the living room one night and he was telling me how happy Herbie was that he was going to have another child. So I told him that he was going to be a father again too.

He was furious. He started screaming and yelling and stomping all over the room. He was positive I was going to give birth to a freak because I was an addict and still using methadone. "I'm not gonna have no addicts for kids," he screeched at me. The next day he dragged me, crying, to a gynecologist who did abortions and had me examined.

The doctor was a nice old man who didn't seem to know too much about modern medicine. "She's pregnant," he said, "but I have to wait a few more weeks before I can do the plumbing." He said it just wasn't a safe time, so he gave me a date for the abortion. "I'm going to give a saline injection because you're too pregnant for anything else," he added.

"I'm on methadone maintenance," I told him. "Is that gonna be a problem?"

"I don't see why it should," he replied. He didn't see why it should because he didn't know anything about methadone, "Just keep taking this methadone and bring it with you to the hospital. The nurse will take care of it for you," he said kindly.

I hated the idea of killing my baby, but Louie was so opposed to it that I knew he could never accept it as his own. I decided to go ahead with the operation.

That was the only black spot in an otherwise wonderful time. Just as Louie guaranteed, Herbie seemed to have everything under control, it didn't seem like anything could go wrong.

And then everything went wrong.

— 13 —

One night in the winter of 1971, Louie and Herbie and Richie Maxton were driving through the Bowery in lower Manhattan, on the way to Herbie's apartment on Spring Street. They got stopped by a red light near Houston Street and immediately three unshaven, filthy bums surrounded Herbie's brand-new Cadillac Fleetwood and started wiping the windshields with their rags. The drunks down in that area do this all the time, hoping that the driver will give them some change. These bums picked the wrong guys in Herbie, Louie and Richie. "Get the fuck outta here," Louie started screaming. "Take a walk. Go wash somebody else's windows, ya fleabag!"

When the light changed, one of the bums was still sprawled across the hood of the car. Louie started screaming at him even louder. Herbie started to accelerate.

The bum made a quick reach into his pocket and pulled out a New York City Police Department badge. He flashed it at them through the windshield. "Police officer," he yelled. "Don't move this car."

The second bum, on the right side of the car, pulled out a pistol. "Keep your hands where they are," he ordered. "This is a bust."

The place just exploded with lights and action. The whole block was sealed off. Out of nowhere men started running toward the car. Police cars came screeching in from side streets. Sirens whined, radios blared. Louie and Herbie and Richie just sat in the car and watched. None of them moved. "If I wasn't so pissed off I would've enjoyed it," Louie told me later. "Those guys were really excited."

The three of them finally got out of the car and produced identification. As the cops started searching the car for drugs, Louie took one officer aside. "Listen," he said in his most charming voice, "I gotta call my wife right away. She's expecting any minute."

The officer tried to stare him into admitting it was a lie. Louie didn't even flinch. "Okay," the cop nodded, "go give her a call."

As usual, I was sitting alone watching television. The three younger kids were upstairs asleep. Paige and Nancy were out somewhere with their boyfriends. In fact, I was waiting for Louie to call, but not for the message he gave me. "The police have me and I'm on Houston Street near the Bowery. Come down here with the kids right away."

"Louie, I don't——"

"Get Billy to drive you down. Call Josephine and tell her she'd better clean house because she's gonna have company soon. Do it all right now." He hung up.

I didn't even have time to start worrying. I made the phone call. "Herbie's been picked up," I said. "Clean house."

They hadn't been married long enough and she didn't have the slightest idea what I was talking about. "If Herbie's been arrested," she asked me, "what difference does it make how clean the house is?" I could hear by her voice she was starting to get excited. That wouldn't help anybody.

I tried to calm her down. "Listen. Listen to me carefully.

Don't get upset, this kind of thing happens all the time," I lied. "It's probably all a big mistake. Herbie's too smart to get caught with anything. They'll have to let him go soon."

"That's right," she agreed in a much calmer voice, "Herbie is too smart for them."

"Right. But just in case, he wants you to take everything he can be arrested for, guns and bullets and dope, and get them out of the house. You have to do that right now. Pack it all in a suitcase and get the suitcase out of the house. I'll come over to help you when I can get some time, but start doing it right now."

As soon as I hung up on her I called Billy D'Angelo. By the time I had the kids up and dressed, he was out in front ready to drive us into Manhattan. I couldn't believe this was happening. Everything's gone again, I thought, he's going back to prison and I'll go back to the streets. I'm gonna lose the kids, the house, everything. I was so frightened. I figured we would have to go through the courts again, the trials, the visiting days in prison, the welfare. Everything was destroyed.

We got there even before the police finished searching the Cadillac. The three of them were standing on the side like this was the funniest thing that ever happened to them. It was a big joke. But it wasn't so funny to me or the kids. The kids came charging down the street crying and they all grabbed him and tried to hold him. They screaming and yelling and kissing him. I came running right behind the kids.

It was obvious from my figure that I wasn't about to have my baby. The cop took one look at me and said angrily, "I thought you told me your wife was expecting any minute!"

"Yeah, she was," Louie told him. "She was expecting my phone call any minute." The cop just glared at him, but there was nothing he could say. Louie took me aside and filled me in on what was happening. The cops had moved in too quickly, there were no drugs in the car. But there was a gun hidden under a seat, and that was a violation of parole. Both Louie and Herbie were also open for a "consorting with a known criminal" charge—Louie for being with Herbie and Herbie for being with

Louie. As we stood there talking the cops finally discovered the pistol underneath the front seat.

"Who owns this?" one of the detectives asked.

Nobody said anything. Then Louie made a guess. "The Cadillac company?" he asked.

The three of them were arrested and charged with possession of a concealed weapon. I took off and went up to Herbie's apartment to make sure Josephine had cleaned up. As I walked in she was busy taking the "Fuck you, Warden" poster off the wall.

The police showed up a little while later and made a complete search of the apartment. They didn't find anything. Herbie, Louie and Richie were down at the court building to spend the night. One of them paid off the cops though, and instead of spending the night in a cell, they sat on a bench in the park across the street from the courthouse. The next morning they all made bail easily.

As soon as they were released, we ran right up to Louie's lawyers to make up some story about why they were all together. Louie finally figured one out. It was the silliest story I'd ever heard. Josephine and I were supposed to be cousins and we'd talked our husbands into having a big family dinner. "Louie," I said, "nobody's gonna believe that stupid story." He smiled.

His probation officer believed it. We put on a real good show for him. I had become a pretty good faker and, with tears in my eyes, I told the P.O. how Louie had gone straight since prison. "Please don't send him back to jail," I begged. "He's been working. He can't stand it back there. I swear, he didn't know the gun was in the car." Then I let the kids loose on him. They were as scared as I was that Louie would have to go back to jail and they really cried. He was finally released. After the show I put on I'm surprised he wasn't given a good conduct medal too.

Herbie wasn't so lucky. He took the fall for the gun and had to go back to prison. Everything had happened so fast I didn't have time to really think about things. All that mattered to me was protecting my Louie, keeping him on the streets and out of prison. I really wasn't overly concerned about Herbie. If he had to go, he would go, and Louie and I could survive very well without him.

I didn't take the whole thing all that seriously, I figured it was just for a few months. Herbie didn't seem to be treating it so seriously, either. The day he went in we all went over to Barbury's Barbershop and he got his hair cut and his last manicure. He tipped everybody $50. Then we went back to Spring Street and he started dressing. Herbie had so many clothes. If he liked a shirt, he bought it in every possible color. He had pants, shoes, a whole wardrobe. As he was getting dressed he kept cracking jokes like "This isn't a life sentence you know, besides I needed a vacation"—stuff like that.

It never occurred to me that without Herbie there was no drug operation, and with no drug operation Louie had no income. In one week Louie's income went from $5000 per week to nothing. Zero. We found out very quickly that there are no unemployment benefits in the drug business.

He was really caught in the middle. He knew that as soon as Herbie got out of prison the money would start flowing again, and he didn't want to risk his place in the big-money operation by getting caught on a two-bit job. But he had absolutely no income, and the bills kept coming due, and the kids still wanted things, and Herbie expected Louie to take care of attorney's fees and his wife and his mother.

The changes I had begun to see in Louie became more radical. He was always nervous, always worrying about something he would have totally ignored previously. He started doing things I just couldn't understand. He came home one night, took off all his clothes and threw them on the bed. "Burn everything," he told me.

He was just starting to get a wardrobe back together again, and he didn't wear anything but $70 shoes, custom-made slacks and shirts and finely tailored jackets. "What am I burning everything for?" I wanted to know.

"Just mind your own business and put everything in the incinerator." I burned up his socks, shoes, underwear, pants, shirt, belt and jacket. He never told me why we had to burn the stuff, and I never found out.

He was also starting to lose his temper at the slightest provocation.

One day, we were driving across the 59th Street Bridge when another driver accidentally cut him off. Louie just went nuts. He caught up to the guy and cut him off and stopped him right on the bridge. Then he grabbed the baseball bat he'd started keeping in the back of the car and leaped out. He dragged the other driver out of his car and smacked him across the legs with his bat. Then he got back in our car and we drove away without a word.

For the first time since I'd left David for him, I was scared of Louie. He'd spend half his day sitting in Herbie's mother's apartment in Manhattan, waiting for Herbie to call from West Street with instructions, and the other half day stomping around our house. "I'm gonna do something soon, Ceil," he kept threatening, "I gotta do it soon."

"Louie, don't start stealing now," I told him. I knew a good thing when I saw it. Not only was he making money with Herbie, he was also getting good drugs. "Just hang in there until Herbie gets out. We'll make it somehow." I wanted to do something besides talk to help calm him down, but I couldn't figure out what to do. I was very calm, I had my methadone and my pills, they relaxed me. Louie had nothing.

Finally I came up with a plan. I decided to share my methadone with him, without his knowledge. I'd done this once before, when I felt he was going out at night too much and I wanted him to stay home, but I stopped after a few days. This time I decided to keep it up for a while. Each morning I dropped a cap or half a cap of my take-home methadone into his breakfast prune juice. At first it made him sick. "Throw that juice out," he'd scream at me, "it's rotten." But after a while he got used to it. The methadone got into his system and he calmed down and relaxed. He even stayed home more.

It took me three weeks to make a methadone addict out of him. At night he would start nodding out and scratching, and I realized he'd picked up a little chippy and I'd better cut him off. He went through withdrawal without even realizing it. His legs hurt, his back ached and he couldn't sleep. Maybe it's from the dust from the cutting, he thought. He even went to a doctor who examined him and found nothing wrong. Thank God, he didn't take a urine sample. The doctor prescribed Darvon and the pains gradually went away. Louie never knew he had been addicted.

After five weeks of legal maneuvering, Herbie was still behind bars and Louie was almost broke. Louie had no choice but to find some work, and he lucked into the perfect job. A friend of his had been tipped off by a contact on the New York City police force that two Cuban smugglers were sailing into town and they were carrying two kilos of cocaine with them. Louie and his friend decided to pull the same junkie trick that I'd worked successfully: They were going to meet the boat and pretend to be New York City cops.

It sounded like a perfect setup. The Cubans were independent, meaning no organized crime family was going to be protecting them. And since drug smuggling is considered a crime, they could hardly complain to the police that they had been ripped off.

Louie and his friend put on their shoulder holsters and carried official New York City Police Department identification, rented for the occasion, when they went to meet the boat.

The Cubans fell for the whole act. Louie laughed his head off when he described how the Cubans begged him not to arrest them. "'C'mon man, geeve us break. You keep the coke. Okay?'" Louie loved his imitation.

"'Nah. I don't think so. Let's lock these bums up.'"

"'We geeve you coke and money. Lotta money.'"

"'There isn't enough money in the world.'"

"'We geeve you five tousand bucks.'"

Dead silence. Louie gave his "partner" a "meaningful" glance. "'That's almost all the money in the world,'" he said. "'Whattya think?'"

His partner nodded. "'All right, let's give these panchos a break.'"

The Cubans relaxed. They agreed to hand over the coke on the spot and show up at the same place the following Sunday with $5000 cash.

Neither Louie nor his partner bothered to show up Sunday. The Cubans were probably home in Havana by then anyway.

Louie didn't want me to know he had the coke. When he thought I was busy upstairs, he went down into the basement and hid it in the crisper. Lucky for me and my habit, I happened to be doing a wash when he snuck down and quietly put it out of sight. He didn't see me, but I watched him as he carefully hid the package between two packs of frozen vegetables.

The minute he walked out of the house I hit the crisper. I knew I had to be very careful because Louie was always trying to out-clever everybody. He would wrap a package a specific way, tape it shut a specific way and set it down a specific way. If he folded the wrapper four times right over left, it had better have been refolded four times right over left or he would know somebody had gotten into it.

I unwrapped this package as carefully as I could and checked it out. As soon as I realized that I was holding a couple of pounds of pure cocaine I gave it a taste. Then another taste. Then I scooped out a whopping teaspoonful, carefully refolded the package, carefully put it back, then I ran upstairs and locked myself into my bathroom. It was incredibly wonderful stuff. I shot it every day for two weeks. I got abscesses from it, but I didn't care. It just ate the methadone away and sent me flying. I was still pregnant, but instead of picking up a belly, I just kept getting skinnier and skinnier. I was actually losing weight!

That package of coke got me back into my drugs. I had the coke, my methadone, and sleeping pills and nerve pills my program doctor had given me. I was feeling wonderful again. I stopped worrying about Herbie, about Louie going back to prison, about paying the rent, and most of all I stopped thinking about the baby I was carrying.

I didn't even care if Louie found out I was using again. If I was going to have his abortion, then I was entitled to use his drugs.

He hadn't mentioned the abortion in a few days, he'd been too busy, but he finally decided that with Herbie in jail and the whole drug operation suspended, this was a good time for it.

He checked with the doctor and made reservations at the hospital. I hated the idea, I wanted to have his baby, but he didn't even want to talk about it. He simply wasn't going to have any drug-freak children. "Next year, when you're off drugs and our new place is built," he promised, "then we'll have another kid."

Every time I started talking about maybe waiting a few more weeks, he changed the subject to the house he was planning to build. "I'm telling you, Ceil, it's gonna make Herbie's place look like the servants' quarters. It's gonna be a palace."

Abortions had just become legal in New York State and the price was $450. Louie paid in advance, in cash. Because I was more than 20 weeks gone the doctor decided the safest method was a saline injection. That's a relatively simple operation in which the doctor injects a saline solution right into the uterus, causing the water sac to break, the mother to go into labor and the fetus to be pushed out of the body before it's ready to be born. It's simple, but painful.

I checked into the hospital two days before the abortion was scheduled. Louie would be in and out three times a day, never staying more than five minutes. "Where ya going, Louie?" I'd ask him.

"I'm going," he'd tell me.

My mother, who stayed at our place to take care of the kids, told me he never came home. I was really jealous, I was laying up in the hospital and he was out running. "Where you been, Louie?" I'd ask.

"I been," he'd shrug.

The worst moment came right after the actual operation when I woke up and he wasn't even there. The operation had been frightening, the doctor stuck this enormous needle right into my stomach. I started screaming, I wanted him to stop.

"It's too late," the doctor said easily, "it's done."

Now I had to wait for the labor pains to start, but the sac hadn't broken. I wanted Louie to be with me. If he wasn't coming to the hospital, I would go home to him. So even before I went into labor I checked myself out of the hospital, against medical orders, and took a cab home.

Louie was there, but he said he was on his way into Manhattan to do some kind of work. I begged him not to go, to stay with me, but he told me he couldn't. "I'd like to, Ceil, but this is business. I gotta pay the rent somehow." He just walked out on me.

We had a second car at that time, an old Ford that had been hand-painted black, that Louie used to make drug drops and deliveries. I grabbed the keys to that car and Paige came with me and I followed Louie. I knew he was taking the Long Island Railroad into the city and I drove like a mad lady to the station. The train was just pulling out as I got there.

I decided to chase the train. I'm speeding down Sunrise Highway, trying to watch the road and drive at the same time, and screaming at Paige to "Watch, watch the train. Look for Louie." She spotted him sitting by the window, reading his usual newspaper. I started honking the horn, I just laid on it, but he didn't seem to hear me. He just didn't pay any attention.

Halfway into Manhattan I felt a gush of water. The sac had broken, I was going into labor. I didn't panic, I just told Paige what had happened. Then I turned the car around and drove back to the hospital as quickly as I could. By the time I got there I was having terrible pains. The baby was being born.

They rushed me right into the delivery room. They couldn't give me any sedative because they weren't sure how it would react with methadone. The pain was just ripping me apart. The doctor had his whole arm up inside of me, trying to ease the fetus out. Finally, after what seemed like hours, I heard him say, "Okay, I got it." He slowly took his arm out: "Here's the fetus."

But the pains continued. I couldn't help screaming. The doctor was trying to figure out what was wrong. He did. "Wait a minute, there's another one in there." And we went through the whole thing again. I was pregnant with twins.

Even after the second fetus was out, there were problems. The afterbirth had been pushed up too far and they couldn't reach it. Eventually, after a lot more pain, they got it out. I passed out.

Louie was sitting in the room when I woke up. "I'm sorry," he said and I knew he really meant it. "I'm so goddamn sorry. I shouldn't have made you go through that. Especially since we had twins. Ceil, I'm sorry." I was really heartbroken.

I checked out of the hospital the next day. Louie had a surprise waiting for me, he had bought a brand-new radar range. My mother cursed him, "You put her through all this, and then you buy her a damn oven."

"Things are gonna be better from now on, Ceil," he swore. "As soon as Herbie's out of jail you and I are gonna go away by ourselves. I'm gonna make this up to you." And, for a little while, he really tried.

For a few short weeks everything was wonderful. Then he discovered I was using drugs again.

He came home from Herbie's apartment one night and found me passed out on the floor, totally stoned out on barbiturates. He went crazy like I'd never seen him before. He started slapping me and throwing me around the room. "You pig," he kept screaming like a madman, "You goddamn no-good pig. I'm not gonna let ya do this to those kids again."

Slap!

"I'm not gonna make them go through this again."

Slap!

"I'll beat you so bad you won't be able to pick up those fuckin' things."

Slap!

I tried to lift my arms for protection, but I was so tired, so weak . . .

Slap!

"If I ever see you like this again, I'm gonna be gone so quick . . . You'll be out in the streets . . . Wish that you'd never met me . . . bitch . . ." I kept hearing bits and pieces of his threats. My face and body were burning. The pain was so distant, so not really a part of me.

Slap! Then a rip.

He grabbed my blouse and ripped it off. Then my pants. He was crazy. He just ripped my bra and panties off my body. He grabbed my hands and pushed them into a set of handcuffs. "I'll show you. I'll show you." Always yelling, one continuous scream. "I want you to see what you look like. I want you to see the spit comin' outta ya mouth." He shoved and pushed me into our big walk-in closet, then he threw me down on the floor.

I lay there completely naked. He took Polaroid pictures of me.

Still screaming. Grabbing, punching, slapping. He picked me up and dragged me over to the bed. I was half-sitting, half-lying across the bottom, nodding and slobbering, dribbling onto the bedspread and the floor. "I'll show you. You wanna see, you're gonna see."

I finally passed out again.

Louie was still there when I woke up the next day. He was physically calmer but still just as angry. "Lemme tell you, Ceil, lemme tell ya good," he warned in a reasonable voice. "There's no way you're gonna put these kids through that again. If you wanna keep using, you go ahead. But the next time I find you like I did last night we're through. And I'm gonna take the kids with me."

I just didn't understand Louie anymore. But he never made threats he wasn't serious about, so I had to cut back on my drug use. I stopped using the pills, they were too easy to detect. But my reaction to my methadone and the coke were very similar, so I kept using both. Louie never found out.

The thing that absolutely petrified him was that the kids would pick up my drug habit. So he started cracking down on them. He wanted to know where they were at every minute, what they were doing, who they were with. He told Paige and Nancy when he wanted them home at night, and if they weren't home by then he went looking for them. When he said eleven o'clock, he meant exactly eleven o'clock. A few times he found them with their boyfriends and he smacked the two of them across their legs with his baseball bat. He was getting to be quite a slugger with that bat. He warned them that if he ever caught them using drugs with their boyfriends, he'd kill their boyfriends. "And I'm gonna find out," he warned them. "You know I'll find out."

To make absolutely sure he would find out, he put a tap on our telephones. I didn't know it was a tap, I just knew he had some equipment set up in one part of the basement and I wasn't allowed to go near it. I tried to find out what he was doing, I'd go sneaking around outside, peeping through the heavy curtains he hung on the basement windows, but I couldn't see in. All I could hear from the other side of the basement, where the washing machine was located, was buzzes and clicks every time the phones rang. But I never realized it was a tap.

The children never stopped loving him. They might have disagreed with him, and been angry with him, but they always loved him. He always had time for them. He was always teasing them. When one of the little ones was writing Herbie in jail, for example, he told her to "Ask your Uncle Herbie if he needs any more white socks."

"What does it mean, Daddy?"

He smiled. It was a reference to the sex life of a male prisoner. "Ask your mother," he finally laughed.

My drugs were helping me get along better with the older girls, too. They liked me because I was still willing to risk sharing what I had with their boyfriends. I tried to be careful though, to make sure that they never got involved. I never wanted them to use hard drugs and had no doubt that Louie would beat me bad if the girls got into anything harder than pot.

The Cuban coke deal took some of the pressure off Louie. But even that got messed up. Louie had cut the coke himself into salable street chunks. Then he took one kilo and drove into the city to make a delivery.

He drove right into a trap. Two New York City detectives were waiting for him when he came out of the Midtown Tunnel. Somebody, he never found out exactly who it was, had set him up. The detectives pulled him over and arrested him for possession of a dangerous drug with intent to sell. Then they offered him a deal. They wanted money.

Louie called me at home. In a very even voice he told me to go into his shoe and take $7000 and bring it to Second Avenue and 32nd Street. "Don't ask me why," he said. "Just do like I tell you."

There was about $18,000 in the shoe. Paige was lying on the bed, reading, while I counted out $7000. She couldn't believe it. "Daddy's got all that money in his shoe?" she asked.

"Yeah. Well, you never know where your father has his

money." But before I left I swallowed eight three-gram Tuinals, to relax me. That was more than enough to relax me, it was enough to knock me unconscious.

"Ma, you'll never make it to Manhattan with all that dope in you," Paige said. "I'll go with you."

I didn't want that. I didn't want her to know that Louie had been arrested. "No, I'm fine, honey," I lied. "I'll make it." The pills started to affect me halfway to Manhattan. I was in a complete daze, I don't remember driving, although I do remember having to back up on the parkway because I missed the exit. Somehow I got to Manhattan, but I couldn't remember where Louie had told me to meet him. And I was so stoned out I was afraid to drive. So I parked the car and took a taxi. "Just drive around Second Avenue," I told him. "I'll tell you when to stop."

Somehow, out of the blur, I saw Louie and the two detectives. I told the cab to stop and tried to step out, but my legs wouldn't support my body. I collapsed onto the street and started crawling toward them. They seemed so far away, but I just kept crawling. I knew I had to get that money to Louie. He needed me, he really needed me, and I couldn't let him down. Finally he was near me. "Hi, Louie," I smiled. "I brought the money for you." I tried to lift up my pocketbook to show him, but it was too heavy. Then I passed out on the sidewalk.

I came to with Louie slapping my face. "Ceil, Ceil, where's the rest of the money? There's only five thousand dollars here."

I was zonked out of my mind. "It's there, Louie, I counted it out."

He slapped me again, trying to keep me awake. "It ain't here, Ceil, what'd you do with it?" He was starting to get really hard with me.

I didn't have the slightest idea where the extra $2000 was. I remember counting it out, I remember putting it in my pocketbook, but I never figured out what happened to it. The only guess I could make is that either the cabdriver realized I was stoned and ripped me off or I was so groggy that I paid him with thousand dollar bills instead of singles. "I don't know, Louie," I said, "I just don't know."

He was as furious as I'd ever seen him. The one time he really needed me and I'd messed up. The detectives agreed to accept the $5000 as a down payment against $20,000 more to be paid the following Sunday. But that didn't satisfy Louie, he was almost insane with anger. "Where's the car?" he screamed.

"I think . . . I don't . . . I lost it," I said.

He slapped me hard in the face. Instead of going home he took me to a hotel and he slapped me for two days. Every time I'd nod out, smack!—he'd slap me again. He wouldn't let me go to sleep. He never slept himself. During the day we'd walk the streets searching for the car—we never found it—and at night he'd scream at me about using drugs and slap me around. I don't really think he was punishing me, I think he was trying to slap some sense into me.

I was so drugged up most of the time I didn't feel any pain. But when I straightened out three days later I was all puffed up and swollen. Louie hardly spoke to me for days. He just couldn't understand why I needed my drugs so much.

The sale of the second kilo of Cuban coke didn't go much better. Louie gave it to a connection to put on the street. Unfortunately, the connection's wife was home alone in her apartment when two strangers knocked on her door. She knew what happened to the first kilo and figured the strangers had to be coppers. She took the kilo and flushed it down the toilet.

The men simply turned out to be on the wrong floor.

Louie was so crazy, he was going to kill the connection and his wife when he found out. Finally he agreed to accept a payoff: The connection gave Louie a brand new Thunderbird and about $10,000 in cash. The total wasn't as much as Louie would have made if the coke had hit the streets, but it was an improvement over the first kilo.

It never occurred to me to ask Louie why we were having money problems when he had $18,000 hidden in his shoe and who knows how much stashed in other places. As I found out much later, there were reasons. Louie had a lot of expenses that I knew nothing about.

– 14 –

I decided I was going to give Louie a wonderful present for Christmas: Me, drug free. It was going to make the start of a new relationship. No more screaming, no more yelling, no more fighting. We were going to be a close, loving family, like we once were, and Christmas was the perfect time to start. Louie loved Christmas best of all the holidays, and I planned to make our first one together in four years absolutely terrific. I was going to make a turkey and lasagna dinner, we would have a big tree covered with dozens of decorations, there would be a lot of presents for everyone, and we would be happy again.

But December started out real bad. Louie walked in one afternoon and said to me, "Put your coat on. We're going for a ride."

His face was all knotted up in anger when he said it. As soon as I looked at him I got very scared. "Why, what for?"

"C'mon," he ordered. "I'm taking you in for your methadone today. I got things to do in the city."

"Okay, Louie," I said. I knew that wasn't his real reason, but I also knew I didn't have a choice. He wasn't asking, he was ordering.

The car was in the garage. "All right, Louie," I started when I climbed in the car. "What's really bothering y——"

"Bitch!" he yelled and slapped me hard across the face. "I warned you, you no-good bitch!"

This time I was screaming right back. "Whattya, crazy? What's the matter with you?" I tried to scramble out of the car, but he grabbed my sleeve with his right hand and smacked me right across the mouth with the back of his left hand.

"Don't try to lie to me. You never could lie." He just kept hitting me and I started crying and screaming and clawing back at him. "I know every fucking thing goes on in that house. Whattya think I am, some kind of jerk? You think I don't know what goes on because I'm not there?"

"Louie! Louie, you're crazy! What are you talking about?"

He grabbed my other sleeve and held both my arms against my body. He didn't say anything for a few seconds, and when he did, he was no longer screaming. "Ceil, I've got seven tapes of you and the girls copping drugs over the phone. And I've never said this to you before, but you make addicts out of my girls and I swear to God I'll kill you." His voice was really calm, almost gentle.

I started shaking my head from side to side, because I really didn't know the girls were using drugs. "I swear Louie, I don't know anything about it."

His hands dropped away from my sleeves. I relaxed slightly. With one swift motion the heel of his hand smashed across my face, pushing me into the door. "Don't lie to me again. Don't lie to me."

"Listen, Louie," I told him, "honestly, I'm gonna do my best to keep the girls away from drugs. Believe me." He didn't say a word. "Believe me, Louie?"

"Get outta the car, Ceil." Then he drove into the city alone.

The Christmas season had gotten off to a lousy start.

As soon as I stopped crying I went upstairs to talk to the girls.

They admitted that they were using a few psychedelic drugs and some pills, but swore they never even tried hard drugs. They didn't believe me when I warned them that Louie had the phones tapped. "Don't believe me, that's up to you," I explained, "but just don't talk about drugs over the phone anymore. Your father'll hurt you if he gets angry enough."

"Daddy wouldn't hurt us," Paige said. "He loves us too much."

"Yeah. But he hates drug addicts even more." It was a ridiculous statement to make about a man who made his living off junkies, but it was absolutely true.

Louie and I really talked it out when he came home that evening. He had calmed down enough to be rational, and I told him I was really going to try to kick. "I'm gonna make things like they were in the old days," I promised him.

I could see by the expression on his face he didn't believe me, but at that point he was ready to try anything. "If you say so, Ceil, I'll believe you. But ya gotta show me. Talk is cheap."

Slowly, we all started to get into the Christmas spirit. Louie was sending me out all day with lists of presents to buy for the kids. He'd give me $300 a day just for presents. When I got home he'd make me sit down and send out cards to people from Queens, from California, people he knew in prison, relatives of friends, I was sending out 30 cards a day. Then, when I finally got our kids' shopping finished, he sent me out shopping for Herbie and his wife and their children. I was beginning to believe that maybe everything was going to turn out all right.

We even found time to drive up and see Mark in Attica prison, just outside Buffalo. Louie was afraid to go in, because he didn't want to be too closely connected with Mark, so he stayed in the motel while I visited. Unknown to Louie, I brought Mark a little Christmas present—about one-quarter spoon of cocaine.

He was overjoyed to see me. Mikey was long gone and he hadn't even heard from her. He didn't want me to mention her name. Most of the time he talked about his case. "I want Louie to find that goddamn doorman and take him to my attorney. Then I want Louie to get the minutes of my trial and have the attorney file an affidavit for an appeal based on what the doorman says. Tell Louie to make him tell the truth. Then I'll get a good trial."

He was convinced he had been given a bad deal. "We beat it, Ceil," he told me. "We had them beat." He was so sure he was going to be acquitted that his mother and sister brought a bottle of champagne to the courtroom for the victory celebration. "I was railroaded," he kept saying. "It was that damn judge, that damn judge." I gave Louie Mark's instructions. The first thing he did when we got home was hire a private investigator to find the doorman. (Eventually he found him in Chicago and had him flown back to New York. It did no good—Mark's appeal was denied.)

Herbie had a much better shot at freedom. He had just about finished doing the time he owed the state on his parole violation, although he still had to appear in court with Louie and Richie on the concealed gun charge. Herbie was really angry about that because he'd told Richie to take the fall for the gun and he'd refused. Herbie had decided to throw him out of his organization because of that.

Louie wasn't at all worried. I was anxious to see what would happen in the courtroom. I'd seen him in operation before. Once he had a violation of parole hearing that he made me go to. All he promised me was that "You're gonna see how justice really works."

The hearing started in a courtroom that was totally empty except for Louie, me, our lawyer, the judge and the court clerks. Everything seemed normally dull. "When's whatever's gonna happen, gonna happen?" I whispered.

"Not yet," he whispered right back out of the side of his mouth.

Ten minutes passed. The hearing continued. The judge kept talking about the law. I was bored stiff. "Soon?" I nudged Louie.

"Yeah, soon," he nudged me back.

Finally, a little while after that, the rear doors of the courtroom opened and this girl walked in. She was wearing a soft black leather miniskirt that just barely ended where her legs met, a thin white halter-top with no bra, and no stockings. Louie leaned over to me. "Now," he said.

Sometimes I have difficulty picking up a prostitute on the street, but I had absolutely no doubts about this girl. Her body was just as sexy as her costume. She had long blond hair that just fell over her shoulders, big breasts and a really small waist. She was wearing bright red lipstick that made her face look like she was pouting. She just took a seat quietly in the back row of the courtroom.

"We'll now have a ten-minute recess," the judge said as she sat down. She stood right back up and walked down the aisle, through that little gate, and walked into the judge's chambers. "The justice is now at work," Louie laughed.

He explained the deal to me. He'd hired this prostitute for the judge. They were now in his chambers working out arrangements for a meeting. A few minutes later the judge returned to the bench and called Louie to the front of the courtroom. "Case dismissed," he said, finishing the deal. Louie thought it was one of the funniest things he'd ever seen. "It was like show and tell," he laughed. "This hooker showed up for the judge and he told us to go home." I think Louie set the whole thing up.

This time it was easier. The judge just called them forward, checked the facts and dismissed the case. Herbie was a free man again, Louie was back in business.

Things were going to get even better than they had been before. Herbie and Josephine had just about completed their house in Bellmore. Louie had promised me that when the house was done, he wouldn't have to go into the city so often, so he could stay home more. I was looking forward to that.

The house was incredibly beautiful. It was in a development, and every house was the same except Herbie's. Herbie's was bigger and better. He had everything custom-made for the house, complete bedroom sets, furniture, he had 12-carat gold bathroom fixtures. I knew they were real 12 carat because Josephine and Louie and I drove to Rockaway while Herbie was in jail and picked up gold-plated fixtures. He came home and told Josephine that wasn't what he wanted, he wanted 12-carat gold, so we had to go back and get them.

The house had at least 11 rooms, plus a full finished basement. They had a swimming pool, a sauna, a gym, round bathtubs with Grecian pillars all mirrored behind them. They had big wrought-iron gates, a garbage compactor, a refrigerator where you could get ice from the front of it without having to open the door. They had three different phone numbers and who knew how many telephones. The place was absolutely beautiful.

We were all having so much fun together. Herbie had these two Doberman pinschers, $1700 each, and they were being attack-trained. Well, we had a little dog too, a mutt-poodle. Louie would go with Herbie to watch the Dobermans being trained, and then he'd come back and try the same things on our little dog. He'd put him on the chain and lead him around the living room for 45 minutes. "Louie," I'd say, "leave the poor dog alone. He's not an attack dog."

"Yeah, but you should see Herbie's dogs. A guy puts a blank in the gun and shoots at him and the dog keeps coming."

I had to laugh. "And you expect that little dog to do that?"

He didn't answer. He just kept walking the dog around the living room.

Christmas was going to be the very best time we'd ever spent together. Everything was going well and the kids were happy and we were together. I wanted it to be a time for all of us, alone. But a few days before Christmas Louie told me he had invited Herbie and Josephine and Herbie's mother over for Christmas dinner. I loved Josephine, but I was selfish. I wanted my family to be by ourselves. "Louie," I told him, "I don't want to cook for them. I just wanted us to be together for Christmas."

He pointed his index finger at me and yelled, "Look. This is my house and if I want to invite the whole fucking Army, I will! And you'll cook for them!" This was the way he was brought up. The man ordered. The woman cooked.

"I'm not cooking, Louie."

"You're not, huh?" Slap. "You sure?" Slap. "You don't wanna cook?" Slap.

I managed to pull away from him. "I'm not cooking for no more of your friends if it's the last thing I do."

He grabbed me and pushed his hand under my chin. He started choking me. This was prison Louie, just going crazy. "You got a big goddamn mouth . . ."

He started choking me and screaming and warning me about what he could do to me. I reached behind my back and picked up a knife from the counter. I really don't know what I was going to do with it, but I needed something to protect myself. Before I could move, he grabbed the knife out of my hand. The blade slid along my hand and sliced my fingers. The blood started gushing all over my clothes, all over Louie, all over the floor. I was too shocked to even move.

Louie stared at the gushing cuts. He hated the sight of blood. "Get your coat," he said quietly. "We better go to the hospital."

They ended up putting 14 stitches in my fingers. I just didn't know what to say to Louie, and I guessed that he didn't know exactly how to apologize. Finally, when we reached the house, he turned and looked at me. I was ready to accept whatever excuse he offered.

He smacked me in the mouth. "You still think you're not cooking? You'll cook. You'll put a rubber glove on that hand and you'll cook with it, and you'll cook for anybody I tell you to cook for. You understand?" I couldn't even look at him. "You understand?" he asked a little louder.

"Yeah, Louie," I said in a tired voice, "I understand."

Louie bought Herbie a big color television for Christmas. Herbie bought Louie a diamond pinkie ring. He gave me a $500 gift certificate to Saks and each of the girls a $100 certificate. Philip got an electronics set. And I cooked for both families.

Christmas turned out nice, believe it or not. The kids got everything they could have possibly wanted. I gave Louie about a dozen different things—a piece of luggage, nice cuff links, underwear, shirts, hand-painted ties, whatever I thought he needed. He was just rebuilding his wardrobe after the four years in prison.

Louie gave me only one thing. When I saw the package, I was very disappointed; usually he lavished gifts on me, and this time there was only a small package. But when I opened it up I found a magnificent diamond watch. There were at least 18 small diamonds. And even more important, a card that read, "I really do love you very much, Love, Louie."

I loved him too. I loved him when he was gentle and I loved

him when he beat me. I loved him when he put down $7000 in cash for the furniture for the new house, and I loved him when he made me go through that terrible abortion. I loved him through the better and through the worse. There were times when I hated what he was doing, like he hated my drugs, but I never hated Louie. Not the real Louie that I knew was always there. We had something special.

He realized that too. Just before New Year's Eve, 1971, we had a long talk about us, about my drugs, about our future. In his own way Louie tried to apologize to me about the way he'd been acting. "It's just the drugs," he said. "You don't know how seeing you all drugged up rips me apart." I did know, and I understood much more than he thought I did. Louie felt responsible for turning me into a drug fiend, and because he loved me he couldn't deal with that. He tried to believe it wasn't his fault, but deep down he knew it was true. When we first went together I was just a know-nothing Long Island housewife taking some pills, and with him I'd turned into a hard-core junkie. "It's all your fault," my mother kept telling him. "It's your fault she's a bum!" He believed that and he felt really guilty. So he hit me, because he didn't know any other way to deal with it. In the world he'd grown up in, that was the way to solve things.

"What's been going on lately," he said, meaning the beatings, "that's over. You just stay away from the drugs and everything's gonna really be good. For the first time in my life, I don't have to worry about money anymore. Hey, I'm even starting a savings account with my own name on it." He laughed when he told me that. "Imagine that, a real savings account." He stopped abruptly. "But listen, I don't want you telling Josephine 'cause I don't want Herbie to know. Our business is our business and you tell her too much. Too many things have been coming back to me."

"I won't tell her," I promised.

"Ceil, we're gonna have enough money to last us forever."

This time I laughed. "Forever, Louie?" I never thought in terms of forever.

Louie was trying to set up a legitimate front. Besides opening a bank account, he had some papers drawn up making him the owner of Billy D'Angelo's gas station. Billy had started spending a lot more time with Louie, acting as a chauffeur and errand boy. That was another thing Louie told me not to tell the Sperlings.

The drug operation was back in business as soon as Herbie's two feet hit the streets. Just like always before, Louie was here and there, in and out. I'd see him when he got up and I'd see him when he came home at night, although occasionally he'd let me drive him to a drop or pickup. I'd have to stay in the car. I went on six or eight—one I remember took place in a McDonald's parking lot. I saw Louie give this guy a shirt box full of money that Nancy had wrapped. When he was out working, or out of New York on a pickup or delivery, he would call every few hours. Louie tried to make up for all the phone calls he missed while in prison. We played and we partied, it was sunny California all over again.

The kids spent much more time with him than I did. During the day he'd take the girls to the barbershop with him and they'd hang out together all day, and at night he'd take Philip along on his pickups and deliveries.

"Ma, you shoulda seen what happened yesterday," Philip would tell me. I still learned more about Louie from other people than I did from him. "We drove up to the Bronx and Daddy made a drop and this guy handed him a brown paper shopping bag and said there was a hundred gees in it. Daddy gave it to me to hold on my lap and I looked inside. There was all this money tied together with pieces of string.

"Then we went downtown to Little Italy and we met Richie Maxton standing on a street corner. Daddy gave him the paper bag and said"—Philip dropped his voice very low when doing his imitation of Louie speaking—" 'It's a hundred balloons.'

"Richie Maxton asked, 'A hundred grand?' and Daddy said, 'Yeah.' Then Richie took the bag and walked away with it. After that we went into Chinatown and Daddy bought me a whole load of fireworks."

But even though Louie spent more time with the kids, I knew them better. One of the gifts Louie bought Nancy for Christmas was a plastic flower-making kit. It was a wonderful gift for a creative 14-year-old. It was also a wonderful gift for anyone who liked to get high. The kit contained a gluelike solution that, when a wire frame was dipped into it, hardened into a plastic flower. As Nancy discovered, this solution was also terrific for sniffing and getting high. It didn't take me long to discover this was what she was using the kit for. She spent hours in her room with the kit, but she never seemed to make many plastic flowers. One afternoon I noticed her eyes were all glassy and her speech slurred. "What are you doing in there?" I asked her.

She shrugged. "Just making flowers, you know."

"Nancy, I'm not that stupid."

She giggled. "Ma, I've been sniffing this great stuff. Wanna try it?"

I certainly did. I wanted to try anything that would get me off. And Nancy was right, I did get high quickly. It was a glue-sniffing high, which I liked, but I didn't do very often because I knew how bad it was for my brain. When we straightened out, I told her I didn't want her sniffing anymore and explained why. Finally I took the set away from her.

Nancy wasn't about to listen to me. When Louie came home, she showed him the few flowers she'd made and he was so pleased he went out and bought her another kit. "The kid's really talented," Louie told me.

"Yeah, Louie," I agreed sadly. "She's good." As much as I wanted to, I couldn't stop her. She really got off on that crap. In fact, one night I came home and she was sitting upstairs on her bed crying hysterically. "What's the matter, honey?" I thought she'd hurt herself.

She was hallucinating. "There's a man sitting on your door," she sobbed, "and he keeps spitting at me. Make him go way, Ma, please!"

Louie was no help. The day after we'd had new carpeting laid all over the house he walked into the kitchen and said quietly, "Now, listen, Ceil, I don't want you to get upset and start yelling at Nancy. It was an accident."

I had no idea what he was talking about. "What accident? What happened?"

He was very calm. "She's fine. It was just a silly little thing. I walked into her room while she was making one of her flowers and she got so excited she spilled it all over her face and the new rug."

I went to clean up the solution as best I could. But inside I had to laugh at Louie. "You dummy," I thought, "you catch her sniffing junk and you don't even know it."

One of the reasons Louie never really understood what was going on behind his back is that he never really spent time listening to the kids. His time was his most valuable possession, and when he was with them he used it for fun and games. He rarely disciplined them and he never refused to buy them anything they asked for.

He could afford the presents. Herbie had put him on a guaranteed $5000-a-week salary, no matter how many cuts he actually made. I was so excited that I forgot Louie's warning and by mistake told Herbie's wife how fast our savings account was growing.

Herbie heard it from her.

Louie heard it from Herbie.

I heard it from Louie.

When Herbie found out about the account, he chewed Louie out up and down. First he wanted to know where Louie was getting enough money to build up a big account, second he wanted to know why Louie was stupid enough to put his own name on the account, and third he wanted to know what Louie was going to tell the Internal Revenue Service when they asked where the money came from. Mostly he wanted to know about the third, the one that would lead right back to him.

"From the gas stations," Louie explained. On paper he owned three service stations in the Bronx. It was an accommodation he had with the real owners. Herbie seemed satisfied with that explanation.

Louie worked hard for his money. He was cutting almost every day, sometimes in our basement, sometimes in the back of his gas station, sometimes in other apartments "somewhere" in the city. When he wasn't busy cutting, he was picking up or delivering. That meant he had to start traveling again.

The second week in January he put gas in the Thunderbird, took the clothes out of the dry cleaner and made sure there was plenty of food in the house. "Herbie's sending me to Miami for a few days," he told me. The plan was easy: He was taking an attaché case filled with cash to Florida to make the buy, and Sonny Gold was bringing the goods back on the train, dressed like a bum. "Now don't go yelling at Herbie for sending me," he finished, " 'cause I have to go. That's what he's paying me for and that's all there is to it." I ironed his underwear, he packed his own bags and he was gone.

He called me from Miami every few hours. "The weather down here is great," he said. "I really miss you a lot," he said. "I love you very much," he said. "Don't forget to put my undershirts in the wash," he said. "I'm really unhappy here without you," he said. "Kiss the kids for me," he said. "As soon as I get back we're gonna go on vacation out to California," he said. "Miami is a pretty nice town," he said. "The deal came off good," he said.

I believed every single word he told me. That was my fault. I'd forgotten Louie was still the best liar I'd ever known.

$-15-$

Louie was going to be in Miami for three days and Nancy wanted to have her junkie boyfriend from Queens come out to Bellmore and stay with us. I decided this was my chance to get even with Louie for always going away and agreed, as long he slept in Philip's room.

So I put Nancy, Philip, Gay and Susan in the car and went to pick him up at the Long Island Railroad station. The first thing the kid says is he has no drugs and won't stay over unless he has drugs. "I'm not gonna be stuck out there and get sick," he says. "Come on, let's go cop."

That was fine with me. I hadn't been involved in street drug sales in months and, in some strange way, I missed the down-head of that life. "How much money you got?" I asked him.

"I got some money," he told me, "but I don't want to put it out on drugs."

That meant that I was supposed to pay for it. He figured we

had a big house, a big car and expensive clothes, we could afford it. We could, but I didn't want to. "I got an idea, I'll tell you what we'll do. Let's burn the connection." We were going to have an adventure!

We drove into the Puerto Rican section of the Bronx and found his connection hanging on the corner. The connection leaned into the car and negotiated the transaction. Eventually he handed over a bundle, which was thirteen five-dollar bags. "Is this stuff good?" the boyfriend asked.

"Dynamite, man, dynamite," the connection told him.

"You got another bundle?"

The connection smiled. One of his front teeth was completely rotten black. There was an open space where the other one once was. He was really frightening-looking. "I got some more."

He gave us another bundle. The boyfriend started to go through the motions of counting out the money. As he did, the connection rested his elbow on the car door. I floored it. We took off.

The connection spun around quickly and slipped to the street. I got to the corner and made a quick right, then a left, then another left. I had no direction, no destination. It was getting late and dark and I just wanted to get out of that neighborhood as quickly as possible. I was so nervous I was shaking at the wheel.

I kept making quick turns. I drove up one-way streets the wrong way. I was really flying. "Keep watching behind us," I warned Nancy, "watch behind us." No one followed.

The whole three-hour trip home everybody in the car was screaming. The boyfriend is happy because he has his junk. Gay and Susan loved the ride. And Philip is screaming because I'm copping drugs. "You don't think you're shooting any of that junk," he yelled at me. "We had that already. I'll tell Daddy . . ."

I tried to calm him down. "It's not for me. I just don't want anybody getting sick. You understand that, right?" In fact, I considered half the haul to be mine. I had no physical need for it, the methadone was keeping me happy, but I wanted to get high because I was mad at Louie for going away.

I did up the heroin as soon as Philip went to sleep, but I didn't even feel it. It was garbage dope, and with the methadone already in my system I didn't even get high. That didn't bother me, that wasn't my purpose in shooting, and I still managed to shoot up most of my share over the next two days. It was something to do.

Louie came back from Florida as pale as he was when he left. I laughed at him, "How can you go to Florida for three days and not even get red?"

He didn't think my joke was funny. "I told you, I went down there to work. And my work is done inside." He didn't even take a day off when he got home, it was right back to work. He was constantly running into the city to make a cut or pick up a package or meet a connection or make a delivery.

Toward the end of January Louie played Paige a game of Frustration and she beat him. Her prize was a trip to California with Louie. Louie said he was going to pay off. I was pretty upset by that. I wanted to go away on vacation with him, and he was taking Paige. Besides, she was growing into a very pretty girl and I was starting to get jealous of her. Louie gave her everything she wanted, and she had no responsibilities. I saw myself when I was her age.

Paige was excited about the trip. She would be seeing all her old friends from our California days. She talked about it for days. By the time the trip came up I felt better about it. On the plane going out there the stewardess thought that she was Louie's girl friend, not his daughter—that's how old she looked. She felt very proud about that. I spoke to them almost every day and one time, after they had been there a few days, I sensed in her voice that something was wrong. But she didn't say anything, so I guessed I was hearing things.

When they came home, she seemed extra quiet and stayed off to herself. Then we got into a fight over something she did or didn't do and I pulled out my usual threat. "I'm gonna tell your father," I warned her. That always worked. The kids tried so hard to please him, and they never wanted him to know when they had done something wrong.

This time it didn't work. She looked at me and her eyes flashed. "Yeah? You tell my father. My father takes me to California and tries to ball me! He tells me he loves me! Yeah, you tell my father!" Then she started crying.

I didn't know what to do. I didn't know what to say, how to act. Louie? Louie trying to make love to his daughter? It wasn't possible. Louie might be a lot of things, I figured, but he wasn't sick and he wasn't perverted.

I got on the phone and started calling around looking for him. I knew just a few places where he might be. I finally found him at the barbershop. "Louie, you better get home, and you better get home now," I told him.

I had never spoken to him like that before. I'd never dared order him to do anything. "What's the matter? What's the matter?"

"Louie, just get home." I hung up.

He came home and I told him what Paige had said. We went upstairs into our bedroom to talk about it. He never blinked an eye, he just denied the whole thing. "That's not the way it happened at all," he said. "It was in the middle of the night and I rolled over and I thought it was you."

I was crying, I was hysterical. Not my Louie. Not to my daughter. I tried to buy his story, I didn't even ask him any questions because I wanted so much to believe in him.

Paige came in the room and they started screaming at each other. "What did you tell your mother something like that for? What'd you lie to her for?"

"You didn't do that?" she said.

"You know I didn't do nothin' like that."

They just screamed back and forth. Finally Paige said she didn't want to live in that house any longer, she was afraid of him. "Good," Louie told her. "You can leave whenever you want."

I was caught between them. I didn't want Paige to leave, but I couldn't lose Louie again. I had to choose between them. I chose Louie.

I called David and told him what happened. He had been remarried with more kids of his own. "If you hadn't left me, this never would have happened," he said. But I convinced him he should take Paige because she was his daughter. We met him somewhere on the highway and Paige changed cars and went home with him.

I was sick about the whole thing. I just didn't know who to believe. I wanted so much to believe Louie, but I'd seen him lie so often, and so well, I just didn't know what to think. I couldn't really function around the house, I just kind of lay around and moped. Louie warned me not to say anything to Josephine and Herbie about it, but I had nobody else to talk to.

They were over the house one night and Louie was upstairs. I told Herbie what happened. Then, without thinking about it, I added, "Break his legs for me or break his arm. Hurt him for me, Herbie, please." I started crying again.

Herbie and Josephine didn't say very much, but I could see they were both disgusted. "Don't worry about it," Herbie told me, "I'll take care of that degenerate."

I knew he would, too, and I was glad about it. I wanted Louie to have some pain. I thought maybe that would bring the old Louie back, the Louie I knew before he went to prison.

I never had a chance to find out. In the middle of a delivery our life fell apart. Louie had three kilos of heroin, one of which he was going to drop with a customer of his named Mark Richter. Herbie had warned Louie that he didn't trust Richter and ordered him not to make deals with him. But Louie figured he was smarter than anyone else, so he did what he pleased. He climbed into his Buick Skylark, left two kilos with Billy D'Angelo in the apartment he used for cutting and drove to the city to make his meet with Richter.

Richter was waiting for him on 55th Street between Second and Third Avenues. Louie parked the car, walked over to Richter's car and handed him the heroin.

Richter was supposedly buying and selling on the spot. He was the middleman: Louie would give the junk to Richter, Richter would pass it to his customers and Louie would be paid in full immediately. In theory. In fact, the whole thing was a setup. The customer was an undercover cop. As soon as Louie handed over his package of dope and Richter made the sale, the action began.

Cops started closing in from all angles. Louie was trapped in the Skylark. He lay down under the front seat, hoping somehow to bluff his way out of this jam.

He almost made it. A few minutes passed. He probably was beginning to think he'd beaten them. And then he looked up to see this tall, dark-haired guy, wearing cowboy boots, standing over the car, holding two six-guns out in front of him. "Whattya doin' down there, Louie?" the cowboy yelled.

Louie had to know he was through. "I'm just lying here," he yelled back.

"Well, whattya doin' that for?"

"Whattya mean, what am I doing that for? I'm just doin' it. It ain't illegal for a guy to lay on the floor if he wants to."

"That's right. But, listen, we wanna talk to you," the cowboy told him, "so why don't you just sit up and come on outta there?"

Billy sat in the apartment waiting. When Louie didn't come back he knew something was wrong. Louie had once told him that if any problems came down, he was to immediately contact Herbie Sperling. This was definitely a problem. He called Herbie. Herbie told him to clean the apartment up and then meet Sonny Gold on the corner of 48th and Broadway and give him everything he had. Billy did exactly what he was told.

Louie called me as soon as they let him near a telephone. "Ceil, you're not gonna believe this," he told me in a shaky voice, "but I got busted by a damn cowboy on Eighth Avenue."

As soon as I heard him say "busted," I got scared. Again, I thought, again.

He kept talking. "He was wearing these stupid high cowboy boots and he had long hair and he was carrying two big six-guns. Six-guns on Eighth Avenue! These guys are nuts!"

"What guys, Louie? Who is he? Where are you?"

"BNDD," he said. The Bureau of Narcotics and Dangerous

Drugs. Federal cops. This was a big bust, a superbig problem. Louie gave me a long list of the things he wanted me to do. I wrote them down and, as soon as we hung up, I started following through. I cleaned house quickly. Everything went out. I contacted an attorney. I tried to reach Billy D'Angelo about two dozen times. I called a few other business people, but not Herbie, specifically not Herbie.

They gave Louie a good going-over at the station. They questioned him up and down, but he was always a good answerer. He didn't tell them anything. He gave them his mother's address in Queens and nothing else. He didn't help them at all. They took all his belongings from him, including his safe deposit box key. Inside that safe deposit box was Louie's real rainy day account, money I didn't even know was there. Louie knew he had to get to that box before the cops.

He was bailed out first thing the next morning, Valentine's Day, 1972, for $25,000. The money was put up by the barbers at the Barbury Barbershop. One of the barbers even put his house up as partial security. Somebody was backing them up, probably Herbie, but they signed for the bond.

Louie was more nervous than I'd ever seen him, really hyper. First thing he did was take Philip to our bank and they closed out the savings account. There was $2007.30 in the account. He left the $7.30 cents. Then he went downstairs to the safe deposit box and cleaned that out. He knew it was only a matter of time before the Feds got a court order and opened it up. The box was stuffed with jewelry and cash. He carefully wrapped the jewelry in a white sweat sock. Then he began counting the cash. And counting. And more counting. Philip counted it out with him, $150,000 in cash. One, five, zero, thousand dollars, more money than I ever dreamed he had stashed away.

When he finished counting, he stuffed it into a plain white envelope and told Philip to stick it inside his shirt for safekeeping. "That's the money for the house," he said.

Louie was moving very quickly now. He had a lot he wanted to accomplish, and he seemed to know his time was limited. On the way home from the bank he stopped at a florist. Louie was always sending flowers and no matter how bad things were, he was going to send me Valentine's Day flowers. From the florist he drove to a good friend named Alice's house. He took the envelope with $150,000 in it from Philip, stuck it in his own belt and went into the house alone. Philip sat and waited. When Louie returned to the car, Philip didn't see the envelope anymore.

Finally he came home. He was so nervous he was shaking. He just couldn't sit down. "That stupid kid," he cursed Billy D'Angelo, "he's going to get me killed." I had no idea what he was talking about. His conversation just rambled from subject to subject, without any pattern. "Ceil, the money is so quick in the drug business it's just unbelievable—"

"I seen it, Louie," I agreed.

"—but you just can't fool around, you know, you just can't mess around."

Early in the afternoon Herbie came over to the house and the two of them had a big fight. "I told you what to do," Herbie screamed at him, "but you're too stupid to listen to me." Louie was walking through the house and Herbie was following him and waving his finger. "I told you I didn't want you dealing with Richter, I told you that. Didn't I tell you? Didn't I tell you?"

Louie just kept walking. "So I made a mistake," he said. "A mistake, that's all."

"Yeah, a mistake that's all, huh? A mistake?" They just walked and argued. Herbie stayed about a half-hour, then he just stormed out the door. Louie seemed to be twice as nervous. Even after Herbie left he kept pacing.

He walked into the kitchen. "I love you so much, Ceil," he said. "I hope you know that."

"I know that, Louie. I love you too."

He just rambled. "Soon as we get back from California I'm gonna take a life insurance policy. That's the first thing I'm gonna do."

He kept watching the clock. Getting more agitated.

"I understand about your drugs, you know that, Ceil. I mean,

I really do understand how it is. I finally can see it. You should know that I don't blame you at all. It wasn't you. I just didn't give you enough support when I should have . . ."

I didn't know what was wrong. I didn't know how to help him. And Louie just didn't know how to reach out for help. He had been so independent for so long, he didn't know how to need anyone else.

Sometimes he was contemplative. "The thing that I did most wrong was not spending enough time with you. I think you could'a taught me things . . ."

Sometimes he was angry. "It's all that damn stupid kid's fault. Stupid, stupid, stupid."

"What'd Billy do, Louie? Tell me."

He just shook his head from side to side. "He just didn't think."

And sometimes he would perk up and start planning. "This house ain't all that much if you wanna know the truth. 'Member the fun we had in California? We could go back out there and . . ."

I was really frightened. This was a Louie I'd never seen before. This was a Louie that he'd hidden for the seven years we were together. This was a small, frightened, tired man.

About four o'clock in the afternoon he put on a clean shirt and told me he had to go out and do something for a while. "Now listen to me," he said, " 'cause this is important. If Herbie calls, you don't know where I went. You don't know what I'm doing. Anything. All I said to you was I had to go into Rockaway. That's all you know. Make sure you don't tell him anything else and you don't tell Josephine anything else. Right?"

"Right, Louie."

Philip wanted to ride with him, but Louie refused. "No, son, you can't go with me this time."

I walked him to the door. He reached into his wallet and pulled out a pocketful of cash. "Take this in case you need some money." Then he gave me a long, open look of love and pulled me close. "Remember, I love you." I kissed him very hard.

He walked down the front sidewalk to our new Lincoln. It

was a repainted hot car we'd gotten only three days earlier for $4000. "A steal," Louie had laughed. It was, it truly was.

Just as he was climbing into the car, the florist delivery truck pulled up. The driver walked to the front door and handed me an enormous Valentine's Day bouquet. In the center was one flower with a red heart-shaped leaf and a yellow stem coming from its middle. It was Louie's favorite flower. I never knew the name, but he always told me it meant love and good luck.

Louie sat in the car and watched as I read his card. "I love you more than anything. Love, Louis." Then he drove away.

I didn't understand what was going on. So I just stood at the door for maybe ten minutes after he left, just staring into space, trying to make some sense out of the day. The pieces just didn't seem to fit together. And the puzzle became more complex when Philip walked out of our bedroom carrying Louie's personal telephone book. "Hey, Ma," Philip said, "look what Daddy left behind."

He held it up to show me. That book was the most important thing Louie owned. It was his business book and he had never left the house without it before. I took it from Philip and put it in my pocket without opening it. This belongs to Louie, I thought, and he wouldn't want me looking in it. I planned to give it back to him when he came back that night.

I had no idea what was going on. I didn't know where Louis was going. Only months later did I find out he went to Billy's apartment. He told Billy, "I'm in a lot of trouble. Things don't look good for me." Billy didn't understand what he was talking about and Louie didn't have time to explain.

Herbie called. "Where's Louie?" he wanted to know.

Billy handed Louie the telephone and listened to his part of the conversation. "I'll be right down," Louie finished and told Billy he was going to Herbie's apartment on Spring Street.

A few minutes later Billy followed him to Spring Street. He walked in just as Herbie was yelling at Louie: "And when the kid delivers it I find extra packages and they ain't supposed to be there!"

Louie tried to explain. "I was doing this for a gift for you. I'm doing this for a surprise."

Herbie didn't want to hear it. "I don't need that kind of surprise. If I want something like that, I'll buy it."

Billy had no idea what they were talking about. He listened for a while, talked to Herbie, then left.

Louie didn't come home that night. I sat alone in the living room, waiting for the telephone to ring. He always called. No matter where he was, no matter what he was doing, he always called. Always. Every few hours.

The phone didn't ring. I was really scared. Something had to be wrong. I got through that night by getting really high on my methadone and my pills.

I called Herbie for the first time the next afternoon. "I haven't heard from Louie since yesterday," I said. "Do you know where he is?"

"No," he told me abruptly, "I'll let you know if I hear from him or I'll have him call you." Then he hung up. Herbie couldn't be bothered, he had his business to do.

That afternoon I made sure I had a good supply of drugs on hand. I gave money to Nancy and told her to cop from her friends for me, and I went out and made some rounds of old connections myself. I also searched the house inside out. There were no drugs hidden anywhere, but I did find a little cash that Louie left.

Another night passed. No Louie. No phone call. I kept calling Herbie. "I'm frightened," I said. "I think something's wrong."

"Nothing's wrong," he tried to reassure me. "You know Louie, he's around. He'll be back." I didn't believe him at all.

The third day passed. I did my best to stay stoned. I'd do my methadone in the morning and speed in the afternoon and night. I was really wrecked out of my mind. I was constantly picking at my skin. I imagined at one time that Louie had given me crabs and I had them all over my body, and that's why he'd left me. I tried to pick them off my body—I picked two moles off my face. I just couldn't stop. My body was spotted with scabs where I had been picking.

The kids were worrying too, about me as well as Louie. They would come home from school and find me locked in the bathroom. "Ma, what are you in the bathroom for?" Gay cried. "You're in the bathroom too long. Are you taking drugs again?"

At night I hallucinated. I heard Louie downstairs, telling another woman that he was going to come upstairs and throw me out of the house. I heard that! I really heard his voice. I heard every word. In my mind, he was there. That's how crazy I was.

Six days passed. I called Billy D'Angelo and told him about the $150,000 Louie had taken out of his safe deposit box. "I don't even know where that money came from," I said, "and I don't know where it is."

Billy knew exactly where that money had come from. "Louie was stealing from Herbie," he told me.

"What?" I couldn't believe I had heard him right.

"Louie was stealing from Herbie, Ceil. He was cutting eight times and only giving Herbie seven cuts. The rest he was selling on his own. That's where that money came from." Herbie found out about it, he added, when Louie had been busted. The stuff Billy handed over to Sonny Gold had been cut eight times. Herbie figured it out. "He's really angry at Louie," Billy finished telling me. "When his guys find Louie, they're gonna break his legs."

I was really happy when Billy told me Louie was stealing. I felt that since he was stealing and since he had been found out, maybe he did take the money and run. Maybe he was afraid. That made me feel like he might still be alive.

Then I started thinking about what would happen if Herbie caught him. I knew how tough he could be. Two weeks earlier I'd asked Herbie to break Louie's legs, but that was all. I just wanted to punish him for what he did to Paige, I didn't want him really hurt. Now, I didn't care about that, I just wanted him back. I called Herbie. "Let me tell you something, Herbie," I warned him, "I know what I told you, but if you do find my husband and one hair on his head is moved, you're gonna be sorry 'cause you're gonna have to deal with me."

Herbie laughed at me. "What do you mean, Ceil? You know how much I like Louie. You know I wouldn't hurt him. He's like my brother, I love him, I wouldn't do anything to harm him."

Eight days passed. I had been stoned for one week. I put an ad in the *Long Island Press* and in the *New York Daily News.* "Louie," it read, "the children and I love you and need you. Please call me or come home." There was no response.

Ten days passed. I called Herbie again. I had no one else to turn to for help. This time he told me to come over to his house. Finally, I thought, finally Herbie is going to help me. Right from the beginning I had expected him to help because when he had been in prison Louie took care of Josephine and his mother. Louie was running to Spring Street every day, giving them money, running errands, following Herbie's orders, and now I expected Herbie to do the same thing for Louie's family.

Billy D'Angelo was already there when I arrived. It wasn't help Herbie had in mind. He wanted to lecture us. He took us both into his unfinished basement and made us sit on empty crates. The place was cold and dirty and shadowy. Herbie stood up in front of us like a teacher scolding naughty children. Then he started pointing at me and screaming questions. "Did you know the kid was stealing from me?" I knew, Billy had told me, but I didn't answer him.

He didn't wait for an answer. "He's like my own brother. I give him everything. I tried to chase him from the barbershop. I didn't want him hanging around there with those other guys. I told him he didn't know shit about the drug business. But I like the kid, I like Louie, so I give him a job. I tried to let him make money, and this is what I get. He steals from me." He paused, then said it again. "He steals from me.

"He was making plenty. I was giving that kid five thousand dollars a week, and if he needed more all he had to do was come to me for it. He didn't have to steal off me."

I didn't know what to say. The drug business was Louie's business, all I wanted to know was where was my husband.

Then he started on Billy. "Look, he got this kid involved. I don't even know this kid and he's got him cutting for him?

What is that? What was he doing? C'mon Ceil, you tell me, what was he doing?"

I said, "Herbie, I don't know Louie's business."

Then he wanted to know what Louie left in the house. "What's over there?" he asked me. "You think he left anything stashed in the house?"

I told him I knew Louie didn't leave anything stashed in the house. He wanted to know how I could be so positive. I finally told him. "Louie didn't keep stuff in the house because I'm a dope fiend myself."

He didn't say anything, he just looked at me. I think he was really surprised because as close as the four of us had been, the Sperlings had never even suspected I was using drugs.

"That's right, Herbie, I'm an addict, and Louie hates that fact. So he doesn't keep anything in the house."

I think that shook him up a little, but he covered up pretty good. He started yelling at us again and telling us how good he had been to Louie. "I loved that kid," he said again. Herbie was right, he had treated Louie very well. There was no reason for Louie to be stealing from him. But for Louie that was part of the game. It was Louie's grown-up version of stealing the safe from the local movie theater and hiding it in his basement. It was the fun part.

When Herbie was pretty sure that neither Billy or I knew anything about Louie or about any more drugs, the meeting ended. I went home and got just a little higher.

Two more days passed. I knew for sure that Herbie had no intention of really helping me. I decided I had to call the police. But first I had to call Herbie. I still needed somebody to tell me what to do, and there was nobody around but Herbie Sperling. "I'm calling the police," I told him, " 'cause something's definitely wrong."

Herbie didn't want that. "No, listen, don't call the police, Ceil. That's stupid. I'll send a few of the boys to look for him. But don't call the police." Other than our meeting and the few phone calls, the Sperlings just shut us off. Herbie I could understand, but not Josephine. We were best friends. When we weren't together we were always on the phone, three, four times a day. All of a sudden, nothing. I needed help. I needed someone to talk to. I needed someone to tell me what to do. "Don't call the police" was all the help I got.

I never slept. I just kept speeding. I'd stay up all night washing clothes, and ironing, and cleaning drawers, and picking up little balls of wool off the rug. The kids told me they were going to cut holes in the basement curtains and charge their friends a nickel to watch their mother going through her maniac act.

I was completely out of my mind. Nancy would get stoned with me and sometimes at night we'd huddle together in bed and feed each other's insanity. "I think I hear somebody at the door," she would say, and then I would hear it too. It was pitch black in the house and she'd whisper, "Ma, I hear somebody coming up the stairs, I'm frightened. Ma, I'm frightened."

We'd hold each other and listen for the footsteps.

"Look, Ma, I see him over there and he's blowing bubbles. No, wait, there's two of them."

I was always scared, endlessly frightened, totally zonked. From hour to hour I'd pick up the telephone receiver and say loudly, "Hello, police department" into the empty phone. I was trying to scare off whoever was in the house.

Once, when the kids were in school, I went upstairs to take a bath and I was so frightened I took these two real swords that Philip had on his wall and brought them into the bathroom with me. I put them down right next to the bathtub. Then I arranged two mirrors so I could lie in the tub, look in one mirror and see the front door reflected in the second mirror. And every time I took my eyes off the mirror for an instant I'd think I saw a flash out of the corner of my eye like somebody was coming in, and I'd grab one of the swords.

Two weeks passed. I was skin and bones because I wasn't eating. Paige had moved back into the house, and she started getting stoned with us. My house had completely stopped functioning. The kids were taking care of themselves. I was alone and I was so scared. I just didn't know what to do. I wanted my Louie! I needed him to tell me what to do. Finally I realized that Herbie wasn't going to help, only the police could help, and I called the police department. I told them Louie, my husband, had disappeared. I told them he was a salesman. I told them he owned three gas stations in the Bronx. I told them I loved him very much.

They were very polite and promised to investigate, but that wasn't enough for me. I needed to do something myself to find Louie, and I remembered his address book. I started with the very first name in the book, Marlene Anker, and began working my way through the entire book. It gave me something to do. It gave me some sort of temporary sanity. I went through that book, page by page, phone number by phone number, and I opened up a whole new world.

And after seven years I realized I never knew Louie at all.

– 16 –

"Is Jerry there?"

"Yeah. This is Jerry."

"This is Mrs. Mileto. I'm Louie Mileto's wife. Louie Mileto, you know, the tall skinny guy. I haven't seen my husband in a week and I'm worried about him. Have you seen him?"

"That bastard? They ought to find him in the trunk of a car. He better watch who he's dealing with. He thinks he's so slick. You tell him he better stay out of the drug business."

"But I don't——"

Click.

"Is Sharon home?"

"This is her."

"This is Mrs. Mileto, Louie Mileto's wife and——"

"His wife? What are you talking about, his wife? Louie and I have an apartment. We've had this apartment for six months already. He left his wife years ago."

"No, really, I'm his wife——"

"What do you want, some more money off him?"

"Let me tell you something. Louie lives at home. Louie has always lived at home. And he's missing and I'm worried."

"You still have the kids?"

Click.

"Could I speak to Kathy please?"

"Speaking."

"I'm Louie Mileto's wife and——"

"I didn't know he was still married. See, we have an apartment together on East 81st Street and——"

"An apartment? I don't understand."

"Look, lady. Why don't you leave him alone and mind your own business. He takes care of his kids——"

"But he's missing! Don't you understand, he's missing!"

"Yeah. Sure, lady . . ."

Every phone call revealed bits and pieces of different lives Louie was leading. It was like going through a maze, trying to fit corners together, trying to understand the whole layout. I needed Louie to explain it all to me. I needed him to hold me and tell me none of it was true, that our life together hadn't been his biggest lie of all.

"Is Penny there?"

"Yes?"

"This is Mrs. Mileto, Louie Mileto's wife——"

"You mean you're the ex-Mrs. Mileto."

"The ex? No, I'm the only Mrs. Mileto."

There was a long silence on the other end of the line. "Well, I do know Louie. I was just with him a month ago. We stayed at the Hilton for three days . . ."

The three days Louie was supposedly in Miami. No wonder he didn't get tan.

". . . and we have a daughter, Jill. She's five years old now——"

"You have a daughter? You and Louie have a daughter?"

"Well, actually we don't have her anymore. Louie made me give her up for adoption when he came out of prison." She laughed. "You know, this must make us kind of related."

"No," I screamed, "this doesn't make us related." She met Louie, she told me, when he was living out in Ventura with his five kids from his first marriage. She was 18 years old.

". . . and I sent him money when he was in prison, five hundred one time, three hundred another time, it was all the money I had in the world. And I told him I'd wait for him."

There were just so many Louies. It was all so difficult to believe, so difficult to understand. I needed my drugs to help me through this. I was learning to hate Louie. After all we had gone through, I was finally beginning to really, deeply hate him. And, of course, I still loved him. I kept calling.

"Lorraine, please."

". . . Louie only comes up to the apartment once in a while, but he pays the rent and the phone bill."

I was beginning to understand why he always needed so much money, and how he spent it so fast. He was supporting four different women. "Louie's no john," I said. Then I hesitated, "At least I never knew him to be."

"Oh, no, Mrs. Mileto, Louie and I don't have anything to do with one another. He just uses my apartment. He takes care of a lot of business up here. When he comes up here he gives me and my boyfriend money to go out and have dinner. But listen, there's nothing going on between us . . ."

She knew Billy. She knew Herbie. She knew everybody. They were using her apartment to cut. Louie's secret life wasn't so damn secret.

". . . and he always talks about you and the kids and how much he loves you."

"Have you seen him lately?"

"No, he hasn't been here in a while. He has a key of his own, but I always know he's been here because half the soda in the refrigerator is gone."

"Please call me if . . ." Between the drugs and the phone calls and worrying about Louie, I was insane. I called a Colorado number and when a girl answered I started screaming at her. "What are you doing with Louie? He's *my* husband. Leave him alone, can't you, just leave him alone!"

"Ceil, are you all right? This is Betty," the California voice said.

I stopped. "Betty who?"

"Betty Mileto. Your niece. What's the matter?"

"Louie's gone and . . ."

Once I thought I'd found him. I called some hotel in Florida and heard a party going on. "Is Louie there?" I shouted.

There was a lot of screaming in the background directing Louie to the phone. "He's here," the voice told me, "he's coming to the phone."

I held my breath.

"Hi, Louie here," a voice I'd never heard before said.

The wrong Louie. The more calls I made the more I wondered if there really was one right Louie. Obviously I didn't know him. He put on a magnificent performance for me, but I never knew him. The more people I spoke to the more I realized Louie tried to be everything to everybody. He was playing with everyone in his life, getting the maximum from them in return for a minimum of giving. Even his friends really didn't understand him. Georgie Farber, who I'd known since the California days when I was bringing in grass, was one of the last people to see him. "Yeah, Ceil," he sighed, "Louie was here a few weeks ago and he needed to borrow five hundred dollars for the rent."

"Money for the rent!" I couldn't believe it. "Georgie, we had two thousand in a savings account and a hundred and fifty thousand locked in a safe deposit box and Louie was making five thousand a week. Are you sure he was borrowing?"

"He was borrowing, Ceil. I'm not that rich I don't remember five hundred bucks. All I know is he was really frantic over the money. He had to have it right away, too. I mean right then and there. He made me go out and borrow the money off a loan shark."

"I don't understand."

"Who does?" Georgie interrupted. "Louie was tough to figger. He was always moving quick, always speeding, even when he wasn't doing coke."

I couldn't believe that. "Louie was doing coke?"

"Didn't you know that, Ceil? I thought everybody knew that. Yeah, ever since he got involved with Herbie he's been snorting."

Even Louie had given in to the drugs. Even Louie. It was so hard to believe. Louie was gone forever, that I was positive about. I didn't know if he was dead or alive, but I knew he was gone. Sometimes I really hoped he was dead for what he was putting me and the kids through, but other times I prayed he was alive, even if he was alive with another woman.

I searched over my mind for some clue. Why? Where? What was his strange behavior that last day about? The answer should have been obvious after everything Herbie had done. But my mind was so stuffed with drugs and fear I just couldn't think straight, so I just kept wondering, imagining. What was he so frightened of? The police? Herbie? Me?

Me? I didn't want to think about it.

I thought about it. It made sense. Just, maybe, Louie wanted to leave me for another woman, but he didn't know how. I know he felt responsible for me, and for my children, and he didn't know how to get rid of that responsibility. There were other women, the phone calls proved that. Susan had even told me about one of them. "Daddy saw his girl friend today," she told me once. "She had long black hair and was really pretty." I thought she was just telling me a child's story. I couldn't believe Louie would bring my daughter with him to meet another woman.

But I was learning a lot about Louie I wouldn't have believed.

Maybe there was no other woman though. Maybe he just took the easy way and disappeared with the $150,000.

Maybe he had an accident, a real accident, and was hurt and couldn't contact anybody.

Maybe he's lying shot up in a ditch somewhere.

I missed him so terribly much. Even my drugs couldn't stop me from thinking about him all the time. The kids were managing to get along, they were unhappy, but they were surviving. Nancy was using a lot of drugs. Each morning before she left for school I'd give her a short pop in the back of her legs be- cause her veins weren't too good. Paige was starting to use more often. Philip somehow kept going to school, doing his homework, playing sports and trying to see that Susan and Gay were fed and clean and going to school. I had stopped functioning.

There was absolutely no trace of him. His private investigator friend flew in from California to make a personal search. He looked for both Louie and the new Lincoln. Like everybody else, he found nothing. When he was leaving to go back to California he told me, "Let me know when you hear something, but either Louie took the hundred and fifty thousand and left the country with it or he's dead."

"I hope he's dead," I told him, "because after what I've found out about his other women, if he's not, I'm gonna kill him." I meant it. At least I meant it when I said it.

Money was beginning to become a problem. I managed to scrape by for over a month on the money I'd found stashed around the house, but once the food ran out, the bills arrived and the rent came due, I was absolutely broke. Herbie wasn't helping at all. The only time I even saw him was when his yacht sailed by our house. The thing that really hurt was Josephine, my friend. She never called. I once sent Philip over for money, and Herbie's mother slammed the door in his face. "Tell your mother we're not supporting you," she told him.

The phone got shut off. The meat market wanted its $60. I couldn't get our clothes out of the cleaners unless I paid them $40. I couldn't even give the kids lunch money for school—I didn't have it. Herbie's son was giving Philip money every day so he wouldn't starve.

Finally I went to see Louie's friend Alice, one of the last people he saw when he had the money from the safe deposit box. Philip was almost positive Louie had the envelope with him when he walked in her house and didn't have it when he came out. That had to mean she still was holding it. I called her and lied to her, "Louie called and told me to get the en- velope from you."

"Where'd he call from?"

"He made me swear not to tell. He just told me to get that envelope from you and hold onto it."

"Are you sure it was Louie?"

"Sure I'm sure," I said, starting to get angry. "Don't you think I know my own husband's voice?"

She kept asking me questions, then she said, "I can't give you the package until Louie gets in touch with me."

I went to see Herbie. I told him straight up. "She's got a hundred and fifty thousand of my money and I need it. I don't know where Louie is and I need the money for home."

Herbie called Alice, who he knew through Louie, and ordered her to get right over to his house. I sat there fuming, waiting for her. As soon as she walked in the front door I leaped out of the chair and grabbed her by the collar. "You bitch," I yelled, "you bitch. Your goddamn friend has been sleeping with everybody in Manhattan. He's got all kinds of apartments all over the place and me and the kids are sitting here and starving and you won't give me my money? You won't give me my money?"

Herbie pulled me off of her. "What's she talking about? What money?"

"The package. I want that package you said Louie gave you. That's my money and I want it." I was really crazy. I would have killed her for the money.

"Herbie, I never said anything about a package," she lied. "I never saw any money."

Philip was standing there with me. I made him tell the whole story. "Daddy had a hundred and fifty thousand. He went into her house and he didn't come out with it."

"That's a lie," she screamed right back. "Louie never gave me noth——"

I didn't let her finish. She had the money. She *had* to have the money. So I went after her again. I started pulling and punching, but Herbie picked me off her before I could do any damage and shoved me into his living room. He was livid. "Lemme tell you something, Ceil, you better calm yourself down. If she's got the money, I'll find out about it and then you'll get it. But otherwise you leave her alone! Stay away from her! You don't touch her again! Got it?"

I understood. And I listened to Herbie, I didn't go near her. I also never saw a penny of that money.

The strain was pulling me apart. There was absolutely no way I could cope with everything happening around me, and I retreated deeper and deeper into drugs. It was like I was on the street again, every time I got hold of some money, I copped. Louie's father would lay $100 on me, I'd cop $100 worth of speed. Billy gave me $50, that was $50 worth of pills and dope. And whatever I bought I'd go through immediately. In one day. I spent entire days swallowing, shooting and smoking. I never, never slept. And my every thought was of Louie. No matter how zonked out I was, it was always Louie.

The kids took care of themselves, the older ones watched the younger ones. They survived on their own. The only problem was Nancy, who was starting to hit the local bars. Although she was only 15, she looked much older, her friends were older and she had no problem getting served. "It's fun, Ma," she told me. "You should go with me. It'd make you forget about Daddy." That was exactly what I wanted to do, forget about Louie. So one night, I went with her.

It only took me a few hours to pick up a tall, good-looking 24-year-old named Hal Lyndal. I was terribly lonely, I needed a man and Hal was a man. At the end of the night I was so stoned I made him take me home. Once I got him there I wouldn't let him leave, and he just moved right in. It was that quick and that simple. By that point, in my own mind, I had decided that Louie had run off with another woman, and this was my way of getting back at him for it.

Philip was terribly upset when I walked in with Hal. There was nobody who could take Louie's place. "You better get out of my house," he warned Hal, " 'cause my father's gonna come home and kill you." It took him a long time to accept Hal, but eventually he came around.

Hal fit right in. He liked kids, drugs and he had $1500 in the bank. I told him I was going to make him a Long Island speed connection, and he'd be able to support us with his drug earnings. So he gave me some money for drugs and overdue bills. I bought drugs with it, enough for me and him and Paige and Nancy.

Hal smoked pot when I met him, but I quickly turned him into a dopie. As soon as he woke up in the morning I would shove a matchbook under his nose and tell him to sniff it. He did and he was gone for the day. He was really fascinated by the whole scene, and I took advantage of it. I told him to quit his job. He quit his job. I told him to take money out of the bank. He ran to the bank and took it out. I told him to go cop, he left and found some drugs. I'd never really dominated anyone before and I was enjoying it.

Eventually I managed to call every number in Louie's address book. Some of the people I spoke to loved him, others hated him; others had borrowed from him, but more had loaned to him; the book was almost evenly divided between men and women, people who knew about his wife and family, people who couldn't believe he was married. But there was one thing in common: Nobody knew where he was, nobody had seen him. Louie just walked out of the house one day and disappeared off the face of the earth. He was absolutely, totally, completely gone. He walked out and left his license, his registration, his address book and every stitch of clothes except what he was wearing. And that was the last time anyone had seen him.

For two months I didn't hear a single word about Louie. In those two months my life and my family had fallen apart. I was into drugs, Paige was into drugs, Nancy was into drugs, the rent wasn't paid, the bills were overdue, a 24-year-old man was living with me and taking drugs, the phone got shut off and I was broke.

It was all Louie's fault for leaving. He was the cause of all my problems. There were times when I was sorry I'd ever met him. I hated Louie all over again.

Then the police found what was left of him.

PART
IV

I knew Louie Mileto better than anyone else in the world. And I never really knew him at all. But there was a time when we laughed and we loved and he made me the happiest woman alive. Now I wanted somebody to pay for taking him away from me.

The government of the United States of America wanted to put some of the same people in prison. Not for Louie, they told me, but for drugs. I could help them do it.

And maybe if I helped them, I'd wind up just like Louie.

– I 7 –

"The police were here, Mum," Paige told me. "Four detectives from upstate New York were looking for you." It was a Wednesday morning and I'd been out trying to get some money. When I came back, the house was packed with kids. I didn't mind; it made me feel good to hear loud, friendly voices and laughter.

"What'd they want?" I knew I had probation in the Bronx and had broken some laws in Manhattan and on Long Island, but I'd hardly even been upstate, much less committed crimes there. So I couldn't figure out why they were looking for me. I didn't have too much time to wonder about it, though. Almost as soon as Paige finished telling me, they rapped at the door.

"Mrs. Mileto?" I counted the four of them. Four.

"Yes?" I was really speeding at that moment. It never even entered my mind that they were there because of Louie.

They identified themselves as detectives from Monroe County. I made them show me their badges. "May we come in?"

I didn't want them in the house, not with all the evidence of drug use casually lying around. "What do you want me for?"

They were very calm and at ease. "Actually, we're not here about you," the spokesman, a small, stubby man, said. "It's about your hubsand."

I forgot all about the drugs and opened the door. My heart just started thumping uncontrollably as I led them into the kitchen. My wait was over, finally I found Louie, everything was going to be all right. I sat them around the kitchen table. "You want some coffee?" I asked. I was trying very hard not to jump ahead of them. I was being very cool, very smooth.

"Mrs. Mileto, I think you'd better——"

"Where is he?" I interrupted. "What jail is he in?"

"You better sit down, Mrs. Mileto." One of them got up and offered me his chair.

I didn't want to sit down. I wanted to know about Louie. "No, I'm not gonna sit down. Where's Louie?"

This stubby detective was persistent. "Mrs. Mileto, I really——"

"What's the problem, huh? Where you got him?" I was starting to both yell and cry. What were they waiting for? Tell me, tell me now. "He'll make bail, anyway. I don't care what you got him for. You're not gonna——"

They kept trying to tell me "No, Mrs. Mileto," but I wouldn't let them. I continued to scream that Louie was too good for them, that they couldn't keep him locked up, that he'd be on the streets in 24 hours. I didn't want to listen. I was too busy telling them.

"Mrs. Mileto, we've found Louis's body."

I screamed. I screamed for a very long time. Just loud shrieks, howls, coming from deep inside my body. They weren't human sounds, they were animal cries. It was the release of unbelievable pain.

I had believed Louie was dead from the day he disappeared. I didn't believe them at all.

As soon as I started screaming the kids came running out of their rooms. The police tried to herd them back in. "Everything's all right," they said. "We just have to talk to your mother for a few minutes."

Philip didn't want to be told what to do. "Ma, what's the matter!"

I didn't know what to do. Louie was dead. How could Louie be dead? Louie *couldn't* be dead. "Philip, go tell Herbie. Tell him they found Daddy, but he's dead. Tell him to come over here." I was crying, I was hysterical, but Philip was still cool. He didn't even flinch. He just went outside and got on his motorcycle to ride across the canal.

The girls just went back into their rooms and closed the doors. They couldn't believe it either. Paige went with the little ones.

I was angry at the detectives, I hated them. "You're crazy," I challenged them, "Louie's not dead. Where's the body?"

No one of them spoke.

I felt more confident. "Where's the body?" I demanded in a louder voice. "It can't be him. I want to go see him. I want to see if it's him."

"You can't identify him, Mrs. Mileto," the stubby detective said very quietly.

"What do you mean I can't identify him? Why? Why not?"

They really didn't want to answer. "He's already been buried," one of them said.

"When?" I demanded. "Where?"

I really had to drag every answer out of these four detectives and I couldn't understand why. "We believe he was killed on the fourteenth of February, Mrs. Mileto, and we found him two days later."

"I want to see the body. I don't care what you have to do, but I want to see the body." I could hear myself ranting and raving but I couldn't stop. "That's not my husband, I'm telling you, Louie isn't dead. He can't be dead. Until I see the body, I won't believe you, do you understand, I *don't* believe you."

The small one with the voice finally had no choice. And only then did I understand why he had been so hesitant. "You won't be able to identify the body, Mrs. Mileto, 'cause there really isn't any body left."

"What?" I sat down.

"He was axed to death, Mrs. Mileto. Whoever killed your husband didn't want anybody identifying him. They really did a job on him, that's why it took us two months to figure out who it was." He paused. "You want me to go on?"

I nodded dully.

The detective didn't hold back any longer. "First they beat him up. They beat him really good. They beat him so good they knocked some of his teeth back into his throat. Then they took him and put him in a meat locker. He died in the freezer, he froze to death."

"He probably didn't even know it," one of the other detectives interrupted. "He was unconscious when they put him in the locker. He just never woke up again.

"But killing him wasn't enough. They took him out of the locker and axed him up. Finally they put the remains in the trunk of a car, drove it upstate and set it on fire." He stopped, then he lowered his voice and said softly, "There's nothing to see. Believe me, there's nothing to see."

Somehow I managed to ask some questions. The detectives believed he was first beaten up in the area of Spring Street in Manhattan. They figured Spring Street because he was known to hang out in the area, and that was the heart of the meat packing district, one of the few places where you'd find meat lockers big enough to put a man Louie's size in. "His hands were severed at the wrists. That's a warning to other people that he was caught taking what he shouldn't have been taking.

"We have reason to believe he was stealing drugs. We hope you can help us determine exactly why he was killed, which would make it easier to find his killers."

There was nothing for me to say. I just sat there.

"Tony, get her something to drink," the stubby one ordered. Tony found a bottle of Scotch and poured me one full glass. It didn't help, nothing could help. They'd killed my Louie, my wonderful, happy-go-lucky Laughing Louie, my we-stuck-

Stuckey's Louie, in-and-out Louie. They finally stopped him. But they didn't just kill him, they brutalized him. They cut him up, destroyed him, tore him apart. "How—" I started to say, but not a word came out, just a small rush of air. I cleared my throat and tried again. "How, how do you know it's him then?"

The detective explained things very professionally. "The teeth that had been lodged in the throat were identified by your dentist. He knew the caps on the teeth, he remembered putting them in.

"We also found a few pieces of the clothing you told the Nassau County Police Department your husband was wearing when he left. A piece of green suede sweater was found stuck to the stomach, and we found a little piece of brown leather from his jacket.

"It's a positive identification, Mrs. Mileto, there's no question about it."

Philip walked in just in time to hear the detective make that statement. "No it's not Dad, Ma, Herbie says it's not." He was crying now. "He said not to worry about it. It's not Daddy."

I put my arms around him. "Where's Herbie?"

"He said he's coming over later, but that we shouldn't worry. He said not to worry. It's not Daddy, is it? Daddy's not dead?"

"I don't know, honey, I'm not sure." I *was* sure. I just refused to give up my last connection with sanity, the hope that the thing they found wasn't Louie.

"We know a lot about your husband, Mrs. Mileto, we've been investigating him for quite some time now." The detectives knew all about the drug operation. They named names, places, an occasional date, and even showed me photographs of everybody—Louie's friends, their wives, mothers—in front of the barbershop. "There's a lot of questions we'd like to ask you when you have some time to think. But for now we'd like your permission to search the house," the stubby one continued in the same quiet voice. "It may help us get a lead on the people who did this."

"You can search. There's nothing here." I slowly got up from the table and walked upstairs into our bedroom. I opened Louie's drawers and just looked at his clothes, his jewelry, the bits and pieces of his life that he left behind. Bits and pieces—that's what I remember of the rest of that day. I remember sitting on two small steps holding Philip and Gay, letting them cry it out. Susan didn't cry, instead she got angry. She just walked out of the house and slammed the door. She was mad at Louie for dying and she never forgave him for it. Never.

I remember walking over to Herbie's. He never did come to our house and I needed to talk to him. "They're coming to search the house, Herbie," I told him.

"Don't involve me," he said, "I'm a friend of Louie's and that's it. We don't work together or anything like that. Don't you tell them we worked together." He stopped. "Besides," he continued almost offhandedly, "it can't be Louie because they didn't give you a death certificate."

"Oh, do I need a death certificate to prove my husband's dead?" I really didn't know. "These people aren't going to come to my house and make up this terrible story. Nobody would do that."

"You don't know that, Ceil, you don't know what these people want from you. But until you have a death certificate, there's no proof that he's dead. Call up any lawyer, he'll tell you."

"He's dead, Herbie," I said flatly. "I believe them."

I didn't want to, and the next day I went to my dentist's office to make sure he had positively identified Louie from only two teeth, and he had, positively, but even at that moment there was no doubt left in my mind.

"I'm going to let them search the house," I told Herbie.

"Let them search the house," he shrugged. "That's your business. Just remember, Louie and I were friends. We never worked together."

I walked back across the canal. The whole thing was too horrible to comprehend in a few hours. The reality was just too much, understanding was just sinking in. I wasn't angry, I didn't hate anybody. I was so unhappy, but I just didn't have the energy to really hate. Besides, I didn't know who to hate.

The detectives stationed a guard on the house and left. They had been there about two hours. That really wasn't as long as it seemed.

Billy D'Angelo showed up before the search team. He had been crying too. Right to the end Billy had loved Louie and admired him. Later I found out that he had helped bury him, but that was later. Now he wanted Louie's address book. "Louie's father wants to see it," he explained, "the telephone book. He wants to notify some people."

I didn't want to give it to him. "Billy, this was one of Louie's most personal things. I want to hold on to it."

He was persistent. Finally he finished his argument by asking, "Don't you trust me anymore, Ceil?"

I did trust him. Only Billy hadn't deserted us. He had been showing up at the house every few days with food and any extra cash he could spare. "You're right, Billy. I'll give it to you, but give me your word that you'll bring it right back. You'll get it right back off him, 'cause this is important to me."

He promised. He lied. He returned a few hours later without the book. "Herbie took it off me," he said, unable to even look at me, "and he burned it up. I'm sorry, Ceil."

"Herbie! Herbie burned it! What the hell was Herbie doing with that book?" I was furious. "You told me that Louie's father wanted the book. Why did you lie to me, Billy, why?"

"Ceil, you don't understand—"

"What is there to understand, Billy? Tell me, what should I understand? That was Louie's book and you gave it to Herbie? Herbie who hasn't come near this house since Louie died? Herbie who wants us away from here? You were Louie's friend, how could you just give it away?"

He had nothing to say. He just stood there, his head hanging down, listening to me screaming at him.

"You were his friend, Billy," I said softly. "Louie loved you. And you did this." I made him leave.

The search team showed up at the house in the afternoon and began an attic-to-cellar, backyard-to-canal search. They really tore through the house. They went through every piece of Louie's clothing, every drawer, every closet. They tore out the wall insulation, and they found Louie's measuring scales and his plastic sealing machines. They found my works and I showed them my methadone to prove I was an addict. They really got excited when they found Louie's basement phone-tap and taping system. "Now we got everybody's voice," they thought, but all they really had were tapes of Paige and Nancy ordering drugs.

Their skin divers in the canal found four sets of works, wrapped in plastic bags, that I'd thrown away four different times that I decided to give up drugs, and two pairs of hand-cuffs that I'd thrown in there when Louie threatened to cuff me to the bed again.

They really did a professional job. They carried out loads of papers, rent receipts, phone bills, notes, anything in Louie's name or handwriting. They took almost all my jewelry and Louie's jewelry, explaining, "If any of this stuff was stolen we might be able to trace it back, and maybe that would help us find his murderer." So I gave the jewelry to them, and all the papers, and the tape recorder, and anything else they wanted. In return they gave me receipts. I got receipts for everything. I *still* have the receipts.

While the search team was working two detectives were questioning me. "Are you sure Louis wasn't beaten in the base-ment and then taken to Manhattan?"

"Are you crazy?" I couldn't believe they would ask such stupid questions.

"How did you and Louis get along?"

"Fine, like every other married couple, we had some times, you know." It didn't take me too long to realize they were try-ing to intimate that I had something to do with Louie's murder.

"Who are Louie's friends?"

"He had a lot of friends. I don't want to get his friends in trouble."

"But you can help us find his murderer. We know he was into something, we know he didn't work in a gas station——"

"He worked in a gas station." Over and over and over.

"Why did you wait two weeks to report him missing?"

"Louie used to take off on little side trips . . ."

"You can really help us by . . ."

"I don't know anything about that and even if I did . . ."

"But why do you . . ."

"You people think you can come in here and . . ."

Louie's father and brother showed up in the middle of the afternoon. They went into our bedroom and started packing his clothes.

"Mrs. Mileto, we're trying to find your husband's killers but you're . . ."

"I know you want me to say . . ."

The phone started ringing continuously. Friends from all over the country were calling in.

"If you could only tell us who he worked with . . ."

"Ceil, we're gonna take this new sports coat that Louie just got and . . ."

The kids started crying. They needed attention too.

"Hello, Ceil? I just heard. Georgie just called me, I can't believe it . . ."

"Just a few more questions, Mrs. Mileto . . ."

"We're just gonna pack up a few things, Ceil . . ."

"I want to spend a few minutes with my children."

The neighbors stood in their front yards, watching the skin divers in the canal and the cars pulling up to the house. It was like the circus had come to town, and I was performing in the middle ring.

The police left about 8:30 P.M.

Louie's father and his brother left soon after.

The phone stopped ringing.

And, finally, the house was quiet. Me and my children were alone, and we cried. We cried for my husband and for their father, for the wonderful years we'd been together, for the things he gave us, for the way things used to be. And we cried because of the pain we felt.

Louie's brother returned to talk about funeral arrangements.

"We want to move the body down to Calvary," he told me politely but firmly, "and we'll give you the death certificate if you'll sign the papers so we can move the body." I knew he hated having to ask me for anything, Louie's family had no use for me once they found out I was an addict. "My mother will pay for the funeral, and when you get some money you can pay her back."

I almost laughed. Louie left no insurance of any kind, there was no money in the bank and nothing hidden in the house. "I have no money. Where am I gonna get some money?"

"Well, you have that diamond watch Louie gave you for Christmas," he said. "Give it to me and I'll see if I can sell it for you."

I wanted to keep the watch, but I figured I needed the cash a lot more. I gave it to him to sell and eventually he got $600 for it. Little by little, all the bits and pieces of my life with Louie were going out the front door.

"You're welcome to come to the funeral," he explained, "but I don't want you saying anything to upset my mother. You just sit on the side with your kids and don't say anything."

The story of Louie's death made the early papers, and more calls and telegrams started coming in. Now even our neighbors and the kids' friends were coming over to tell us how sorry they were. We didn't hear a word from Herbie, though, not even a phone call.

The kids stayed off to themselves. Nobody talked to each other in the house. Every time we looked at each other we started crying. Louie was gone, Daddy was gone, it didn't seem possible. Hal was around, wanting to help but feeling like an intruder. There was really nothing he could do.

The house finally cleared out after midnight. The kids went to bed and I was alone, really alone, for the first time. I sat and listened to the quiet, the settling sounds the house made, the water flowing by in the canal, and I thought about my Louie. He was a hustler, a crook, a liar and a grand actor. But he was also the most wonderful, most loving man I had ever known. I sat and I thought about our whole life together, the trips across America, Mark and Mikey, the good years, the years in jail, the year since his release. And I smiled. Sitting there all by myself, in a dark house, just thinking about him, he made me smile.

I went upstairs and got very, very high.

–18–

Seven of us rode to Louie's funeral in the front of a pickup truck. I couldn't afford to rent a limousine and no one offered to rent one for us, so we all squeezed into the front seat of Hal's El Camino, and he drove us to the cemetery. By the time we got there our clothes were badly wrinkled and we looked just as terrible as we felt.

Susan didn't even want to go, she wanted to go to school. She refused to believe that her father was dead, and she didn't want to hear us talking about it.

He had a closed coffin. I just stared at that big brown box. I couldn't believe that was Louie. I knew he was dead, I knew the remains of his body were in there, I just couldn't believe it. I had no money, but my father-in-law gave me $20 and Philip went across the street and bought a wreath that read "Beloved father, from his wife and children."

There were about 70 people there. His whole family, their friends, our friends. A lot of people I didn't know, so I just stood in the background with my children. His mother was there, but we didn't speak. We couldn't, we had never even been introduced. Louie and I were together seven years, and I'd never met his mother. Until the funeral, I'm not even sure she knew he was married. Louie kept telling me he was going to introduce us, he kept promising, but he kept putting it off. I think he was afraid of it. My mother never approves of anybody, he told me. That was his excuse. I thought it was strange, but I didn't mind, that was Louie. And as long as I had him, I didn't need to meet his mother.

She took the murder very hard. She was hysterical, continually screaming, "Louie! Louie! They killed the kid, they killed the kid" over and over.

His father was crying too. Him I knew. He came over to me and put his arms around me and cried and told me how sorry he was. I held on to him and told him how sorry I was. He was shaking.

There was a lot of crying, Italians let their emotions out and this was a time for it. The only reason I didn't get hysterical was my drugs. I had been speeding since the day the detectives came to my house.

The service was short and simple, and then we went back to our big, empty house. On the way home, squeezed into the truck, I decided I had to go back on welfare. It was the only solution I could come up with.

A few days later one of Paige's friends offered to drive me down to the welfare office to register. I needed the lift because Louie's Lincoln had never been found and the drop-off jalopy was missing somewhere in Manhattan, so I took his ride.

And this kid took me for the whole ride. On the way to the office the police moved in on us. The connection wasn't stupid, as soon as he saw red flashers he handed me what I thought was one plastic bag of little white pills. I shoved them into my panty hose.

That one little bag turned out to be two bags and a grand total of 190 amphetamines, good enough for a possession charge. The kid never opened his mouth to claim the pills, he let me take the whole weight for the charge. Two days after Louie's funeral I was back in jail on a drug charge.

My mother bailed me out, $500 worth.

That was the real beginning of my life without Louie. I just couldn't pull myself together. One month passed. Two months. Time just drifted slowly by. At the hearing on the pill charge I was sentenced to 90 days in the Nassau County jail. The judge said I was incorrigible. Besides, I'd been late for my court appearance and made him late for his golf game.

As soon as I went back into jail the house was gone. The welfare department took over and put all the furniture and all the kids in storage. Paige and Nancy went to live with David's mother in Queens, and Philip, Gay and Susan were put into a children's shelter. I was told I could get everything back, kids and furniture, if I was drug free when I came out.

I didn't have much choice, drugs weren't too easy to come by in Nassau County jail. I spent my first week on the inside trying to kick my methadone habit. But instead of bringing me down, they shut me off completely. My body physically craved the drug, I couldn't relax, I couldn't even close my eyes. I walked my cell for three days until another inmate told me I could get some medicine at the hospital, but I could only get into the hospital if I was bleeding.

I let her cut my arm open with a piece of glass.

I got enough Valium and chloral hydrate out of it to knock me out for two days. That was enough time for my body to adjust to no drugs.

The thing I remember best about Nassau County were the "pay" telephones. We "made" them by sticking a pillow in the toilet and jumping on it so it would suck up all the water in the bowl. Then we'd wash out the bowl with brown soap and a rag. When the bowl was dry, we could talk to the men in the cells upstairs through the pipes and through the men's own washed-out toilets. We really formed friendships with the men upstairs. We talked about everything people on the outside talked about, except we talked through dry toilets. What do you do all day? Where you from? You married? What did you do on the streets? What drug do you use? Have you got a good lawyer? Can you bail me out? One guy that used to call me all the time wanted me to send him up a pair of my underpants on the food cart. I asked him what he needed them for and he said he wanted to wear them. That was the end of that friendship, I didn't need to know any more weirdos.

We called them "pay" telephones because if a guard caught anyone wtih her head buried in a bowl she "paid" by being locked into her cell for a few days. That meant no going to work, no walking the corridor, no cigarettes from the commissary and no special privileges. They were expensive calls and, like most everybody else, I paid for a few.

The only visitors I had were Hal, a few times, and Herbie's lawyer, once. "Herbie just wants to see how you're doing?"

I knew Herbie well enough to know he wanted more than that. "I'm doing okay," I told him.

He coughed. "He'd also like to know if anybody besides your own attorney has been up here to talk to you. You know, any government people or police officers, anyone like that."

I had to smile. Herbie was beginning to sweat a little. "You mean, he wants to know if I told anybody Louie was working for him, right?"

He didn't really answer me, he just mumbled some sort of protest.

"I should make him worry for what he's done to me. But you tell him that I haven't talked to anybody. Nobody's been here, nobody's asked any questions. But after you tell him that, tell him that I could use some help." That wasn't meant as extortion, I didn't want to talk to anybody. Besides, who would care what I had to say. I just wanted Herbie to give me some money.

The attorney slammed his attaché case shut. "Okay, I'll ask him," he agreed. "I'll get back to you." I never saw him again.

As soon as I finished my 90-day Nassau time, the Bronx authorities picked me up and revoked me on violation of probation. The Bronx sent me to Riker's Island to finish up the weeks I had left.

There was no frame to my life. Time had absolutely no meaning. In jail, out of jail, there was no difference. I have only bits and pieces of memories of that time. I remember Christmas 1972. Nancy and I got into a cab and rode by Herbie's house to see how he had decorated. He didn't just have Santa Claus, he had Rockefeller Center. He had Santa Claus and eight reindeer and a sled piled up with presents. As we were looking at the happily lit house we saw Herbie pull up in his Mercedes. He climbed out with his arms filled with gift-wrapped presents. It was going to be a big Christmas at his house. We just sat there, staring out of the cab, feeling awful.

I celebrated the New Year by getting busted again, this time for selling cocaine. It was a bad rap. I'd given some to this kid who said he was sick, I never sold him anything. That was enough for Hal Lyndal. He couldn't take my drugs anymore, and he packed up and finally left for good. I didn't blame him.

My mother bailed me out again, giving her a grand total of $3500 in bail money invested in me. I went to welfare and talked them into getting me a place in Long Beach, on Long Island. I wanted Long Beach because Hal lived nearby, and whenever I managed to clean myself up for a few days I called him and he'd take me out. He was ready to marry me as soon as I got cleaned up. I wanted to marry him too. Why not? But I just couldn't kick the drugs.

The kids all moved into the Long Beach apartment with me. It was the first time in the months since I'd gone to jail that the six of us were together. The place was a 24-hour party. When the speed connection left, the barb connection would show up. Philip was shooting craps on the floor. He had his own bedroom, Nancy and Paige had their own bedrooms, and Gay and Susan shared a bedroom with me. It wasn't Bellmore, but it wasn't Brooklyn either.

They all missed Louie as much as I did. Philip spent a lot of time thinking about his last trip with his father. "You know, Ma," he told me once, "when I had all that money in my hand I was thinking of slipping a few hundred out of it. I'm really glad I didn't, because I would never want to think that maybe

Daddy had the money on him to make a payoff, but that he didn't have enough because I robbed him, and that's why they killed him."

Susan, my little one, missed him worst of all. We went to visit his grave a few times, and each time she would have a fit. She'd pick up rocks and throw them at us and warn, "You better not start that crying all over again. You better not cry!" She stayed mad at Louie for dying.

Things continued to get worse. The house was always packed with people I hardly knew, sleeping all over the place. Drugs were everywhere. Paige and I both got pregnant. We went in for abortions one right after another. I had no qualms about this abortion. This was Hal's baby, not Louie's. I didn't care.

The only thing I had been reasonably responsible about was seeing my probation officer, because I couldn't handle going back to jail. But in March 1973, I missed one Tuesday and called to tell her I couldn't come in. "I was in a car accident," I said, "and I'm all black and blue." That was true, but not the way I made it sound. I had been in a car accident, I was stoned out in the back of Nancy's boyfriend's car, and he was barbed out, and he hit another car. And I was black and blue, but not from that accident. I got the black and blues a few nights later in a hamburger joint, when I was so stoned I kept falling down. "I can hardly walk," I honestly told my probation officer, "so I can't come in."

She understood. "I'll come to see you then," she said. She showed up with three other people, her supervisor, plus two young agents from the Bureau of Narcotics and Dangerous Drugs. "This is Jack Bruns and this is Teddy Burke, they want to talk to you when I'm finished."

I shrugged. I didn't care. I sat politely and answered all her questions. I was pregnant seven different times. No, I never had venereal disease. No, I didn't use drugs. Yes, the children were in school. She went right down her list of questions and I gave her the proper answer for each and every one.

Then she left me alone with Bruns and Burke. The three of us were sitting around the kitchen table. I didn't know exactly why these agents had come. I guessed it had something to do with the coke case. I'd just finished trial on it and there had been a hung jury.

"Mrs. Mileto," Burke began, "we're going to tell you directly. Your life is in danger. There are some people who are planning to kill you. We're going to give you a choice: Either you come into protective custody with your children, or we'll be forced to put you in what's called a safe house, which amounts to the same thing."

"This is for your own protection," Bruns added. He was younger than Burke, and nice-looking in a common way. Burke was taller and had wavy black hair and was really handsome. I wondered if he was married. "If you don't want to cooperate with us," Bruns kept talking, "you don't have to. That's your choice. But we have all the proper authority to take you and your family into custody."

"One way or the other," Burke interrupted, "you're going. Either willing or unwilling, but you're going."

I began to pay some attention to what they were saying. Going? Who was going? They weren't talking about any coke case. "What?" I said. I wasn't sure exactly what I was hearing.

Burke ran it down for me one more time. "Evidently you have some information that certain people consider dangerous to them. They're willing to kill you, and your children, to make sure you never talk."

I had just started noticing his green eyes when he started talking about someone killing me and my family. I couldn't believe what was happening. It was too fast. In real life things didn't happen this way. People just didn't come into your kitchen and tell you somebody was planning to kill you. That was a scene from one of those gangster pictures Louie loved so much.

Of course, in real life they also don't come into your kitchen and tell you your husband's been chopped up with an ax. "What are you talking about?" I didn't even know what questions to ask.

"Herbert Sperling," Bruns said.

Now I knew they weren't serious. "No, not Herbie," I laughed. "I don't know anything about Herbie at all."

"Mrs. Mileto," Burke said. "We've been watching Sperling for a long time. We believe that Sperling may be planning to kill you."

Kill me! That was impossible. I didn't believe Herbie could even think about something like that. In all the time I knew him he'd done nothing to make me believe he was capable of anything like that. "Listen," I told them, "I don't know anything, nothing at all. I swear it, I don't know anything." I didn't think I did. Aside from bits and pieces of telephone conversations, and little jokes, and a few meetings, what did I know? Nothing that could help the government.

"Do you know Herbert Sperling?" Bruns asked.

"Sure I know Herbie," I told them.

"Then you can help us."

I just didn't see how. So I knew Herbie. I'd never seen him sell any drugs. The only thing I'd ever actually seen was him giving packages to Louie and Louie handing him back big amounts of money. "I don't understand," I half mumbled and now I was starting to cry too. "Why would Herbie want to kill us? He knows I don't know anything. Besides, we were friends. He knows I wouldn't talk."

Burke explained. I had stopped noticing his good looks. "He's afraid you'll want to get even."

"Even! Even for what? This is getting outta hand. What are you talking about?"

"Mrs. Mileto," Bruns, the younger one, said evenly, "we think it's possible that Herbert Sperling was responsible for your husband's death."

– 19 –

At first I didn't believe them. Herbie and Louie were best friends. My mind was racing. Herbie was going to make Louie a partner. They worked together, played together, watched football together. I didn't know what to do. Even our kids were close friends. It didn't seem possible. Herbie was rotten, but murder Louie? Kill me? I couldn't believe it.

"Did you know your husband was stealing from Sperling?" Bruns asked me. And then the whole thing began to make sense. If these agents were right, Herbie, or Herbie's men, did find Louie. And they beat him to death.

Louie knew about it too. He must have. "The kid's gonna get me killed," he kept saying on that last Valentine's Day, "the kid's gonna get me killed." And Billy, Billy told me that Herbie was going to hurt Louie if he found him. I thought that was just Bobby's mind working. Until the agents planed the thought it never occurred to me that Herbie was involved in Louie's death.

"How long have you known about this?" I asked the two agents.

Burke answered. "We've been looking for you for almost a year."

I started to tell them that I shouldn't have been too hard to find, I'd been in jail a lot of that time, but I didn't finish my sentence. Right in the middle of a word I realized what they were telling me, and I burst into tears. "I'm scared, I'm scared, I'm scared," I kept crying. "I don't wanna get cut up, I don't want them to cut me up."

"That's why we're here," Burke cut in, "to make sure that doesn't happen.'"

I lifted my head. "You don't know Herbie, you don't know how powerful he is. If he wants to kill me, you can't protect me. He'll get me and he'll cut me up like he did Louie." I went on a crying and screaming binge.

Burke and Bruns did their best to calm me down. They were total professionals. "Mrs. Mileto. Ceil, we're different from city cops. Our whole job is to protect your life," Burke told me, his voice never rising above his mild tone. "Believe me, we can do it. We've protected hundreds of people and no one, absolutely no one under our protection, has ever been touched."

He told me what the government was offering. In return for my help they would move me and the children to a different city, "almost anywhere you want to go," give me a complete new identity, a place to live, a small car, a monthly allowance and safety. "If you're still strung out," he continued, "we'll put you in a hospital to detox. We'll help you in every way we can, if you'll help us."

"But I don't know anything," I cried, loud, "I don't know anything."

They showed me photographs of friends and acquaintances of Louie's, people I'd seen in the apartment, or in clubs, or at affairs. "Do you know who this is?"

"No," I lied.

"How about this guy?"

"No," I lied again.

"Him?"

"No, I don't know anything. I told you, I can't help you." I was just too scared to cooperate. I was speeding my brains out, and I knew they could revoke my probation and put me back in jail. I knew they could take my kids away from me. But I was just too frightened.

Then they told me about Patsy Parks. "Did you know her?" Burke asked. Louie had told me about her. She was a very pretty model that had gone out with Richie Maxton a few times. "She's dead," he said bluntly. "She was subpoenaed into court a few months ago. But she went to these people for money to get out of town. Instead they stabbed her to death, threw gasoline on her and set her on fire."

Bruns took over. "These are tough people you're dealing with, and they've got a major drug business to protect. They're not gonna let you, or your kids, get in their way. Don't even think about going to them for help."

"You owe a lot of time," Burke cut in, "and you're gonna do that time if you don't cooperate with us."

"Do you know Alvin Gibbons?"

"No."

"Do you know Richard Maxton?"

"No."

"Johnny Hooks?"

"No, I told you I don't know anything."

"Mrs. Mileto, I want to tell you something . . ." The front door opened and Paige and Nancy walked in. "Don't tell the kids who we are," Bruns ordered. "Tell them we're from the probation department."

I went into my bedroom with the girls and closed the door behind me. I needed their help. I needed someone, anyone, to tell me what to do. "Those guys are feds," I told the girls, "and they're here about Daddy." I gave them the whole story as quickly as I could. "They told me Herbie's gonna kill me," I started crying again, "and I don't know what to do."

"Are you crazy?" Nancy said. "Don't say a word to them."

"Let's get outta New York," Paige said. "Don't tell them anything or we'll all be killed." They were scared, but they didn't cry.

We hugged each other very tightly, and I went back to sit

with Burke and Bruns. "I can't help you," I told them. "I just can't."

They didn't let up. Another hour passed. Philip came home. Then Gay and Susan. Still more questions, more warnings, more pleas. All of us, the kids, the agents and me sat around the kitchen table. I liked the agents, they were calm, considerate and professional, but I was still too frightened. I was having nightmares of being chopped out and left in a trunk, like Louie.

After at least five hours of constant discussion, Bruns sighed, "If that's the way you want it, that's the way it's going to be. You don't want to cooperate with us, that's your decision, but we're going to subpoena you into court as an uncooperative witness.

"We're also going to put you and your family into what we call a safe house under a material witness warrant—this is for your own protection. A safe house is something like a jail, you can't leave once you're in, but you'll be safe and you'll be together. It's not too pleasant, though."

"It's your say, Ceil," Burke said. "Either way you're gonna testify. Whether you want to cooperate or not, you're gonna testify. And if you get up on that stand and lie, and believe me, we can prove you know more than you're admitting, then we will prosecute you for perjury and you'll do time."

Bruns took over. "All you have to do is say the word and you'll have a good, clean place to live, the rent will be paid, you'll have money in your pocket, identification, you'll have food, and you won't have to worry that every time one of the kids leaves they might not come back."

"How about it?" Burke asked. "Let us put you in protective custody. Do it the easy way."

Bruns urged, "Do it for Louie. The people who killed him are walking around free men. He's dead. And they killed him."

It was the toughest decision I ever had to make. If I testified, Herbie would kill me if he could find me. If I didn't testify voluntarily, he'd kill me anyway. Life against death, freedom against prison. The government really didn't leave me any choice.

I walked back into the bedroom with Nancy and Paige. "I'm gonna answer their questions," I said.

"But Ma—" Nancy started.

"I don't have any choice. I don't think what I know can help them, but I have to tell them. Herbie's gonna kill us anyway if he finds us, so we might as well talk. Besides, what did Herbie ever do for us anyway? He deserted us after Daddy disappeared. I'm gonna tell them what I can."

I hated Herbie. The pieces all fit together so easily now. I knew why he didn't want me calling the police to tell them Louie was missing, why he didn't want me to tell them Louie worked for him. And it was obvious why he didn't come near us when we really needed help. I hated Herbie. It was easy to do.

I sat down at the kitchen table again. I cleared my throat. And I said, without any warning to the agents, "The first time I found out Louie was into heavy drugs was when we were living in Elmhurst. I found some cocaine in his drawer, mixed in with his underwear."

Both agents sat bolt upright. They knew I had made my decision. "Did you ever see any money passed from Louie to anyone else?"

"I saw him give money to Herbie and other people."

"Do you know Alvin Gibbons?"

"Yes, I knew him through Louie."

"Do you recognize the man in this picture?"

"Yeah." I told them who it was. "That's Alvin."

"Get a coat please, Mrs. Mileto, we'd like you to meet our boss." They hustled me into Manhattan and I found myself sitting in the office of the director of BNDD in New York.

He was a charming man who reminded me a little of Alfred Hitchcock, the movie director. When I was brought into his office I was just coming down off my speed and I was very nervous, but he made me feel right at ease. "You're still an attractive young woman," he said, "and you can make a good life for yourself outside of New York. We can help you do that, if you're willing to help us."

"I'll try," I answered, "but I really don't know anything. Louie didn't tell me too much about what he was doing."

"You probably know more than you think you do. It's up to us to ask the right questions. Like how were you able to live on the scale you were living? Louie supposedly owned a gas station."

"Louie worked for Herbie," I told him.

"Herbie?"

"Herbert Sperling." The government always wanted very precise answers.

"How do you know that?"

"Louie, my husband, Louis Mileto, he told me he was." This was more of a conversation than a complete examination. I figured they were just testing me, trying to find out how much I really knew. I was beginning to worry that they would just say thank you, put me in a car and send me home when they found out I really didn't know anything. And after they'd finished telling me how dangerous I was to Herbie, I didn't want to be any place where he could find me.

"How much was Herbert Sperling paying your husband?"

"Five thousand dollars a week."

"What did your husband do for Herbert Sperling?"

"He cut drugs for him."

"How do you know that?"

"My husband told me that's what he was doing."

"Is that the only way you know that?"

I thought for a minute. "I saw his cutting tools." I thought some more. "And Billy D'Angelo told me too."

"That's no good," Burke, with the great green eyes, said. "You can't talk about things other people told you. Everything's got to be your own knowledge."

I told him I understood. The questions went on and on. "When did you see your husband make that delivery?" the director asked after I told him I'd gone on drops with Louie sometimes.

I couldn't remember when it was. I told him so.

"When you're trying to remember dates," he explained, "try to remember small things. Were you wearing a coat?"

I thought about it. "I was."

– 230 –

"So it had to be in the fall or winter. Do you remember where you went from the bar where Louie made his delivery?"

That I remembered. "We went Christmas shopping."

"See how easy it is," he smiled. "So now we know it was in November or December." The interview went on for almost two hours, question after question. Sometimes I thought they had the information and they were just using me to check its accuracy or using it to check my accuracy, and sometimes I thought I was telling them things they never knew before. Toward the end of the interview they started showing me pictures again. I identified as many as I could. Then they showed me a picture of Billy D'Angelo. "Do you know who this is?"

I just sat for a second. Billy was a nice kid who had just gotten in over his head, he wasn't like Herbie or Richie or Johnny Hooks. He wasn't a professional. I liked him; I didn't want to be the one to get him in trouble. Then I thought about what Burke and Bruns had told me, that Herbie might kill anyone who could tie him to Louie or to the drug operation. Billy would have to be one of the first to go. He was still involved with Herbie. My kids would see him at Herbie's house, or I'd see his car there when I went by. "That's Mama Rosa." I smiled. "Billy D'Angelo. He worked for Louie, he helped Louie cut once in a while." Maybe I was helping Billy.

I told them just about everything I knew. It didn't seem like too much to me. I was positive I didn't know enough to hurt Herbie. But they thought differently. They really got excited about some of the information I gave them. Finally the director turned to Bruns and Burke and said, "All right, let's get her into custody. Let's get her out of New York right away."

He looked back at me. "Mrs. Mileto, from this minute your life is going to change completely. I know this is going to be difficult for you to understand and to get used to, but you'll have to forget your past. Everything that's happened to you is over. Finished. You won't be able to contact anyone you know, and that includes family and friends. The same goes for your children. They have to understand that they won't be able to contact any of their old friends."

That sounded terrible. "You don't mean forever, right?"

"I mean forever. Ceil Mileto is dead. She doesn't exist anymore after today, except for the trials you'll be testifying in. You and your family and everything you want to take with you will be moved anywhere you'd like to live in the United States. I suggest you pick some place you've never been before, a big city would be better than a small town, but we'll move you anywhere, you just have to tell us where. When we need your testimony, you'll be brought back to New York and protected by our agents and federal marshals."

He sounded like a recorded announcement. He just kept talking in this same voice, just reeling off all these facts. I listened, but I didn't really believe. It didn't seem possible that somebody could change their whole identity so easily.

"When you arrive wherever you pick, you'll start a whole new life. You'll be given new identification, new school records for your children, a new past history. There will be absolutely no way you can be traced."

"That sounds hard to believe," I said. I was still afraid of Herbie. If he wants to find me, I thought, he'll find me.

"Mrs. Mileto, there are hundreds of people, just like you, federal witnesses, living all over the country, having good lives but using new names and new pasts. Now, you'll be given money each month to live on, I think you'll be getting something just over a thousand dollars a month, and that's it. That has to pay your rent, your food bills and whatever else you need." He finally stopped speaking. There was an old-fashioned-looking feather pen on his desk, and he picked it up and stared at it for a minute. "I know I'm giving you a lot of information in a very short period of time, but unfortunately we have no choice. We don't want anyone to know we're taking you into custody. We want your appearance in court to be a complete surprise, if possible. We also want to minimize any danger to you and your family.

"I don't want to lie to you, there is always some danger. In your case, quite a lot of danger, I understand. That's not going to go away after the trials over, either. For the rest of your life there will always be the chance that someone may try to kill you. If you follow our suggestions, we can almost guarantee you it will never happen. It hasn't happened yet and we've been in business for a long time. With your new identity, you'll be safe. However, if you feel nervous or in any way apprehensive about your safety, we'll put an around-the-clock guard with you starting right now. That's up to you too." He looked up at me from his pen like he wanted me to answer.

I had no answer. "I don't know now," I told him. "I'll have to see how I feel." I couldn't feel a thing right then. I was numb. How do you react when somebody tells you your whole life is over? You have to start again? That you can't even contact your own mother? "Just get us out of New York," I said—or something like that—"and we'll be safe enough, I think." I tried to decide right then and there where I wanted to be moved to. California was wonderful, but there were too many memories of Louie and maybe too many friends. "Just send us some place warm," I asked, "maybe some place in the South. Except for Miami, I've never been anywhere down there."

The director stood up and reached out with his hand. I took it and we shook. "Okay, some place in the South. You'll be leaving tomorrow. Until then these agents"—he nodded at Burke and Bruns—"will stay with you."

It was just after 9:00 P.M. when we walked out of his office. It had been both the shortest and longest day of my life. So much had happened, so much had changed. One minute my future was filled with nothing but drugs, jail and probably an early death, and a few hours later I was given a chance to start all over again, in a new city, with money, with my children. But it wouldn't be Ceil Mileto. It would be somebody else.

And all I had to do was talk about Herbie. Herbie, Louie's friend. And possibly even Louie's murderer. It was dangerous, but I was starting to feel good about it. This was my chance to get back at him, and I intended to do just exactly that. Now, finally, I had something to live for.

As soon as I got home I called the only person in the world, besides my kids, who meant something to me, my mother. I explained to her that I was going into protective custody. "I have to, Ma, there's people trying to kill me."

"But where," she asked, "where are you going?"

"I can't tell you that. I just want you to know you won't be able to contact me." I felt so sorry for her. After all I had done to her, after the way she continued to help me, I was just going to take her grandchildren and disappear from her life forever. And besides us she didn't have very much.

She was against it. "Are you crazy, Ceil? Don't get involved. These people will kill you, just like they killed Louie." We argued for a while, and then she happened to remember that a package had arrived at the house, addressed to me, two weeks earlier. It had been postmarked California—but the name on the return address was one of Herbie's New York lawyers.

That was really strange, I thought. What could one of Herbie's lawyers be sending me? I asked her if she knew what it was.

She didn't. "It was just a square package. I didn't accept it because I didn't know when I'd see you again." That was her way of saying she didn't know when I'd be straight, or when I'd need bail money, again. "So I sent it back to the post office."

I couldn't figure out what it could possibly be. Then the warnings I'd been given all day sunk in. I decided it was an attempt to kill me. I turned white. Burke, I think, asked me what was the matter. "My mother received a package," I said softly, "with the name of one of Herbie's attorneys on it."

By the time the agents checked with the post office the package had been marked undeliverable. They never did find out exactly what was in it, but they figured it was probably a bomb. I was asked if I wanted my mother placed in protective custody with me and the kids. If I felt her life was in danger, they were going to take her, whether she wanted to go or not.

I had to laugh. "Let me tell you something," I told them. "My mother would not allow you to put her in custody. She would put up such a stink you wouldn't believe it. She would rather die than go into custody."

The kids didn't want to go into custody either, although Paige quickly decided she was in love with Teddy Burke's curly hair. Philip was furious I'd agreed to work with the government.

"You're gonna get us killed," he yelled at me. "You should know better than to talk to the cops, Ma. Daddy wouldn't like this one bit."

"Daddy's dead, Philip," I told him, "and this is our chance to get even with Herbie for everything. And all we have to do is tell the truth. Just because Daddy brought us up with a code about not talking, are you gonna stand for this? Are you gonna let Herbie get away with this?"

"I don't care," he yelled angrily, "I know Daddy wouldn't want us to talk. He hated cops. You shouldn't talk to them. Don't talk to them!" He started crying.

I started crying too. I didn't know if I was doing the right thing, I never knew if I was doing the right thing, but it just seemed like there were no alternatives. The federal agents really made me believe my life was in danger. "Philip if they just shot him and threw him out on the road, that's different, Daddy told us that could happen. But they hurt him really bad. Why'd they have to cut him up like a sausage and put him in a trunk and set him on fire? They didn't have to do that."

"I don't care," he cried. "I don't wanna go, I don't wanna go."

Nancy didn't want to go either. She didn't want to leave her new boyfriend. So she started crying too. "I don't care what you say, you can't make me go. I'm not going." Her boyfriend, Charlie I think his name was, came to the apartment with a big load of barbiturates he had just picked up. He was stoned. I chased him out, but I had to promise her she could let him know where we were and he could come down to stay with us. "If he loves you, he'll come," I told her.

Paige refused to talk to me at all, she just went into her bedroom and closed the door. When I came into the room, she ignored me.

The two little ones weren't talking to me because I was a drug addict, but they were entranced by Bruns and Burke. Teddy Burke was the agent who arrested Louie in Manhattan that last day, he was the "crazy cowboy with the six-shooters" Louie told us about, and Gay and Susan made him act out the arrest for them. Teddy did a pretty good imitation of Louie: " 'What are you bothering me for, man, I'm just laying here on the floor of my car.'"

"Well, whattya laying on the floor for, Louie?"

"'It's a free country, ain't it?'" He had the kids laughing hysterically. Somehow all of us got through the night, although I had help from some of Nancy's boyfriend's pills.

The next morning we got dressed and left. We didn't even have to pack. The agents told us to take enough just for a few days, because the BNDD has men who specialize into going into houses and packing up for people leaving for protective custody. They also warned me not to tell the kids where we were headed until we were actually on the plane. "We had an experience with a family of seven," Jack Bruns explained, "who told the kids their destination before they left. Everybody in the neighborhood knew where they were going before they got there. We had to change all the plans."

So I did exactly that. In the morning I told everybody we were going back to California. Once we got on the plane I told them the truth; our new home was Savannah, Georgia.

It was a long plane ride and the kids were really unhappy. I figured things would get better once we reached Savannah and got settled in our new apartment. But it wasn't going to be quite that simple.

We were met at the airport by federal marshal John L. Chrysler. The Federal Marshal Service is the branch that actually provides protection, BNDD just investigates and makes arrests. John L. Chrysler was exactly the opposite of Bruns and Burke, he was a heavyset, crew-cut, sunglass-wearing marshal who spoke with a deep southern accent. I disliked him immediately.

"Where's my identification?" I asked him.

"I'm sorry, ma'am, I really don't know," he twanged.

I got upset because the government had made a big deal about how important our new identity was. "You have to establish a new identity right at the beginning," I was told, "and then stick to it." Teddy Burke and Jack Bruns even made us pick out our new name before we left Long Beach. The kids went through the phone book, they argued over choices like Mafia and Bono and finally settled on Monet because it was French and they like the way it sounded. We were the Monet family. But we had no identification to prove it, and the marshal looked at me like I was crazy when I asked him about it. I was told the identification would be waiting for us, but I figured it had to be only a slight mix-up and would be taken care of. Besides, I didn't want to fight with the marshal. I was trying to cooperate. "Okay," I asked him, skipping the identification, "what hotel are we staying at?"

He tightened his mouth like he was trying to remember a difficult answer. "I don't rightly know that either, ma'am. We jus' gotta find one. See, they don't tell us too much, just pick ya all up and bring ya all down, you know." So he brung us. He piled the six of us into his car, plus the dog that Susan demanded she be allowed to bring with her and drove off toward Savannah.

It was a terrible ride. I was all mixed up. In New York they made it sound like they had a place waiting for us. Instead they had this one not-so-bright marshal who had to hunt up rooms for us to stay in. If they messed up the first thing they had to do, how could they protect all our lives? The kids were hot and cramped in the car and kept nagging and fighting. The dog had crapped all over his kennel and walked in it and then walked in the car. We were all exhausted and hungry because we hadn't eaten in hours, and we had no idea where we were going.

I was starting to get very scared again. I'd felt safe with Burke and Bruns, but I didn't see how this marshal could do anything at all to protect us. I knew we were safer in Savannah than we would have been sitting in our apartment in Long Beach, but right at that minute that didn't make me feel too much better.

Marshal Chrysler finally stopped in front of a small motel that seemed to be in the middle of nowhere. "This is it," he said.

"It" was nothing. A small motel. "The Home Sweet Home Motel." I couldn't believe the place. "It's jus' right outside of the town," he drawled.

"How far?" I asked.

"Jus' about fifteen miles, ma'am." If he ma'amed me one more time I was going to choke him.

We registered as the Monet family. They gave us two rooms

with two television sets and no cooking facilities. Paige and Nancy immediately claimed one room and announced no one else was allowed in it. Susan's dog ran outside and she started chasing it. Gay and Philip got into a fight.

Marshal Chrysler had no idea what was happening. He picked us up and dropped us off, as he was supposed to. "Now Mrs. Monet," he explained, "ya'll 'sposed to stay here till we find a place for you in town. I got thirty-eight dollars for you and ya'll pay your own hotel bill and buy your own food from that. Now if ya'll got any problems or there's anything you don't unnerstan', just call this number I'm givin' ya and ask to speak with Mr. Mayhew. He can tell you everything else. Hope ya'll enjoy your stay in Savannah, ma'am."

I just stood there like an idiot and watched him drive away. I couldn't believe what was happening, the BNDD had lied to me from beginning to end. They promised me everything and gave me two rooms in the Home Sweet Home Motel 15 miles outside Savannah, Georgia. About the only thing they were right about was us being safe there, no one in the world could find this place. Being a government witness wasn't anything like the government promised.

Nothing went right. The television went off at 1:00 A.M., and we were used to watching it all night in New York. The dog wouldn't stop barking. The air conditioning didn't work. Gay and Susan wanted to sleep with me, but Susan also wanted to sleep with Philip and Philip refused to sleep with me. The kids were screaming and fighting.

The $38 went almost immediately. We were eating doughnuts and milk for breakfast, no lunch and cheap hamburgers for dinner. The only luxury I bought was a jug of Strawberry Hill 99-cent wine so I could get high and sleep. But there were times when we had nothing to eat and were completely broke.

Mayhew turned out to be less help than Chrysler. He was just an older version, the main difference was that he had a thicker drawl. "We have no food and no money," I told him.

"Well, what would ya'll like me to do, ma'am. This is Sunday."

I said, "I'd like you to get your ass over here and write me a personal check out of your own checking account, so my children can eat!" If I had any money, I would have just put the kids in a car and disappeared. I was so mad at the government for lying to us.

"I'm sorry, ma'am," he drawled, "I can't do that. Ya'll jus' gonna have to manage on what ya got till the check comes in." The Marshal Service had raised our weekly allowance to $100 to cover our food, motel bill and anything else we might need, but we hadn't gotten any checks yet.

"When are our clothes coming down?" I pleaded. "We're running out of clothes to wear." All I wanted from him was just a little help.

"Don't rightly know, ma'am." There were a lot of things he didn't rightly know. "We're here to protect you. Anybody bother ya, ya let me know, hear!"

We were all miserable. I kept getting sick because we had no drugs and my system was kicking everything out. The kids were going crazy being cooped up, the Home Sweet Home didn't even have a pool. We were fighting all the time, always bored, and even the two trips we took into Savannah didn't help. We had no clothes, no clean underwear. We just had to get out of that place.

I couldn't take it any longer. I called Jack Bruns in New York. When I told him what was going on, he started yelling at me for not calling sooner. He really got mad at the federal marshals. They were supposed to be giving you more money, he said. They were supposed to take you to a doctor when you were sick. They were supposed to make sure you got everything the government had promised. "Ceil, I'm sorry," he said. "We'll do something about it immediately."

"Just get us out of here, Jack," I asked. "Please."

Two days later we were on our way to our new apartment in Atlanta.

$-$ **20** $-$

Our apartment in Atlanta had three bedrooms, a living room and a nice kitchen. We had no television set, no radio and no clocks, but it was a gigantic improvement over the Home Sweet Home. Even Susan's dog liked the place enough to stop crapping on the floors.

When we arrived in Atlanta, the marshals told me my monthly allowance was being raised to $400, plus they gave me another $300 cash for linens, pots and pans, and any furniture I needed to buy.

But we weren't getting along with the Marshal Service at all. They were really angry at me for calling New York. Every time they gave me anything they made me feel like I had to beg for it, like I was stealing it from them. I understood that the government had saved my life, and my kids, and I was grateful for that and I didn't like to complain, but nothing was happening the way it was supposed to. They told me in New York I'd be getting about a thousand a month, I was getting $400. They told me in New York that I could have my furniture as soon as I wanted it. But when I asked for it, I was told, "The government only makes one complete move. You'll have to wait until you're finished testifying and permanently relocated." I just didn't know who to believe.

Almost as soon as we got settled in Atlanta the marshals told me I'd have to go to New York to be briefed on the upcoming cases. I was wondering when they were going to need me, because except for the few hours I'd spent with Bruns and Burke and the director, I hadn't been questioned at all. The government still didn't know exactly how much I knew. Honestly, neither did I.

I was looking forward to testifying. Bruns and Burke told me my testimony was "key," that I was the only one not connected with the drug group that could tie everybody together. "You're going to be a big surprise to them, Ceil," Teddy Burke told me, flashing those big green eyes, "and they're really gonna be angry. That's why you're so important to us."

"And important to them, too," Jack Bruns interrupted. "If they can prevent you from testifying, we'll have a hard time making our case stick."

They'd been preparing the case for two years. They'd been watching Herbie, and Louie, and even Billy. I was the missing link to tie the whole thing together. It wasn't so much the facts about the drug operation I knew that made me important, it was that I could put everybody together, I actually saw drugs and money and buys and sells, and I wasn't a member of the ring. My testimony was totally admissible in court, as long as I only told them what I knew from seeing it myself.

I left the children with a federally provided housekeeper and flew back to New York under the name of Monet. The government was very careful about keeping my real name a secret, even the marshals didn't know who I was. Life with Louie had always been a series of adventures, and his death was putting me in the middle of another one.

U.S. attorneys George Hacker and John Boeheim began preparing me for the trials, and this was even before anybody had been arrested. "There are going to be times when you'll have eighteen or twenty different defense lawyers examining you," Boeheim explained, "and you're going to have to be able to stand up under their questioning. All we want you to do is tell the truth as you remember it, don't make anything up, don't try and add things you think might help. Just the truth as you remember it."

"Isn't it true, Mrs. Mileto," Hacker said in a harsh tone, "that you were a drug addict during this whole period and you were so stoned most of the time you really can't remember anything?"

Who did this guy think he was? "Of course not. That's a lousy——"

"And isn't it true that you hate Herbert Sperling because he wouldn't give you money after your husband disappeared?"

"No! That's not true. And I'll——"

"Come on, Mrs. Mileto, you really don't remember anything do you? You're admitting these things because the government's given you an apartment and money and a new——"

"It's not true!" I was really starting to get angry.

"Good," he smiled, "and believe me, that's absolutely nothing compared to what the defense attorneys are going to ask you. They're going to rake you up and down trying to destroy your credibility. You just stick to the truth and keep your answers short."

Boeheim took over. "One more thing, Ceil, and this is really important. You can't ever mention the fact that Louie was murdered. We're not charging anyone with the murder and, frankly, I doubt we ever will. This is a drug case. If anything about the murder gets into the trial, the defense may get a mistrial. Is that really clear?"

Painfully clear. Whoever murdered Louie was going to get away with it.

Then they outlined the government's plan. They were developing as much evidence as possible against as many people as possible, then they were going to make one clean sweep. They were going to arrest everybody in one night. "There aren't two dozen people who know about this," Hacker warned, "and one dropped word could blow the whole thing, so you don't tell anybody anything."

Then they began to question me hard for the first time. We covered my whole life with Louie in New York. They asked hundreds of questions. Did I ever see Sonny Gold do this? What about Alvin Gibbons, did he do that? Who was at Herbie's house when this happened? Did I ever see Richie Maxton give drugs to Herbie? "No." Think about it for a minute, they told me. "No, I never saw him give Herbie any drugs. But I did see him hand over gobs of money."

"Good," Boeheim said, writing everything down, "whatever you remember."

He asked me how Billy D'Angelo fit in. He was Louie's helper, I told him, and, I remembered, the cause of Louie's death. "He's probably cutting now." I really didn't know for sure. "Herbie bought Billy an Italian restaurant, a pizza parlor, on Long Island right after Louie disappeared, and I seen——"

Boeheim interrupted. "Nothing about Louie, Ceil. It's important. Remember that, huh? You could get the whole case thrown out."

"Sorry," I told him. "Anyway, he bought him this restaurant and I seen him there a lot after the place closed. I'm sure they're still keeping drugs in the iceboxes." I didn't add that I'd gone there to see Billy stoned out of my mind, a few times for some money.

They asked me for names and addresses. I told them how Herbie had destroyed Louie's address book, but before that how I'd called every single number in there, looking for Louie. The government had all my phone bills and every number outside the 516 area code, Long Island, was recorded. They traced the names through those numbers.

They showed me the hundreds of surveillance photographs they had, most of them taken at the barbershop. I identified everybody I knew in the pictures. Louie was in a lot of them. The government had really done a good job getting these pictures. I remember laughing at Herbie because he used to joke that "the feds got a camera behind this mirror" in the barbershop. He'd stand in front of the mirror and wave into it and tell me to smile, "C'mon Ceil, they're watching us." The feds were watching, but they weren't behind the mirror.

Jack Bruns walked into the room, and he showed me one of the surveillance photographs and said, "Pick me out in this picture."

I looked at the picture carefully. Richie, Louie, Herbie and a bunch of the others were outside sitting on the trunk of a Cadillac. "You're not there," I decided.

"See, Ceil, you're not as smart as you think you are," he laughed. "Who else do you think they'd put in the trunk of that Cadillac?" He told me that he lay inside the trunk, with a tape recorder, for seven hours listening to them making dope deals. "They were sitting right on top of me, for seven hours, Ceil, seven hours," he said. "I was afraid to cough. I couldn't straighten my legs when they let me out."

As they questioned me they also filled me in on information they'd picked up during their investigation, "Louie was very well liked on the street, but he was known for being cheap," Hacker said. "He'd never go into a bar and buy a round because he didn't drink. He only drank Coke." I knew that. "Herbie used him as a gofer, go for this, go for that, the way Louie used Billy D'Angelo."

I laughed at that. I didn't believe that was true. Herbie was paying him $5000 a week, and he could have gotten an errand boy for a lot less than that.

"See this guy," Hacker continued, pointing out a short, skinny man in another photograph. "That's the guy who took Louie's place. He was a real nut. One night he took a machine gun into some after-hours place and shot it up. They had him killed because of it."

Boeheim picked up. "They really blew that job though. They found him with his girl friend and they didn't kill her. They thought they did, they grazed her in the neck and then threw his body on top of hers, and he bled so badly they thought she was dead."

They had everybody, absolutely everybody, and they let me

know it. They had mothers, wives, girl friends, friends, bookies, every connection. They had been watching them, tailing them, building cases against everybody, including people I'd never seen or heard of. It was difficult to believe that they had piled up all this evidence without anyone getting onto them.

The only thing I had difficulty remembering was dates. I was so high so often that the days used to run together. So they jogged my memory, just like Burke and Bruns had done. "You found the dope how long after you moved into the house?" "Louie gave this money to Herbie how long after you found the dope?" "Now think, was it near Christmas? Did you do any shopping for presents around this time? Try to put the pieces together, Ceil, you have to try."

I did try. I tried the best I could. We spent four days in a small room in the Holiday Inn out by LaGuardia Airport going over point after point, question after question. We covered the same areas two, three, four times, and each time we did I'd remember something else I had totally forgotten, and that memory would, in turn, lead to another memory.

I was under armed guard every minute I stayed in New York. Jack Bruns and Teddy Burke were there during the day, during the questioning, and I had two other guards overnight. When I first got there I didn't like the idea of having guards around all the time. I changed my mind pretty quickly.

Jack and Teddy had just arrived for the morning detail, this was my second day there, and I was taking a shower. All of a sudden someone's at the door to my room, trying to get in. I didn't know this, and I started walking out of my bathroom. The first thing I saw was Teddy running across my room with his gun in his hand. "Get back in there," he shouted at me. Jack Bruns, meanwhile, had circled around through the adjoining room. I ran back into the bathroom and locked the door. I stood inside, wet and scared.

From inside the bathroom, I heard Teddy tear open the front door and grab the guy. It was only some drunk trying to find his own room. I wished I could have seen his face when Teddy opened the door and pointed his gun at him.

That was enough of a scare for me. After that I did whatever the agents told me, and I was very happy they were there.

Over the months I really learned to respect the BNDD agents, particularly Jack Bruns and Teddy Burke. They had long hair, dressed casually and spoke like normal, sharp guys, not like the crew-cut gung-ho federal marshals I'd met in the South. I always felt confident when I was with Burke and Bruns. They knew what they were doing, they knew what they were looking for, they knew how to act. I didn't feel the same way about the marshals.

I told that to the director before I went back to Atlanta. "The marshals are gonna get me killed," I said. "You watch! You know what the ones who're supposed to guard me in New York did? They had to drive me into Manhattan and they got lost and they drove right by the barbershop! And this one guy I knew from Louie, Bozo, he just looked me right in the eye. He recognized me. So now they know I'm with the government."

The director seemed sympathetic. I told him I wasn't getting the money I'd been promised. "I've got five kids to support, that gets expensive."

"They're wrong down there," he said flatly. "You're supposed to be getting $1080 a month to cover all your bills and expenses. I'll make sure that you get that every month from now on." He also explained that the BNDD couldn't have all my pending cases squashed, but that the government was going to contact the proper legal authorities and tell them I was cooperating with a federal agency. "Usually the judge suspends sentence in cases like this," he explained. "I don't think you have anything to worry about."

I hadn't been worried at all. I figured that was part of our deal.

He was a nice man, a calm man, and it was easy for him to tell me I had nothing to worry about. I had a lot to worry about. I had to worry about this drug dealer who might want to chop me up and put me in a freezer. "Thanks," I said, "now I can stop worrying." We both laughed.

Then down in Atlanta, something terrible happened.

By the time I got back, Paige had fallen in love with a boy

named Andy and was staying over at his apartment. She'd fixed up his roommate, Lonnie, with Nancy and they'd hit it off, so both girls were happier than they'd been since we left Long Island.

I liked both the boys. They were polite and nice, and they were both into drugs. They did a lot of morphine, pot, downers and occasionally acid, but no heroin. That was all right with me, I could get high on anything they could. Besides, it had been very difficult to make any sort of drug connection in Georgia. One time I managed to rob a huge bottle of barbiturates from a black doctor's office when the doctor was with another patient, but otherwise none of us had been able to score anything at all.

Eventually, Paige and Nancy decided they were in love and wanted to move in with Andy and Lonnie. I was against it, and we really battled about it. They kept moving out, I kept moving them back in. Finally, after going through this four times, I gave up. Paige was 16 and Nancy was 15. I was married and pregnant at 15, and I *knew* I knew everything. I couldn't tell them anything.

We started spending every night in their apartment, getting high on pills and morphine and an occasional tab of acid.

For some reason morphine was very easy to get in Atlanta, and Andy was really a morphine junkie. He was shooting it up like crazy. One night he was lying on his bed and he asked me to hand him his needle, because he was too stoned to get up and get it. I gave it to him, and he loaded it up and got himself off. I watched him, then I went home and went to bed.

I had no idea the kid had a stomach full of barbiturates. He was a real junkie, I just assumed he knew better.

Nancy woke me the next morning with a scream. "Ma," she cried hysterically, "come over to Andy's apartment. Hurry up, we can't move him, he won't wake up!"

I ran across the street. He was still lying on his bed, exactly where he'd been when I went home. His right arm was draped around Paige's neck, holding her close to him. She was just lying there, her eyes bulging open, her whole body shaking. "Mama," she whimpered in a low, tight voice, "I can't move his arm. I can't move him at all."

"I know, honey," I said softly, "I'll help him." I took his right arm and slowly rolled him over on his back. His arm just hung in the air. I lifted up his eyelid. It flopped closed. I put my hand on his chest. I didn't feel a thing. "My God," I whispered, "Oh Christ!"

I slugged him in the chest as hard as I could! His body didn't even move. I punched him again, and again. I opened his mouth and started breathing in. I took some breaths for him, then punched him again. "Get some ice cubes!" I shouted at Lonnie. I punched, I breathed, again, again, again. When Lonnie came back with the ice cubes I put them under Andy's armpits and in his crotch. I was trying to get some reaction, some sign of life.

I punched him one more time, this last time as much in frustration as in anger. The kid was dead. "He's overdosed," I said almost calmly. "He's overdosed on morphine."

"Whattya mean he's dead," Lonnie almost laughed. "You're crazy, Andy can't be dead. Not Andy. He's my roommate!"

Paige was truly terrified. She couldn't help thinking about being trapped by his arm after rigor mortis set in during the night. "Nancy, take your sister back to my apartment," I told her. "Then get back here and help us clean house."

"C'mon Ceil," Lonnie said lightly, "he isn't really dead, is he?"

I knew this wasn't the time to fool around with these kids. "Yeah, he's dead," I told him, "and we have to get this place cleaned out before we call the police."

We got every trace of drugs out of the apartment. We took all the pills, the morphine, the works, the pot, over to my apartment. Then I called Teddy Burke and told him what happened. Finally we called the police.

The police made an investigation to determine if Andy had been murdered. They took Paige in and questioned her, but they couldn't make a case because Andy was a known drug user.

I felt really terrible about that. I didn't feel that his death was my fault, he loaded the needle, he shot it himself and they were his drugs. But none of that made me feel any better. He was a nice kid and he was dead and there was absolutely no reason for it.

The funeral was very bad. Paige and Nancy were both hysterical. Neither girl had ever been so close to death before. It had always been a distant thing; like Louie, the person just disappeared. That was death. This was the first time they had to deal with it close up.

Andy's sister was the worst at the funeral. She kept screaming at me that I murdered her brother. "She's the one," she kept yelling, "she's the one who killed him."

I tried to talk to her, but she didn't want to listen to me. She was a good kid, a little younger than Andy, and we had spent some time together at his apartment. "I had nothing to do with it, he overdosed himself."

"You're a murderer!" she screamed. "You murdered him!"

I pressed two barbiturates into her hand. "Take these to calm down."

She threw them at me.

Two nights later she walked into the bar I had been hanging out in. She was a totally different person. She acted like nothing had ever happened. "My cousin just came into town," she told me. "He drove all the way from Mississippi and he's exhausted. He missed the funeral and now he can't sleep. Can you help him out?"

After Andy's death I didn't want to be seen near any drugs. "I don't have any pills," I told her.

She pushed me on. "C'mon Ceil, you can get 'em."

I didn't want to take the chance. "No, I don't have any. If I had them, you'd be welcome to them, but I don't."

"We'll buy them off you."

I was starting to get angry. "Look, I don't have any. How many times do I have to tell you, none, zero, no pills. I'm sorry."

"Thanks," she said in a nasty voice and walked out. I finished my drink.

She was parked in front of my apartment when I went home to check on Susan and Gay. A young kid with a crew cut, tattoos, and wearing a white T-shirt was sitting in the front seat with her. "This is my cousin from Mississippi," she said. "Can't you please get him a couple of pills?"

Then he asked for himself. "I'd sure like to get some sleep, ma'am. If you got any of them pills I'd appreciate it one big load."

I just stood there looking at them. They weren't going to quit until they got their pills. "Park in front of my house and go ahead in and wait for me. I'll see if I can get you some." I had stashed a few underneath a neighbor's milk box, and I went over and took two Seconals.

They were all sitting on the couch when I walked back in, talking to Susan and Gay. I handed him the pills and started down the hallway. This cousin from Mississippi hops up and follows me down the hall. "Lemme give you a couplea dollars," he said anxiously, "lemme pay you."

Now I was a little frightened of him. "I don't want your money. Just get yourself a good night's sleep."

"Take it," he ordered.

I turned around and faced him. "I don't want any of your money. Is that clear?"

"Okay," he said, "then take this." He pulled out a policeman's badge and a small gun. "You're under arrest."

The place exploded with cops. Andy's sister came running down the hall, screaming, "You bitch, you killed my brother. I set you up. You bitch—" One cop had to hold her away from me.

"You can't arrest me," I kept saying, "I'm a federal witness. You can't arrest me . . ."

"We don't care who you are lady, you're under arrest for distributing a controlled substance."

Gay and Susan started crying as soon as the cops ran into the apartment.

Paige was screaming at Andy's sister, "Are you crazy! My mother didn't kill your brother. You stupid jerk—" She went after Andy's sister and the cops grabbed her. One of them smacked her to try to calm her down, but as soon as I saw him hit her, I went after him. I couldn't control myself. I really tried to hurt him.

That crazy girl was still shouting, "You bitch, you killed my brother."

They got me in the police car and started questioning me. They wanted to know who my connection was. I figured I'd help them, so I just made up a name. "He's right over there by the pool now," I told them quickly. I was playing Louie. "Too late, you missed him, there goes his truck." I had them running in all directions after figments of my own imagination.

They brought me back to the station house and tried to book me. They wanted me to sign some paper acknowledging that I'd been told my legal rights when I was arrested. "I'm not signing anything," I told them angrily, "not after that police brutality." I figured a few threats from the streets of New York City would shake them up. They started to book me and I explained very carefully, "Get in touch with federal marshal Mayhew right away and tell him you have Cecile Monet because I'm a government witness and you can't do this to me." I didn't have the slightest idea what Mayhew could do, but I felt I was somebody important and deserved to be treated that way. I was really beginning to believe everything that Bruns and Burke and Broeheim and Hacker had told me about the importance of my testimony. I figured I was too valuable to be locked up in some local-yokel jail.

When I saw Bruns and Burke, who were coincidentally in Atlanta at the time, walk in with worried looks across their faces, I knew I was right.

"Teddy, what's gonna happen?" I asked as soon as we were alone. "Do I have to go to jail for this? I didn't sell no narc no pills."

"Did you hand it to him?"

"Sure."

"Ceil, that's the same thing. Whether you accepted money or not, it's still considered a sale."

I started to get scared. "What's gonna happen to me? You're not gonna leave me in here?" I couldn't believe they'd let their soon-to-be star witness rot in a jail cell.

Jack Bruns tried to calm me down. "It's all right, just relax, we can work something out. We'll be able to get you bail, but you're going to have to spend the night in jail."

"No, I don't want to." I started crying once again, "C'mon you guys, you can get me out of this, you know I don't sell drugs." I was pleading with them. I started begging. I never wanted to spend another night in a cell as long as I lived.

"It's too late," Teddy said, "there's nothing we can do about it tonight. You're just going to have to make the best of it."

It was crazy. Over the last few years I'd done so much I deserved to go to jail for, but this time I didn't deserve it, I wasn't guilty of anything.

I didn't sleep the entire night. I just lay on my cot, thinking about so many things. But everything led right back to Louie. Louie Mileto, he got me into that cell, he got me into everything. Louie got me to California, to Long Island and cross country. Louie got me into expensive clothes, jewelry and drugs. As I lay there, sweating in that lousy jail, I thought, all that I am today, a scared drug user, hidden in some hick city in the South, I owe to Louie Mileto.

And even then I loved him.

– 2 I –

The next morning the Marshal Service arranged it so I would be released in $5000 bail. They posted bond and guaranteed my appearance. Jack and Teddy were in the courtroom and after the hearing they drove me back to my apartment. The night of the big bust was getting very close, Jack explained, and they had been assigned to stay with me and make sure I didn't get into any more trouble.

I was glad they were there, but I didn't like the reason. "Wait a second," I said, "I didn't do anything. I'm not a kid. I don't need any nursemaids."

"Well, you know——" Jack started to mumble something.

Teddy interrupted him. "It's not exactly what you've done," he said in an angry voice, "it's just that you don't know how to shut up. We're doing our best to save your life and you keep making things tough for us." The more he said the tougher his voice got.

"Teddy," I answered, "I'm not making nothing tough—"

From his tone of voice it was obvious he was saying something he'd been holding back for a while. "Ceil, everybody and their brother knows who you are and what you're doing here. You and your kids have got to learn to keep your big mouths shut or somebody's gonna get killed. Maybe you think the whole thing's a big joke, but Patsy Parks didn't think it was so funny. Or the guy from New Jersey, a case just like yours, who drifted ashore after a week in the water, or anoth——"

"Hey, man, take it easy," Jack tried to calm him down.

"No way, Jack," Teddy said, his voice rising with every sentence. "I want her to hear the way it is. She's got to learn sometime. Ceil, you seem to think that everybody you meet on the street or in a bar is your friend, right? Wrong. That's not the way it is, I'm sorry, but that's not real life. Real life is that most of those people don't give a good goddamn if you live or if you die. This is a small town, and right now your tongue is worth one hundred thousand dollars. That's a whole lot of money, Ceil, one hundred thousand dollars, and there are a lot of people out there who would do anything for that much money. And that includes putting a bullet in your back. So if you don't want to lose that tongue, you learn to shut up, and you teach those kids to shut up! I'm sorry to yell at you, but there's only so much we can do to protect you, and you got to help us!" His face was a deep red when he finished yelling.

I didn't know exactly what to say. "What's this hundred thousand dollars?" I asked. "What does that mean?"

He was calmer now. "There's a contract out on you, Ceil. Dead, you're worth one hundred thousand dollars. They want you very badly. Now, you still feel like playing games with us?"

I didn't react. I just sat there and said nothing. One hundred thousand dollars! It didn't seem possible anyone could want me dead that badly. I knew I was an important witness, but it never occurred to me that I was *that* important! All of a sudden I realized that Teddy was exactly right, I had been treating the whole thing like a big game: I'd been so intent on getting everything the government promised that I'd forgotten that their job was to protect my life. Except for that incident with the drunk in the Holiday Inn in New York, I'd forgotten they were playing with real guns and real bullets. The $100,000 price tag got me very scared all over again. It was a very expensive reminder. "You're right, Teddy," I managed to apologize "I'll be careful from now on."

"Okay, Ceil," he accepted, "I think you will." He relented a little. "That doesn't mean you have to stay in the house all the time with the window shades closed. It just means you have to think a lot more and talk a lot less. Other than that, you can do anything you want. The government's giving you a good deal, you're allowed to enjoy it."

And for the final week we spent down there before moving closer to New York and the U.S. attorneys, we really did enjoy ourselves. We went swimming, fooled around, played games, lay in the sun, drank bad wine and laughed a lot. Philip had bought an air rifle while we were down there, and one night Teddy took it out of the apartment and started shooting it in an open field. "Paige," I whispered softly, "go call the cops and tell them there's some nut in the lot shooting a rifle." She laughed and ran inside.

The Atlanta Police Department didn't send one patrol car, they sent 15. It was hysterical, and these sirens screaming, cars tearing around the block, lights flashing. Teddy grabbed the gun and ran into the house to hide it.

A tall, very muscular policeman was the first one there. "There was a complaint called in about a rifle being fired around here."

"I don't know anything about it," I said. I looked at Paige. "Do you?"

"No, Ma." She looked at Teddy. "Do you?"

He managed to keep a straight face. "A rifle? Around here? No, I didn't hear anything."

The cops searched the lot, but naturally they didn't find anything. After they left Teddy looked at me and said, "Okay, Ceil, you're Miss Mafia, I want to see how smart you are. Let's see you find that rifle."

I went directly to my bedroom, lifted up the mattress and picked up the rifle. "Here."

He was really surprised. "How'd you know it was there?"

"That's where I used to hide mine." He didn't think it was as funny as everyone else did.

I liked Jack Bruns, but it was Teddy Burke I developed a serious crush on. He was cute, smart and single. I took advantage of his job and made him take me everywhere. Wherever we went I tried to convince him that he should take me out. "I can't do it," he kept telling me, "I'm on a job."

I paid no attention to that. "Why can't you take me out? Aren't I good-looking enough for you?" This was one of the few times in my whole life that I was the complete center of attraction, all by myself, and I took full advantage of it. I became a real brat.

"Of course you're pretty enough," he told me, "and if these were different circumstances I'd definitely take you out. But I can't now."

"Why not?"

"Ceil, leave me alone!" He was really getting exasperated.

The next move we made was from Atlanta to a bungalow colony in the Catskill Mountains, far enough from New York to be safe, close enough so I could be driven in every day to confer with the U.S. attorneys. Jack and Teddy had given me some confidence in the BNDD, and when those people were around I felt pretty safe. Living with a death sentence over your head is very frightening, but also fascinating. For the first few weeks after I was told about the contract I was terrified by anything the slightest bit out of the ordinary. I would wake up in the morning and wonder if this was the day my killer was going to find me. I thought about the best and worst ways to be killed. I told the kids I didn't want them wearing black to my funeral, I wanted them to be happy.

But after a few weeks of living like that I became a little more confident. Not reckless, but confident. I realized I couldn't live the rest of my life in fear. If they were going to kill me, I decided, then they would kill me, and all the worrying in the world wasn't going to stop them or help me. All I could do was to be careful, listen to my guards and keep my mouth shut. The only thing I kept worrying about was being cut into pieces. I wanted my death to be quick.

The government put me with another witness in the bungalow colony, the first time I'd met anyone else living like me. The name I knew her by was Lucy, her real name I guess, and she was a South American also involved in the drug bust. At one time she had been a very big drug dealer herself, but she was working for the government in order to keep herself out of jail and to free her brother, who was in jail for killing a cop.

She had known Louie very well, so immediately we had something in common. "He was a great guy," she told me, "and he was crazy about my own little daughter. He kept telling me how much he loved you and the children. He always said that."

She didn't know they weren't his children until I told her. He'd always claimed them as his own.

Lucy had been working with the government for two years. She was out on the street for a while, wired for sound as she made her deals, but eventually it just got too dangerous for her. The day one of the dealers gave her the kiss of death and said "Let's see who they get first" as he climbed out of her car was the day they took her off the streets. Now, like me, she waited, and lay in the sun, and went swimming, and cooked, and waited.

The agents liked her better than they liked me because she was so easy to get along with and was always doing something to help them. One agent had recently been married, for example, and hadn't been with his wife in two weeks. She made him call his wife and have her come up to the colony. Then she stood watch outside, in case his boss should show up while they made love inside.

Lucy had a $100,000 contract out on her too. When the people she had worked with found out she was cooperating, they hired somebody to kill her. They paid him $100,000 in cash. The problem was, the somebody they hired was an agent. He made two arrests in the case.

The agents kept us aware of everything that was happening. They told us who was doing what in the organization, who was on the outs, who was being set up and who knew what about us witnesses. I was constantly surprised at the number of informers, "rats" the agents called them, that the government had on the street. Between the "rats" and the wiretaps, Herbie's operation had been wired for over a year. They knew everything that was going on.

They even put a phoney mailbox in front of the barbershop. The first day it was there Herbie leaned against it and said, "I know there's either a midget or a bug in there." He was right—it was a bug. But he talked anyway.

The kids hated the Catskills. Nancy missed Lonnie badly. Gay wanted to go to Florida to be with her grandmother. Philip had no friends and was really into pot. Paige was depressed and only Susan was happy. Nancy and Philip ran up a huge phone bill—mostly for Teddy Burke. They were constantly calling Atlanta and either using bad credit-card numbers, Louie's old trick, or telling the operator that they were Teddy Burke or his wife, "and I'd like to make a long-distance call and charge it to my home number." Later we found out the phone company was charging them with fraud. There were warrants out for their arrest, and the police were looking for them. The agents eventually had to squash those cases too.

We stayed in the Catskills for two weeks and then we were moved to Birchwood Lake in the Pocono Mountains. Birchwood Lake was heaven. If that was considered a hide-out, I didn't mind hiding out. The lake was beautiful, they had a nice pool and the weather was wonderful. It was so quiet and so peaceful, we'd wake up in the morning and see deer on our front lawn. It was worth the $450 a month I had to pay for it—out of government allowance, of course.

Teddy and Jack convinced me to let the Marshal Service protect me again. They promised they'd selected special marshals—"and besides, you don't even have to let them in the house if you don't want to. Just make them sit out there in their own cars."

I'd always imagined marshals to be strong, tough, smart

people. At least that's the way they appear on television. In Birchwood Lake we had all types. One agent used to sit at the kitchen table and pick his nose when he thought we weren't looking. Another husband-and-wife team used to tell me how to control my kids, and they congratulated me when I hit Susan. Them I made sit outside. Another marshal refused to take the kids anywhere. "I'm not their chauffeur," he said. "You're not?" I asked him. I called his boss and he found out he was.

The marshals knew their business though. If I went to the pool, there would always be two of them sitting right behind me in the car. If I got up to take a walk or get a hot dog, one would always come with me, the other would sit in the car and watch the kids. At least one of them had to stay in the car at all times, because that's where they kept their loaded shotgun.

We'd all learned not to talk about our business by this time, and the other early spring guests at Birchwood Lake were very curious about us. They knew we were special people because our front gate was always guarded and no one was allowed on our property. The marshals cut off everybody's guessing by spreading the word that we were the family of an important foreign diplomat and our guards were U.S. government agents.

We gave our marshals as tough a time as we gave Teddy and Jack. Once we went to a place nearby named Miracle Lake, which hadn't opened for the season, and let all their sailboats loose on the lake. Then we sailed across the lake to some of the closed houses and robbed a few deck chairs.

"Your family's crazy, we gotta get outta here," one of our marshals growled at me when we sailed back with two boats filled with chairs. "Where'd you get those things?" he wanted to know.

"We stole them," I told him. "Now open the trunk up." He didn't want to open, but we all yelled at him, so he unlocked it and carried the chairs back. Even I could see that we were probably not the easiest people the Marshal Service ever had to guard, but we were living under such tension that we needed to do silly, stupid things just to let off some steam.

We knew when we were brought to Birchwood Lake that

the big busts couldn't be too long away, otherwise they never would have kept me that close to the city. I was going into the city almost every day to be prepared for the trials. And in March 1973, the Grand Jury was convened.

A Grand Jury isn't like a regular jury. Its job is just to hear the evidence that the prosecutor has collected and vote on whether he has a legitimate case or not. If they decide there is enough evidence to make a full trial worthwhile, they give out indictments and then arrest warrants. The whole Grand Jury meeting is supposed to be secret, and most of the time the people who are going to be indicted don't even know the Grand Jury is meeting.

I wasn't nervous about testifying in front of a Grand Jury because I'd been in front of one on my armed robbery case, when I got drugged up with Rhonda and we robbed that kid leaving for the army. They had indicted me.

This one was held in the United States Courthouse in Foley Square. The marshals drove me in a three-car convoy, one car in front of the one I was riding in and one car behind us. Two armed marshals rode in the car with me. When we reached the courthouse, they handed me over to the BNDD agents, who took me up to the Grand Jury room.

Before I went in to testify the U.S. attorney talked to me outside the room for a few minutes. He told me not to be nervous. He told me what he was going to ask me, and he told me how much information he wanted me to give to the Grand Jury. Then we walked in together.

The Grand Jury room isn't at all like a regular courtroom. There is no judge's bench or seats for spectators. There's just one long table set up, and the jury box is on the side. There are more than 12 jurors too, but I can't remember how many. The U.S. attorney, the Manhattan district attorney and some other people I didn't know were sitting at the long table. I took a seat at one end of the table.

"Would you tell us your name, please?"

"Cecile Mileto," I said. I was looking right at the Grand Jury. It really looked like a weird collection of people. There were more women than men. There was this one really big fat lady, wearing a red dress, sitting in the second row. She was just layers of fat.

"Do you know Herbert Sperling?"

I told them I did. "My husband used to work for him." There was another juror I couldn't help staring at—a man with a really thin neck, and every time he swallowed his Adam's apple would bob up and down.

"Where is your husband now?"

"My husband is dead." I was very careful not to say he had been murdered, but I wanted to, I really wanted to.

"What did your husband do?" The district attorney was asking me exactly the questions he'd told me he was going to ask.

"He cut drugs for Herbie Sperling."

"How do you know that?"

"He told me." It was all very matter-of-fact. The BNDD agents were standing guard outside the room. I just wasn't nervous, I'd been getting myself ready to testify for months now. I was just glad the whole thing was finally starting. I wished I could see Herbie's face when he found out about this Grand Jury—the day he was arrested.

They only asked me a few questions, then I was excused. The district attorney came out into the hall and thanked me. I said, "That's it?"

"That's it," he told me, at least for now. "I'm sure we've got a good case."

The BNDD agents returned me to the marshals, the marshals drove me back to Birchwood Lake. It was kind of a letdown. We waited almost three more weeks for the night of the big bust.

It came down on April 13, 1973. The Grand Jury handed down a total of 86 indictments, covering just about every single person I'd met or even heard of. On April 13 more than 200 BNDD agents, most of them heavily armed, started a big pickup through New York, New Jersey and even into Pennsylvania and Westchester.

Jack Bruns was assigned with another agent and a New York City cop to arrest Billy D'Angelo. Instead of just busting into his apartment and risking a gunfight, they decided to try to bring him out by calling him and telling him someone had tried to break into his gas station on Fordham Road. They made the call about 2:00 A.M. "Mr. D'Angelo," they told him, "do you own a gas station on Fordham Road?"

"I used to," Billy told them, "but I sold it. The guy's making weekly payments." The agents didn't know a thing about that.

Jack Bruns really thought fast. "Well, this is the New York City Police Department and we still have you listed as the owner. You'd better get down here right away because somebody tried to break into the station and the burglar alarm is waking up everybody in the neighborhood."

Billy told them he would call the owner, then he hung up.

Bruns and the two others figured they had to break in. At least they knew he was home. But while they were standing on the corner getting ready, Billy drove right by them in his new car. He was on his way to the gas station.

The agents took off after him. They caught up to him and pulled him over. Billy didn't resist at all. But while they were making the arrest, the New York City cop opened the trunk of the car and found about 60 pounds of white powder. He started dancing and shouting. He thought it was heroin. "Is that your car?" Bruns asked him.

"It's my wife's," Billy said.

Bruns asked him again. "Is that your car with that stuff in the back."

Billy gave him the same answer. "It's my wife's car. You can't arrest me for it." Billy didn't realize he was involving his wife in the operation.

Bruns did and he was trying to help Billy out. "Well then," he told him, "let's all go back to your house, so I can arrest your wife."

Billy *still* didn't catch on. Instead he got really nervous. "Arrest my wife? What for? She ain't done nothin'."

"If that's her car," Jack Bruns explained really carefully, "then that's her stuff in the trunk. So we got to arrest her."

Billy finally understood. "No, no, that's my car. That's my stuff."

"That's what I thought you said in the first place," Bruns told him. It didn't really make any difference, the white powder turned out to be quinine, used to cut heroin.

Jack Bruns told me Billy was really scared to death. On the ride back to BNDD headquarters on West 57th Street, he started babbling about other people involved in the drug operation, naming names and places. Bruns just sat and listened. He couldn't believe Billy knew so much and would talk about it.

Later Teddy and Jack told me about some of the other pickups. Agents found one guy with a hooker in a midtown hotel. When they handcuffed him and dragged him out of his room, his pants kept falling down.

They couldn't find Alvin Gibbons or Richie Maxton or Benny Mallah.

They found Johnny "Hooks" Capra at his house in Westchester. I'd been to that house once when Josephine's house was being built. She wanted marble tiles and Johnny Capra had a connection in that business, so we drove up to Westchester. It was a beautiful place, but the thing I remember best is that the wall going down into the basement was covered with a kind of stucco paint. When it was still wet, Johnny's wife, Connie, had drawn a big heart and written "Johnny and Connie" inside. I liked her, and I felt bad for her. She almost convinced the agents he was at an all-night card game. After an hour they were ready to give up, but then they heard him moving around upstairs. He was hiding in his bedroom.

Teddy Burke was assigned with another agent to pick up Herbie. They waited outside his house till 4:00 A.M. when he finally pulled into his driveway. While he was parking the car, Teddy came around the side and put a gun to his head. At the time the other agent threw himself on the hood of the car and held his cocked gun in Herbie's face. He warned him, "Don't move or I'll blow your brains out."

Herbie was very cool. "Get that cowboy off my car," he told Teddy. "He's shaking like a leaf and he's liable to shoot me." Without taking his gun off Herbie, the agent climbed off the car.

"Federal agents," Teddy told him. "You're under arrest." He started reading Herbie his rights.

"You're kidding? For what?" Herbie asked. They told him. He started laughing. "Are you guys kidding? I'm a salesman. I make a hundred-eighty a week."

It was Jack's turn to laugh. "Yeah? Then how come you're living in a two hundred fifty thousand dollar house. How come you have three new cars, including this Mercedes? How come you got two boats and your wife has a huge diamond ring?"

Herbie looked them right in the eye. "Hey! I'm a good salesman!"

They searched the car and found a small ax and an arsenal of guns. "Hey Herbie," they asked him, "what are you doing with all these guns and this ax?"

He gave them a disgusted look. "When I get out of this," he answered, "I'm telling you, I'm gonna write this renting company some nasty letter. They're not supposed to leave guns in their cars!"

They finished reading him his rights, let him say goodbye to Josephine and brought him down to 57th Street and Eleventh Avenue to join the growing crowd. Both Herbie and Johnny Hooks were held in $1 million bail. Johnny Hooks had them laughing when they brought him in. He took one look at the roundup and asked, "What are you guys, crazy? You got everybody here. Now what are you gonna do? You're out of business!"

They managed to arrest 65 of the people indicted.

They even got Sonny Gold. When they started to question him, he waved them away. "Don't insult my integrity, please. There are three things I hate in this world: hookers, pimps and rats. So do me a favor, huh? I'm an old man, I'll do a hundred years anyway, but don't ask me no questions because I'm not gonna tell you anything." Louie would have been proud of him.

I thought about Louie when Teddy and Jack were telling me about the raids. If he had lived, he would have been right at the top of their list, because even without me, they had strong cases against a lot of people. They had movie film, taped phone recordings and witnesses. I just happened to know the people at the top, which made me an important witness. But Louie would have been put away again. I don't think he could have taken it; I know I couldn't have.

Once the bust was finished the real preparations for the trials began. I was driven into the U.S. district attorney's office in Foley Square every day to be prepped for my testimony in the upcoming trials. It hadn't yet been determined how many different trials I'd appear in. Wherever the government thought my testimony would be valuable they planned to use me.

The trip in from Birchwood Lake took almost two hours, and as soon as we got near the city, the marshals would make me lie down on the back floor of the car and take me into the building through the judge's entrance. They weren't worried about me being seen with government guards anymore; they were worried about somebody ambushing the car and trying to kill me. When we left the building, usually close to eight at night, they made me lie down again for the two-hour ride back to the Poconos. As the trials got closer, the marshals got more careful. And more nervous.

But even with all the traveling, I still had it better than a lot of other witnesses. Some of them moved from motel to motel room every few days for their own safety. "These are pretty desperate men," one marshal told me. "Some of them are going to jail for the rest of their lives. They got nothing to lose by trying to kill the people who are going to send them there."

One of those people they wanted to kill turned out to be Billy D'Angelo. For some reason the higher-ups figured he knew too much and wouldn't hold back. A contract was put out to have him knifed to death in jail.

Teddy Burke felt really bad about it because he knew from my testimony that Billy really wasn't one of them. "They're going to kill your friend D'Angelo," he told me. "The contract came across the prison wire today."

"Oh, no, Teddy, you can't let that happen. Not to Billy, I told you about him, remember, Mama Rosa. He's just a kid. You gotta get him outta there."

"I'd like to, Ceil," he said, "but I can't. There's nothing I can do." I could see he was really upset about the whole thing.

"There's got to be something you can do, you can't just let them kill him." I started begging him to pull Billy out. "He's a kid," I said all over again, "he's not one of them. You can't just let them kill him."

"I swear, Ceil, there's just nothing I can do about it. You know I would if I could."

I knew that was true. I tried to figure a way out for him. There was only one way, I realized, and that was if he agreed to become a witness. "He'll talk, Teddy, I know he will. And believe me, he knows much more stuff than I do. Do yourself a favor. Go get him."

Teddy agreed to try it, but he didn't think it would do any good. "He's been inside with them too long. They got him all psyched up. He won't break down for a while, and by that time he'll be dead." At first Teddy was right, Billy played very tough. He didn't want to talk, he was too scared.

I was sitting in a room about ten yards away from the room he was in. Teddy kept walking back and forth between the rooms. "It's no good, Ceil," he told me, "he won't say a thing."

"Tell him I'm talking," I suggested, "that might open him up."

Teddy shook his head no. "We can't tell him you're involved. You're our surprise witness. If we tell him and then he goes back and tells Herbie, your life is going to be in more danger than it is now. And that's too much."

I tried another direction. The kid didn't seem to want his life saved. "Ask him how long he was cutting for Louie." I was going to try to save Billy's life in spite of Billy.

Teddy made the round trip. "He says he never cut for Louie. Look, Ceil, it's not gonna work, let's put him back in the cage."

"No, no, wait." I had to think of something. "Okay, okay"—I was talking really fast—"you go back and you tell him, you ask him, what was he doing driving Louie to Philadelphia in June. Ask him what he went up there for." I was hoping Billy would be so convinced that they knew everything he did that he would just give it up and start talking.

It worked. "He says he drove Louie to Philadelphia for a pickup," Teddy told me with a big, wide smile on his face.

"Louie had twenty thousand dollars on him."

I felt really good. Maybe I could save Billy's life. I started giving them more and more little tidbits of things that only Billy and Louie and I knew about.

Teddy spent an entire afternoon running back and forth between Billy and me. A scrap of information, then another scrap of information and he started talking, until finally the floodgates opened and he was telling the agents everything they wanted to know.

As soon as he started talking, the government realized that he would make a very important witness, so they made a deal with him too. In return for his testimony they would inform the judge on his case about his cooperation. He agreed to plead guilty to the indictment, and was put on probation. He was given a total new identity after the trials were finished and relocated somewhere in America.

Once he agreed to the deal they told him I was cooperating and let us see each other. We hadn't seen each other in over a year and we had a short, wonderful reunion. We just put our arms around each other and cried. The whole thing was so unnatural, the two of us sitting in a hotel room, protected by armed guards, testifying against people we'd known for a long time. "It's a long time since Big Bear," I laughed.

He didn't say very much.

"Remember the time you came over to stay with the kids when Louie and I went back to New York and ate the brownies Mikey and I baked?"

He remembered, but he didn't want to talk about old times. "I loved Louie, too, Ceil," he said softly. "You know that."

"Yeah, Billy, I know that."

"I just couldn't help what happened."

"I know that, too, Billy. I'm not mad at you anymore." He asked me all about the kids and told me to say hello to them "from Mama Rosa." I asked him all about his family.

"My wife just had a little girl." He stopped. "I'd love to see your kids. They were the best family I ever had."

"I'd love to see your little girl, Billy." We discussed all my relatives and all his relatives, Mark and Mikey, other mutual friends. He filled me in on all the gossip about Herbie. Finally I asked him, "Where are you thinking of moving to after all this is over?"

He didn't know. Everything had been happening so fast he hadn't had time to think about it.

"It would be nice if we could live near each other," I suggested. "I'd like to move near you."

His face brightened. "The kids need somebody now that Louie's dead."

"Yeah, Billy, they do." Then I gave him my telephone number at Birchwood Lake, which, at the time, I thought was a very innocent thing to do. Even though I had been specifically warned by the agents not to give that number to anyone, I trusted Billy enough to give it to him.

A few weeks later I realized that was a very stupid thing to do. I realized that after Billy accidentally sold out another witness.

The government was looking for the man who replaced Louie, because they figured he might turn state's evidence and help build their case. Billy managed to contact him and tried to convince him to surrender. Instead this guy threatened to tell the government that Billy was holding back on them if he didn't make a $5000 pay-off. Billy panicked and called some people to try to borrow the money. They figured out exactly what he wanted the money for, and the guy was found dead, with his hands cut off.

When I heard the story I got scared. Billy had my phone number. I could be located. I went running to the marshals. They yelled at me, changed the number and kept a very close watch on Billy D'Angelo.

I never saw him again. We communicated mainly by marshal. I'd get one who'd been guarding Billy for a while, and he'd tell me everything that was happening, or Billy would get one of mine and keep up with me and the kids this way. Billy did so many bad things, but I always liked him. He was Mama Rosa, just a nice kid who didn't think too good. Like all of us.

I was scared every moment after the bust. I had begun to realize how important I was to the government; that made me even more important to Herbie. And I'd seen Herbie at work enough to believe he could do almost anything, including find me.

So, by the time the trial started nothing could really scare me anymore. I had been hardened and toughened. I was ready.

PART
V

Q: *Mrs. Mileto, you do feel you have to testify here, don't you?*

A: *Yes, I do.*

Q: *You have no choice, right?*

A: *No, that's not the reason.*

Q: *You mean, you don't owe the U.S. government anything, do you?*

A: *Nothing.*

Q: *And that's not the reason you are testifying?*

A: *That's not the reason.*

Louie was the reason I testified. I didn't care about getting drugs off the street, I didn't care about Herbie going to jail, I didn't care about "making" anybody's case. Louie was my reason. What they did to him.

− 22 −

The trial began in late June 1973, 16 months after Louie walked out the front door to be cut up into pieces. Herbie and 13 other defendants were being tried together. After all the preparation I really felt ready for anything I might be asked. The D.A.s had told me so many times, don't try to be smart, just answer the questions as asked. Don't invent and don't elaborate. Just answer the question with the truth as best I remembered it. "As long as you keep doing that," they told me, "there's no way the defense can shake your testimony."

I was prepared, but that still didn't stop me from being frightened. Even though Herbie was in prison, I was still afraid of him. Teddy Burke did his best to make the trial easier for me. Over and over he kept telling me they weren't gonna get me, they weren't gonna get me. He kept reassuring me, and I believed in him.

I was one of the first witnesses called. When they called my name and the big doors to the courtroom opened, I started walking straight ahead, trying not to look at anybody. My knees were banging together. I could feel my heart pounding away.

Just as I reached the front of the courtroom I caught my first glimpse of Herbie. I took one look at his face and I could tell he was really surprised to see me there. The color seemed gone from his face. He turned white. He must have known my testimony was really going to hurt him.

He just stared at me. Then he sort of relaxed and leaned back in his chair. He smiled at me, he always had a nice smile. Then he put his hands to his lips and threw me a kiss. I thought I knew what he meant by that kiss. Herbie was saying goodbye to me. It was the kiss of death.

I was trying so hard not to be scared. I knew the courtroom was very well protected. It looked like an army camp. One armed marshal sat right next to the witness stand. Another armed marshal sat at the end of the juror's box. Other armed marshals sat behind the row of defendants, against the walls and in the rear of the courtroom. Outside, the entire floor was guarded by marshals, and I was escorted by armed guards everywhere I went in the building.

With all that, I was still frightened. I tried hard not to show it.

"Raise your right hand, please."

It didn't work. I raised my left hand.

"Your right hand, please," the bailiff asked with a smile. I corrected my mistake. I was sworn in and I sat down in the witness stand. I tried to relax and I looked out at the spectators. The first person I saw was Josephine. She was crying. I felt so bad for her and I think she felt bad for me. I knew what must have been going on in her mind. Slowly, she got up and walked out of the courtroom. I don't even think she was crying for her husband, I feel she was crying for me, seeing me there, knowing Louie was dead.

"Mrs. Mileto, are you married or single?" John Gross, the U.S. attorney, was standing directly in front of me so I had to look at him and nobody else.

"I am a widow," I said. I looked over at the jury. They were staring at me, judging me, I thought. They looked like a very ordinary group of people, there wasn't even a big fat lady, like on the Grand Jury.

"When did your husband pass away?"

I just paused one second. "February of seventy-two." I didn't say another word, but I wanted to, I really wanted to. I wanted to tell the jury how he died, I wanted them to know. I wanted to scream it out. I wanted to be sure the jurors knew that he had been murdered, that he didn't just "pass away." I wanted to make it rougher on Herbie.

I didn't. I had been told over and over I couldn't refer to that because it would cause a mistrial.

John Gross started to ask his next question. "What was your husband's—" but he was interrupted by one of the defense attorneys.

"I can't hear the witness," he complained.

I had been speaking low because I was so nervous. "This is a high-ceilinged room," the judge told me. "You have to speak up. Don't worry about these amplifiers, but do the best you can to speak up."

I nodded. Gross tried his question again. "What was your husband's name, Mrs. Mileto?"

"Louis Mileto," I said very loud and clear.

"Mrs. Mileto, you have some prior convictions, correct?"

John Gross was trying to beat the defense to my criminal and drug record. He wanted to make sure the jury heard about it straight, so the defense would not be able to use it to discredit my testimony. "Yes," I answered him.

He started reading them off. "In 1970 you were convicted of petty larceny, correct?"

"Yes."

"In 1972 you were convicted of possession of drugs?"

"Yes."

"In 1972 you also pleaded guilty to another charge of possessing drugs?"

"Yes." I was starting to feel more confident on the stand. My shakes were beginning to go away.

"In 1972 you were also arrested for petty larceny?"

"Yes."

"In 1972 you were also arrested for possessing two pills in Atlanta?"

"Yes." My record was now part of the court record.

John Gross finally moved into the real questioning. "Did there come a time," he asked me, "when you had a discussion with your husband with regard to what he was doing?"

"My husband had told me that he had gone to work for Herbie and that we didn't have to worry about money or him going to jail anymore because he wasn't stealing, that——"

"I can't hear, your honor," the defense attorney interrupted.

I spoke up. "—that there wasn't anything that he couldn't, Herbie and he couldn't buy their way out of." With every question I felt a little more comfortable.

"Did you ask him who Herbie was?" John Gross asked.

The judge stopped me. "Just a minute. We have to have that read. You have a soft voice."

I liked this judge. He seemed like a warm man. "I asked my husband who Herbie was because I didn't know him. He said Herbie Sperling." I tried to look at Herbie, but Gross was blocking my vision.

The trial was nothing like I expected. It was more like a business conference, a lot of men in expensive suits pushing papers and carrying expensive attaché cases. It didn't seem like a big drug trial. John Gross was very well prepared. He moved from question to question, building his case. "Did there come a time when you moved into another apartment in Queens?"

"Yes, in the same building," I told him. We'd moved from a one-bedroom into the bigger place after we got the kids back. Gross covered every point carefully before moving on to the next question.

"Did there come a time in June 1971, when you looked in your husband's dresser?"

This was when I found the coke. "Yes," I answered. The defense attorneys started objecting to every question he asked. I didn't know what they were objecting to, but the judge sustained every one. Finally John Gross got his question in. "He,

Louie, said that I should mind my own business. Stay out of his things, that those were samples for Herbie's customers."

We covered some more material, skipped around some more. I was beginning to feel really comfortable on the stand. I only had to remind myself to answer just what was asked and not to give any more information.

"Do you see Herbert Sperling in the courtroom?"

"Yes, I do."

"Will you point him out, please."

I stepped down. My knees started shaking all over again. I looked right at Herbie and he looked right back at me. He had his smile back on his face. "Right here," I said, pointing at him.

John Gross wanted me to be really specific. "Which of the two gentlemen here?"

"The gentleman in the pink shirt."

Really specific. "There are two gentlemen with pink shirts."

"I'm sorry, the one closest to you."

John Gross said, "May the record reflect that the witness correctly identified Herbert Sperling."

Eventually he reached specific details. "Did there come a time when you saw money in Mr. Sperling's house?"

"Yes."

"When, can you recall?"

"It was after Christmas, the winter of 1971."

"Was this the house on Spring Street?"

"Yes, it was."

"Will you tell the jury who was there and what, if anything, happened."

"Objection!" I didn't know why.

The judge let me answer the question, subject to "connection." That meant that it was just for information and could be used later on when other information was added to it. "Who was there and what happened?" the judge repeated.

I told the jury. "Herbert Sperling, Benny Mallah, Josephine and Louis and myself, and Richie Maxton came up after."

"You mentioned Josephine. Who is she?"

"Josephine Sperling, Herbert's wife." And once my best friend.

Gross had me fill in some more details, then he asked, "What, if anything, were the people doing in the kitchen?"

"Herbie was counting money and piling it according to denominations." As I answered the questions my mind jumped back to the minute I was talking about. I wasn't just remembering, I was describing what I was seeing in my mind.

"What, if anything, happened during the course of that?"

"Richie had come up and given Herbie a paper bag which contained more money and he added it and then it was put in an attaché case, and Benny left with it."

"You say Benny left with it?"

"Benny Mallah."

"Was anything said?"

"Herbie said, 'That's not a bad haul, seventy-five thousand dollars.'" Goodbye Herbie.

Later. "Did there come a time when Mr. Sperling moved to Bellmore, Long Island?"

"Yes."

"Can you describe his house there?"

I started to open my mouth, but the defense attorney cut me off with an objection. Gross tried the question another way. "Were you ever in his house?"

About a thousand times, I thought. "Yes," I said.

"Can you describe it?"

"It was a beautiful home, very expensive."

"Was there a gym?"

"Yes."

"A sauna?"

"Yes." Josephine had come back into the courtroom. She was wearing a little pink suit, and she had lost some weight, and she looked really pretty, as pretty as I had ever seen her look. I wanted to go over to her and hug her. I just felt so sorry for her. And so sorry for me.

"Did there come a time thereafter," Gross eventually asked me, "when Mr. Sperling asked you to come over to his house?"

"Yes, by phone." I had been on the stand for about a half-hour. I felt good about it. Very comfortable. My answers were coming easily. John Gross wanted me to talk about the meeting between Herbie, Billy and me, but the defense just kept objecting. Finally John got his question in legally. And I told them: "He wanted to talk to Billy D'Angelo and myself and we went downstairs and he asked me if I knew that Louie was stealing from him, that he had been cutting out of the packages.

"I then told him that I was an addict, because he asked me if there was anything in my house and I said no, that Louie did not bring things like that home because I was an addict, and he said he hadn't realized how much the kid was stealing at the time."

Eventually John Gross finished his questioning by asking me about the other people I knew. Alvin Gibbons. Sonny Gold. Then the defense took over. I knew exactly what they would be trying to do, trying to make me out as a junkie and a nut, and I sat quietly, trying to show the jury that I was responsible.

They started with the very first question. "Mrs. Mileto, how long did you have the heroin habit that you said you did?"

"Heroin habit?"

"Yes."

"Four years."

He asked me some more questions about my heroin, then asked if I used any other drugs during that period of time. I told him I did. "Cocaine, speed."

"What is speed?"

Speed is wonderful. "It is an amphetamine."

Then they tried to make the jury believe that I was testifying because the government had promised to help me with my cases. "Has anyone from the prosecutor's office or federal agents here told you that they would assist you in any way in that case?"

"I was told they would talk to the sentencing judge, and in most cases the sentencing judge was lenient."

They asked that question about each of my cases. I was starting to get very hostile because they were trying to make me out as a liar. And the more hostile I got, the easier it was to answer their questions. "Isn't it true, Mrs. Mileto, that you feel that you have a license to commit whatever crime you want to commit and the government is going to protect you because of your cooperation?"

I didn't even get angry. "No, that is not true," I said.

The defense attorney harped on the same subject, trying to convince the jurors that I was testifying to help myself. "Mrs. Mileto, when you testified in front of the Grand Jury, you had problems of your own, did you not?"

"Yes, I did."

"And you were trying to help yourself, weren't you?"

"Help myself?"

"Sure."

"Yes."

"And you figured if you cooperated with the United States government, give them all the answers they want, they would help you, right?"

I smiled. "That wasn't my main reason for testifying," I said. I looked at Herbie again. He was sitting there, smiling, sometimes laughing. I knew he understood why I was sitting up there trying to put him in jail. I didn't care how much drugs he sold, I wasn't trying to be a good citizen by taking millions of dollars in drugs off the streets. Why would I do something like that, being an addict myself? I was testifying because of what happened to Louie. And that was the whole reason. All of it.

I wanted him to pay the price.

The trial lasted a total of three weeks. I was on the stand four different times, each time for quite awhile, but even when I wasn't testifying I had to be in the building because John Gross wasn't sure whether the defense was going to recall me. During the trial I stayed at Birchwood Lake, but I was heavily guarded going back and forth to New York. We traveled as a three-car caravan, two marshals in each car, my car in the middle. I sat in the front seat next to the marshal driving, and an armed marshal sat directly behind me. The kids stayed at the lake and were constantly guarded by other teams of marshals.

The kids were just waiting for the trial to be over so we could be permanently relocated. But things got happier for them one afternoon when Lonnie came bouncing up the front walk after hitchhiking all the way from Atlanta. Everybody liked him and he brightened up the place. I had a big battle with the marshals, they didn't want to let him stay in the house, but I won out. He had a little pot with him and we smoked it up the first days he was there. I had been drug-free for so long that I got off on his grass, which was really unusual for me. I hadn't been able to get high on grass since our California days.

The kids didn't come to the trial, but each night I recreated what went on in the courtroom for them. They were as interested as I was, because they knew all the people being tried too. The government brought in a line of witnesses. The girl who lived in the apartment Louie rented for cutting—they got her name and address through my phone bills. Lucy testified. Billy D'Angelo testified. Under the direction of Jim Lavin and Frank Velie the government built strong cases against everyone, but the strongest case of all was against Herbie. He hadn't been quite as smart as he thought he had.

On July 12, 1973, Herbie and ten other members of his organization were found guilty of conspiring to sell narcotics. There were numerous counts against most of them.

I didn't feel any great emotion when I learned that Herbie had been convicted. It wasn't like I'd won a big prize or beaten somebody bad in an important game. I just had a nice, warm contented feeling inside. Herbie figured he was such a big man he could get away with anything. I remember Louie telling me, "I'll be making so much money I'll never have to go to jail again." That came from Herbie and Louie believed it. Herbie believed it too. He thought he was such a big man that he could run over everybody, including me, my children and my husband.

The jury told him he was wrong. And that made me very happy.

The government attorneys congratulated me after the trial and told me I had been their "star" witness. They told me I was fantastic under pressure and that they were surprised how I handled myself under extensive cross-examination. I enjoyed the entire trial. It was a lot of fun being on stage, I admit it.

As soon as the trial ended the government started asking me about relocating permanently. They wanted me to decide where I wanted to move, and they wanted me to decide quickly. I wasn't in any hurry. Birchwood Lake was beautiful and restful and the bills were being paid. So I kept putting the government off.

Lonnie had to leave to get back to Atlanta because his unemployment was running out, and Nancy begged me to let her leave with him. I knew in the end she'd do what she wanted to do anyway, so I gave her $50 for her birthday and another $20 to travel on. They decided to make a cheap adventure of their trip and hitchhike back. A marshal drove the three of us into New Jersey, and I said goodbye to them on the Jersey Turnpike.

With Susan in Florida at her grandmother's and Nancy in Atlanta, only Philip, Paige, Gay, me and a houseful of marshals were left. I wasn't happy about the marshals staying around, but I knew they were still necessary. Eventually there would be more trials, and appeals from those convicted, so my testimony was still important. A lot of people had a lot to fear from me, so my life continued to be in danger. That's what they told me and I had become a believer.

But the marshals had been around so long they began to get a little too friendly. One night, for example, they were driving me back from New York and they stopped at a bar along the route. That didn't bother me, I figured one of them had to go to the bathroom.

I was wrong. They both wanted to go in and have a drink. Or two. Or three. That was fine with me, I always liked liquor, and so the three of us had a few drinks together. What wasn't so fine with me was when we got back into the car the two marshals started closing in on me. Instead of taking his place in the back seat, the second marshal sat up front, pushing me between the two of them. They were ready to party. I guess they figured I'd gone so long without sex that I had to be ready to climb the walls.

I didn't want anything to do with them. When Louie was in prison I'd managed to go long stretches without sex, and I wasn't about to mess around with marshals I didn't even like. So absolutely nothing happened, not because they didn't try.

They were persistent. During the trial one of the marshals guarding the kids gave Paige $20 to come up to his room at the hotel in the Poconos. She told me about it and after we'd both finished laughing I made her give him his money back. But when she got propositioned again, I decided the marshals were starting to get a little too comfortable and the time had come to make our permanent move. If I waited much longer, the way a few of them were leering at Paige, I was going to need marshals to protect us from the marshals.

I didn't know where to move. The marshals wanted us to go to a so-called "safe house" in California, a large place where a group of former federal witnesses lived together under constant guard. I liked the thought of being back in California, but I knew I couldn't live that way. Paige wanted to go to Florida. Philip wanted to go back to Atlanta. Nancy finally called from Atlanta and talked us all into coming back down there. "We can all be together," she bubbled happily, "and it's really a nice place to live!" We all agreed Atlanta was as good—and as safe—as anywhere else.

Lonnie and Nancy put a $50 deposit on a four-bedroom apartment that rented for $190. The marshals gave me my $1080, plus airfare for all of us, and gladly told us goodbye. I kept bothering them about getting my furniture back and getting the new identification I was promised, but they didn't seem to care at all. The furniture would be there—eventually, they told me—and they never did anything about identification. Officially, to the government, we were still the Monet family, but we had no identification and we were back to calling ourselves Mileto.

I was excited about the chance for a new start. BNDD was still looking for Benny Mallah, Alvin Gibbons and Richie Maxton, but they felt none of those three would actually go looking for me. "If they spotted you on the street," one agent explained, "they might do something about it. Otherwise they wouldn't bother." Herbie was the only one who might go out of his way to find me, but he would have a difficult time locating us outside the New York City area. "If you just keep quiet and don't get involved with the wrong people, you shouldn't have anything to worry about."

I still worried. At night, when I was alone in bed, I lay there with my eyes open listening for strange sounds. I wondered if someone was hunting me down. The agents told me the contract on my life had been upped to $150,000, and it's difficult to ever stop worrying when someone threatens to put your children in a meat locker. The thought of being killed scared me, but when death came I knew I could die happy knowing Herbie was going to suffer in jail for most of the rest of his life. If they do kill me, I thought hopefully, they'll give me a hotshot, a drug overdose, to make it look accidental. I'll just go to sleep and never get up. That just didn't seem so terrible to me.

The only thing that did seem terrible was being dismembered. That terrified me. But as long as they didn't cut my hands off, I wouldn't fight them.

The fear of suffering through death never left me, but I'd learned to live with it before the trial, and I couldn't let it control my new life in Atlanta. I really wanted Atlanta to be the start of something new, something good, a life I could finally enjoy. With the money the government gave me I put down a month's security and a month's rent on the apartment, I had a telephone installed and the electricity turned on, I bought clothes for the kids and a bicycle for Gay and I got a used car for $300. And then I waited for the government to deliver my furniture from Bellmore.

And I waited. The government not only had stopped protecting me, they didn't want to bother to fulfill the promises they'd made. They didn't send my furniture and they didn't pay attention to my requests. For three months we lived like squatters in that apartment. Our beds were still in storage, so we had to sleep on the floor. Our refrigerator was still in storage, so we had to eat out of an ice chest and keep running to the store to buy ice. We had no pots, no pans, no dishes, no anything, and every time I called the government for help they fumbled around and gave me another excuse.

Once they'd used me, they'd abandoned me.

The whole time I was in Atlanta I received only one piece of good news. On September 12, 1973, exactly two months after being found guilty, Herbie Sperling was sentenced to life imprisonment and fined $300,000 and court costs. Teddy Burke sent me a copy of the story from the newspapers. Herbie went away just as tough as ever: "Anyone who came here to see me beg or plead is in the wrong courtroom. I'm asking the court for nothing."

He told the judge, "I am and always will be a better man than you. I sentence you to think about me the rest of your life. May God have mercy on your soul."

I didn't feel the slightest bit sorry for him.

— 23 —

We slept on the floor. We ate food from an ice chest on paper plates. And we had no television. But we were together, safe and happy. Things finally seemed to be going right for us. Lonnie and Nancy had decided to get married, and I was working two jobs to help them out—nobody gave them anything when they got married—as well as support my own family. I was working from 7:00 A.M. to 3:00 P.M. in a pancake house with Paige, and from 6:00 P.M. to 2:00 A.M. in a classy bar. In my free hours I kept the house clean, slept and did a little drugs.

I felt confident that I was through being an addict. I didn't have the time or the desire. My continuing confrontations with the government had forced me to take some responsibility, and I finally felt that I could make my own decisions. I did drugs when I wanted to; I didn't need them.

My kids used more drugs than I did. Philip was smoking a lot of locally grown marijuana, and he had discovered that boiled mushrooms make a wonderful hallucinatory drug. He was constantly searching fields for mushrooms and, when he found some, boiling them, drinking the muddy, muddy water and going off on a tremendous trip.

Paige's new boyfriend started dealing drugs, so there was always grass, speed, coke and barbiturates in the house. Nancy particularly liked a new drug called Talwin, which was a morphine extract that is cooked down and shot into the veins. It was a very popular drug for a while because it was easy to get from dentists. We all ended up shooting it up.

Lonnie had become a pill head mostly, but like all of us, he used whatever was around the apartment.

None of the kids were addicts, but they all used. They had grown up around drugs, either seeing me shooting up or working with Louie, so they liked them and respected them, but they weren't frightened by them.

The only thing that scared me was the fact that Gay was starting to smoke grass when I was around. And she was still only twelve years old.

After three months of living off the floors, I decided to try to force the government to get me my furniture. I called Teddy Burke in New York and told him, "Listen Teddy, I've been waiting three months for this stuff. Either you get it here right away, and I don't mean next week, I mean tomorrow or the next day, or I'm calling the newspaper. And I'm going to have a lot to say about the Marshal Service."

"Don't call," he told me, "just hold on. It's been lost and I'll try to trace it for you."

Maybe he tried, but I didn't get any help from him, so I turned to the newspapers. Ed Kirkman of the New York *Daily News* had written a story about the drug bust, so I called him long distance and laid my story out for him. "This is Cecile Mileto," I told him, "and I was a witness in the Herbert Sperling case. My children and I have been relocated by the government, but we've never been given the new identification they promised us. My children are still waiting for their school records to get here. We've been down here for three months, we're no longer in protective custody, and we're sleeping on the floor because our furniture hasn't been returned to us. I'm working two jobs trying to support my family, I can't get any help from welfare, and . . ." And on and on. Kirkman listened quietly. ". . . and I really want to talk to someone. I want some help," I finished.

Kirkman was polite, but not as enthusiastic as I hoped. "I'll get back to you," he told me, "I have to check with my editor to see if we're interested." I gave him my number at home, and my number at work, even though I'd been warned over and over by BNDD never to give anyone enough information to track me down. I wanted my clothes and I wanted my furniture!

Teddy Burke called me back before Kirkman. He wanted to know if I'd spoken to anybody. "All of a sudden you guys are interested again?" I said in a nasty voice, "What's the matter? Afraid of bad publicity?"

"Actually, we'd like to keep you alive," he answered smartly. He wanted to check out whoever I spoke to. "You know Ceil, he might sell you down the tubes. You might be signing your own death certificate."

"Ed Kirkman," I told him. Teddy was right, no harm could be done by checking Kirkman. Teddy called me back the very next day to tell me Kirkman was an honest reporter, but he asked me not to talk too much about the trial.

Kirkman called soon after. "We want the story," he said.

All my furniture arrived in Atlanta the day after Kirkman did. The agents explained that the furniture had been lost somewhere in Virginia, and they had to call special truckers to haul it down to Atlanta. They said it had nothing to do with my contacting the newspapers.

I started unpacking the boxes and couldn't believe what I found. Our leather-covered kitchen table was sliced up. Legs were missing from the dishwasher. The arm of an expensive crushed-velvet living room chair was splintered off. Everything that was there was either torn or scratched. This had been almost new stuff, all of it less than a year old, and it was ruined.

It looked like a pile of garbage, not the expensive stuff it had been.

Half of it was missing. The canopy to Paige's bed, gone. A $450 set of cut-glass bedroom lamps, gone. Two television sets, gone. A living room chair, gone. Somebody's house was well furnished.

It was obvious that everything had been packed in a great hurry. They packed the dirty dishes I had in the sink without even rinsing them off. They packed two Tupperware bowls of split peas but didn't close the lids, so split peas were squashed into everything.

I called New York and screamed. Nothing happened. I called again. Nothing happened. All I got were stories and excuses. No one knew where the furniture had been or who had been in charge of it. "It looks like they left it out in the rain!" I yelled. They didn't need me anymore, so they didn't pay too much attention to me.

I gave my whole story to Kirkman, and the New York *Daily News* ran a four-part series, "Diary of a Mobster's Wife," the week before Herbie was finally sentenced.

After the furniture arrived everything started going downhill again. The furniture had real meaning for me. I expected it to be clean and new, like I was trying to be. Instead it was old and beaten up. It was garbage. Looking at it really hurt.

I started calling my old boyfriend Hal Lyndal in New York and begging him to come down and visit me. I knew it was dangerous to contact him, but I needed a friend badly, and he was one of the few I had left. He came down and took me out. I wanted to marry him and let him support me, but I couldn't go back to New York and he didn't want to live in Atlanta. He went back to New York and we wrote each other for awhile, but the letters became less and less frequent and finally they stopped completely. I'd never caused him anything but pain, so I couldn't blame him for dropping me.

I kept working hard at two jobs, not sleeping too much, fighting to pay all our bills, and now I was starting to use drugs a little more often. My drugs relaxed me, made me feel contented and guaranteed me at least a few happy minutes every day. I was taking a little coke, shooting a little Talwin, dropping some uppers to stay awake and trying whatever else happened to be available. The fear was still with me, but as every day went by I felt a little more comfortable and a little more confident that I was safe.

Then came my first reminder that I would never really be safe, that for the rest of my life I'd always have to look for familiar faces in crowds, that I'd have to stay out of large groups, that I couldn't communicate with my mother and other relatives. I got found.

I was working in the bar one evening when Paige walked in with a guy I'd never seen before. He seemed nice enough and we talked for a while. Then out of nowhere, he asked me, "Do you know who I am?"

I'd never seen him before. "Raquel Welch?" I joked.

He smiled warmly. "I'm Sonny Gold's nephew."

My whole body tensed up. A chill ran right up and down my spine. I couldn't open my mouth. I actually felt my own deep breaths. I felt complete fear. "Sonny who?" I somehow managed to ask. I knew who: Sonny, Herbie's errand boy at the barbershop.

"Sonny Gold from New York. You know him?" He was still smiling.

I tried to smile back, but my mind was racing. I knew I had to run for help. "No," I told him as calmly as I could, "I don't think so."

"I just left Miami. I'm down here on vacation and . . ."

I had testified against Sonny at the trial. I had helped put him away. But this had to be a coincidence. It had to be! Paige was a very pretty girl, this guy was on vacation, it was a coincidence. Nothing more than a silly coincidence. "Excuse me for a minute," I said, "I've got to go to the ladies' room."

I got on the phone to the Marshal Service. "This is Cecile Mileto," I told them very clearly. I told them exactly where I was. "You know who's with my daughter? Sonny Gold's nephew!"

"All right Ceil, relax, can you get his license plate number?"
I went out through the back and got the number. "Now relax,"
I was told, "two agents will be there within a half-hour. Try to
keep them there, and Ceil, try to stay cool."

The twenty minutes dragged by, but the two agents finally
walked in. Cautiously, I identified him with a nod of my head.
The agents sat down at the bar to watch. As soon as the
nephew got up to go to the men's room, I went back over to
Paige. "Don't take anything he gives you," I told her, "and go
home, go home right now. Don't give me any excuses, just go
home."

She thought the whole thing was funny. "Oh, Ma, according
to you everybody's trying to kill me. Will you stop looking over
your shoulder. He doesn't even know who we are."

"Yeah?" I whispered at her, "why does he come up with the
name Sonny Gold if he don't know who we are? Why did he
even mention it?"

She had no answer. "Okay Ma," she agreed quietly, "I'll go
home."

He came back from the men's room and offered to drive her
home when she told him she had to leave. That was fine with
me, I knew the agents would follow them home. She got home
safely.

The marshals did a very fast check job. This kid, it turns out,
hadn't seen his uncle in maybe 18 years. He didn't even know
his uncle had been busted. The only reason he even mentioned
Sonny was because Paige told him we once lived in New York
and his uncle was the only other person he knew who lived
there.

The whole episode really depressed me. It just magnified the
fact that I'd never, ever, be really free as long as I lived. For
the first time I began to understand the meaning of what I'd
done. Until that night, I was most afraid of dying, and now I
realized that living was going to be much harder. My death
would probably come quickly, but all my life I was going to be
looking over my shoulder, suspicious of new people, busy trying to remember the lies I'd invented about my past, and

having awful nightmares about being cut up into pieces. Living, I suddenly realized, was much more terrifying than dying. And I was trapped.

I was very lonely. Nancy was married, Paige had moved in with her new boyfriend, and my two jobs didn't leave me time for friends, male or female. Then Drug Enforcement (BNDD had changed its official name) contacted me and asked me to get ready to come to New York to testify against Benny Mallah, Herbie's accused partner. I didn't want to go; I just didn't want to start that over again. Testifying against Herbie was one thing; the few times I'd met Benny he was very nice. Nancy was happy. Paige was happy. Susan was still in Florida with her grandmother and happy. Gay had her school friends and was happy. And Philip had his 15-year-old girl friend sleeping over. He was playing cards all night, partying all day and getting stoned on pot day and night. He was happy. I was alone and unhappy, and that's when I started thinking about committing suicide.

The first time the thought came into my mind I pushed it out. But then it came back and I began wondering what death would be like. I saw it as freedom. It would be calm and peaceful. I would be permanently free from all my worries. There would be no more Herbies, no more drugs and no more government people pushing and pulling. I would be free forever.

I pushed it out of my mind again; I had to bring up my children.

The thought returned, stronger than ever. Peace. Freedom. Rest. And maybe my children would be better off without me. Four of the five had become drug users because of me. If Louie had lived, he wouldn't have permitted it, he would have beat them first. But I'd failed them, they learned their drugs from me. They wouldn't be in worse shape if I was dead.

I pushed it out of my mind again. I knew the future had to be better than two jobs, not enough money and constant fear.

But how? How could the future be better?

I could do it with an overdose of drugs. That would be the

easiest way, but for some reason I didn't want to do that. Guns? I was too scared. Pills? They were drugs. Cut my wrists? Too much pain. No, maybe not, I'd heard somewhere there was no pain.

I forced the thoughts away, but now they were coming back stronger and stronger. I started thinking about when and making arrangements. Not for real, I told myself, not for real. I wasn't going to do it for real.

I waited until all my children were out for the evening. I wrote a note to the kids on the back of an unpaid bill. I told Susan to behave and stop hitting everybody. I told Gay to please get to the dentist. And I told Philip to stop gambling so much. I asked Paige and Nancy to make sure I was buried with Louie, and I told them to wear bright colors to my funeral because I didn't want them to be sad.

Then I walked into the bathroom and unwrapped one of the new razor blades I'd bought. It was very bright and the light over the bathroom mirror glinted off of it. I touched one point to the tip of my finger and pushed. Then I squeezed the finger and watched carefully as a tiny drop of blood bubbled up on the finger and then fell off and ran down into the palm of my hand. I was high, but not really drugged. I knew exactly what I was doing.

I was making good my escape.

I took the razor blade in my right hand and turned my left hand over so the palm, and the veins, were up. I pushed the corner of the blade into the side of my wrist and slowly pulled it across. There wasn't much pain at all. Blood started seeping out from the new wound. It didn't flow out or pulsate out in big amounts, a thin layer just rolled out and spread over my hand. I moved the razor up my wrist about an inch and again pushed the corner of the blade into the side of my wrist. Again I started pulling it across.

There was no great rush of thoughts through my mind. I didn't think of Louie and I didn't think of the kids. I didn't think about my reasons for doing this. I was working very carefully and I wanted to make sure I did a good, clean job of it.

The blood started flowing off my hand into the bathroom sink. Some of it immediately flowed down the drain, but most of it just stained the sides. It wasn't the deep red I'd expected, it was a lighter color for some reason.

I made a third cut across my left arm. The flow of blood was warm. Then I put the blade in my left hand and pushed down into my right wrist. It was more difficult than it had been, I was quickly losing strength in the left arm. I made the first cut, and the second cut. The blood was now starting to flow more freely from both arms. I just stood over the sink and watched it as it ran out.

Good, I kept thinking, good, good, good. I didn't hate anybody, I wasn't angry at anybody, I just knew this was the right thing to be doing.

It never occurred to me that by slicing my wrists, I was symbolically doing that thing I was most afraid of, having my hands cut off.

I got tired pretty quickly. I couldn't focus. It was difficult to keep my eyes open. I think I remember falling.

Paige found me in a small pool of blood. I don't know how long I'd been lying on the tile floor, but it couldn't have been too long. I didn't hear her scream, later she told me she screamed at the top of her lungs when she found me. But she acted quickly to save my life. She grabbed some towels and bound up my wrists to stop the bleeding. Her new boyfriend helped pick me up and carry me to bed.

Things happened fast. I only can remember bits and pieces. I remember people screaming and doctors and an ambulance. I remember getting a pins-and-needles feeling in both my arms. There was some pain as my arms were sewn and bandaged tight.

Before the night was over I was in the psychiatric ward of the hospital. I lived. I'd blown my attempt to commit suicide too. My life was now a total failure.

The psychiatrists spent a lot of time examining me the next few days, as much because the government was concerned about me as for my own well being. The government had the

Benny Mallah trial coming up, and if I couldn't be certified sane, they were going to lose one of their best witnesses. I spent a lot of time with the doctors talking about suicide, and depression, and my problems, and my children, and Louie. Everything was still Louie. I told myself I did eventually want to get married again, but I could only marry someone exactly like Louie. In-and-out Louie, he'd been dead almost two years and he was still running my life.

It would be another year and a half before other psychiatrists would tell me I had a chemical imbalance in my system, that I was manic-depressive, that I had been that way since I was 11 years old and that my suicide attempts were predictable. But these doctors simply certified me sane and fully able to testify in court and understand what I was testifying to. Then they sent me home.

Almost as soon as I got back to the apartment, the government brought me back to New York to testify against Benny Mallah.

I was the first witness in the trial. "Mrs. Mileto, what was your husband's name?"

"Louis Mileto." It was starting all over again.

"You were married to Mr. Mileto, were you not?"

"Yes, I was."

"You are presently a widow?"

"Yes, I am." They objected to that. I don't know why, I didn't say anything else. I wanted to though, even after all this time, I still wanted to.

"You have been arrested and convicted of some crimes, have you not?"

"Yes, I have."

"Would you tell us what your husband Louis was doing for a living in 1971, in May."

"He was cutting heroin." I wasn't as nervous as I'd been at the beginning of Herbie's trial.

"How do you know that?"

"My husband told me."

"Did he tell you who he was working for?"

There were a few objections. Then I got to name Herbie. "Herbert Sperling."

The U.S. attorney in this trial was Jim Lavin. He covered some of the areas John Gross didn't use me for. "You testified before that you moved from Queens to Bellmore. Can you tell us when that was?"

"The summer of seventy-one."

"Did you pack your belongings from the apartment in Queens to move?"

"Most of them, yes, I did." Benny just sat and stared at me. He never said one word.

"During the time you were packing did you discover anything in your closet?"

"Yes, I did."

"Could you tell us what that was, please."

"A large plastic bag with a white powder in it."

"Did you have occasion to test that in any way?"

"Yes, I did. I put a hole in the bottom of it and took a little bit and tasted it."

"Can you tell us what you thought it was at that time?"

"I thought it was a cut."

He covered every detail. "Con you tell us what you mean by 'cut'?"

"A cut for heroin. I had never tasted pure heroin and I didn't know at the time that's what it was."

Eventually we got around to Benny. Did I know an individual named Benny Mallah? Yes, I did. Was he in the courtroom? Yes, he was. "May the record reflect that the witness has identi- fied Mr. Mallah."

Later I identified Bozo. That's the only name I knew him by. When I pointed him out, he started screaming and yelling. "You never seen me before in your life, you liar. You know you're a liar."

The judge asked him to keep quiet.

"What do you want me to do, your honor?" Bozo kept talking. "The same thing is happening that happened in the Sperling case. You put these junkie witnesses on the stand, the same thing in the Sperling case." Benny just sat quietly.

Benny's attorney tried to do the same job on my character that Herbie's attorneys tried. "You take pills of one sort or another every day, don't you?"

"No, I do not."

"You don't? Tell us when you first became a hard user of heroin?"

"Nineteen sixty-nine, to my knowledge."

Later in the trial I had some trouble remembering dates. "Mrs. Mileto," I was asked, "do you have trouble remembering times of the year?"

I had to smile. "I am trying to forget this whole life," I told him.

He also tried to show the jury that the government was bribing me to testify by paying my rent and giving me money for my bills. "When did you start receiving money from the government?"

Money? That wasn't it at all. "They gave me my life, the government." I said it without smiling, and I meant it.

Benny got on the stand and swore I was lying. "I never saw Louis Mileto in my life," he said. Instead of using me to upset his testimony, the government wanted to use Philip. I was a little unhappy about that because I didn't want him getting that involved, I thought it was too dangerous. But he wanted to testify, Drug Enforcement felt they needed him and I was getting mad at Benny for denying he knew Louie. So I gave permission.

Philip made a terrific witness. Every time Louie's name was mentioned he started crying. And he swore that he'd been in Benny's apartment with Louie.

His testimony was damaging to Benny, so the defense attorney attacked him. "You love your mother very much, don't you?"

He didn't even hesitate. "Yes," he said firmly.

"In fact, you love her so much, you'd even lie for her, wouldn't you?"

Philip stayed very calm. "No, I wouldn't lie. Everything I've said about Benny is true. He knows why I'm testifying."

Benny Mallah was convicted. He was released on bail and is appealing his case.

Bozo was convicted. One by one each of them was going to jail. Alvin Gibbons was caught in 1974. His trial was scheduled for the summer of 1975. Richie Maxton is still a fugitive from justice.

Philip appeared on the stand a second time in Benny Mallah's trial. He was paid over $400 in witness fees and expenses. It wasn't enough; there could never be enough to replace Louie.

– 24 –

The January 1974 issue of *Reader's Digest* had an article about the drug operation called "Night of the Big Bust." Near the end of the story there was one paragraph about Louie and one paragraph about me. "Shortly thereafter"—that was after Louie's body had been discovered—my paragraph read, "Mileto's wife agreed to reveal the inner workings of Sperling's operation to agents. Her testimony—added to that of the others—nearly clinched the government's case."

I liked seeing that article as much as anything that had happened since Louie had been killed. It was proof that I had contributed to breaking up Herbie's ring. It was also a nice reminder about how far I'd come since my days as a housewife and mother living in Queens, New York, and not allowed to leave my house. I used to look forward to the *Digest* coming to my house every month because reading it filled so many lonely hours. My life was one world; everything the *Digest* wrote about was another, bigger and better, world. And now they were writing about me.

If I hadn't learned to keep quiet about who I was, I probably would have given copies to everyone I knew in Atlanta. But I was finally getting smart enough to keep my past private. Unfortunately, the kids hadn't learned that lesson yet. They were excited about the article and the word spread around quickly that I was the woman mentioned in *Reader's Digest*. I tried to tell them that maybe they should be a little careful about who knew we were the Mileto family mentioned in the article, but they thought I was still being paranoid. "Oh, Ma," Nancy complained, "I can't believe you still think everybody's out to kill us."

She found out soon enough why I was nervous. She was at a party with Lonnie when a boy about their age came over to her and said simply, "We know who your mother is and she's gonna get blown away."

"What are you talking about," she asked. "Are you crazy?"

"Some people are coming from New Orleans to blow her apartment off the block." This kid is standing there with a big smile on his face and a copy of the January issue of the *Digest* in his hand, telling this to Nancy and Lonnie. "We know that she's Mileto's old lady and we know that she's hiding out here from the people in New York." This kid's father lived in New York, and there had been rumors that he was connected to the mob. "It's worth a lot of money to give her up," he finished.

Nancy and Lonnie ran right home and told me the story. That was all I had to hear. I got on the telephone and the agents came running right over. They took me, Nancy and Lonnie, Paige, Philip, Gay and Susan, and another couple, friends of the kids, who had been staying with us. The agents checked us into a downtown hotel and put a 24-hour guard on us. We were warned not to go back to the apartment under any circumstances.

We were packed into the room and nobody bothered to tell us we could use room service. So we had a room, but no food. And I wasn't allowed to go back to my job. We ended up going almost two days without eating, waiting for somebody to give us some direction, before we started calling room service and putting it on Drug Enforcement's bill. And once we started, we really got into it. We were eating steaks, roast beef, lobsters, stuffed shrimp, ham and eggs, bacon, we were drinking the best liquor and having absolutely everything we wanted from the hotel pharmacy delivered to our room. One by one, I called every local dentist, told them I was from out of town and suffering from a toothache and that I was allergic to codeine. "My dentist in New York always prescribes Talwin," I explained. The dentist would call a pharmacy with his prescription and we'd have it delivered. So we had plenty of drugs, paid for by Drug Enforcement.

We were running up a bill of over a thousand dollars a week.

The Marshal Service didn't want anything to do with us because I'd said some nasty things about them in the *Daily News* series, so they were fighting with Drug Enforcement who wanted them to guard us and then relocate us.

I was calling Drug Enforcement every day to find out when we were going to be moved. They kept telling me soon.

One month passed. We were still eating steaks and spending the government's money. We spent most of our time playing cards and watching television.

After the second month everybody had gotten terribly bored. The two friends of the kids couldn't take being cooped up anymore. I told them they were welcome to my apartment "if you want to take your chances getting blown off the block because somebody thinks you're me," and they left.

Drug Enforcement carefully investigated the kid who had threatened Nancy and Lonnie, but they couldn't find out what his connections were. They were constantly sending teletypes to the Marshal Service, telling them that I had risked my life, that Philip had risked his life and that we would probably be needed in the future for the Alvin Gibbons and Richie Maxton trials. The point was that we were still valuable to the government and should be relocated and protected.

The third month of sitting in the hotel room passed. Our

apartment was empty, and watched, and the rent was piling up. We were told to decide where we wanted to be moved to. And this move, we were warned, was absolutely our last one.

I still wanted to go back to California. One of the kids wanted to try Chicago because it was supposed to be like New York. There was one vote for Miami and one vote for San Francisco. It's exciting and difficult to decide that a place you've never seen is where you'd like to live for the rest of your life. We argued a lot about it; we had a lot of time to argue. Finally, as a compromise choice, we selected——. I figured I could get work as a waitress there, the weather was nice and it sounded like a fun place to live.

After waiting three months and one week, the Service finally decided to move us. On Wednesday afternoon we were told to pack and be ready to leave Thursday morning.

The move wasn't going to be that easy, the Marshal Service had been waiting too long to get even with me. The first thing they told me at the Federal Building Thursday morning was that the government would not pay my back rent for the apartment, and the landlord would not release my furniture until $920 he was owed was paid. I was furious. I tried screaming and yelling, but no one paid any attention to me. "Once you have an address and pay the landlord," I was told, "we'll move the stuff for you."

I asked the marshal about the $1080 moving expenses I was supposed to be given, to pay for our plane tickets and any extra expenses.

"I got it right here," he smiled, showing me that he was missing one tooth in front. "All you got to do is sign for it." He slid a piece of paper across his desk.

"What's it say?" I had a good idea.

"This is a release form," he explained. "Once you sign that paper, the Marshal Service is no longer responsible for you or your family. If anything should happen to you . . ." He didn't even bother to finish his sentence.

They were really getting even. "And if I don't sign?"

"You don't get the money."

It was my turn to smile. The marshals had tried to get me to release them after we had been relocated to Atlanta, but Drug Enforcement put up a big fight and I got my money without having to sign. But this time I wasn't going to fight them, I really didn't care. I was just as glad to get rid of the marshals as they were glad to get rid of me. The marshals had been a painful necessity; we just never got along with them. With a little care in our new home, we wouldn't need them anyway. And we didn't want them.

"Gimme the check." I signed their paper. I was through with the government of the United States.

That afternoon, we all climbed on a plane and flew out of Atlanta. I wasn't sorry to leave. We were still looking for a new life.

A year later my furniture is still in storage in Atlanta. For $920 I can have it back. The government still owes the furniture one move. A lot of things have happened in that year. I've been on and off drugs and in and out of methadone programs a number of times.

In November 1974, 12-year-old Gay overdosed on a handful of barbiturates at a party. She was rushed to the hospital and they saved her life. In December, I was kicked out of my methadone program for shooting heroin again, and Susan and Gay were taken away from me and placed in foster homes. Philip went back up to New York to stay with his father. I wrote to him, asking him to come back because I was so worried he was too close to Bellmore, but he refused. "Why should I come back," he wrote, "to see you cut yourself up again?" I haven't heard from him in over six months. I don't blame him. I get weekly reports about Susan and Gay through Drug Enforcement, and they both seem to be doing good in their new homes.

Mark Moffett is still in jail, but with parole, he may be getting out in three years. Billy D'Angelo has been relocated somewhere in the Midwest. The agents tell me he's gotten a job and seems to be adjusting to his new life. Lucy had a rough time of it once she was released from protective custody. Her family thought the government had made a settlement with her, and they all moved in and started living off her.

And I'm alone. I've learned to control my fear. The only time I get worried is when I'm on the street and I think I see somebody I know. A few weeks ago, I was taking a bus to my new methadone clinic and I looked across the street and thought for sure I saw Benny Mallah, who's out on bail waiting his appeal. I got really scared and just froze up. I stayed on the bus until it reached the end of its line.

Drug Enforcement keeps me informed of any developments in the cases. They want me to testify in an upcoming trial, but I haven't decided whether I should or not. After all this time, I don't feel I owe them anything. I think they used me and then they abandoned me. The Nassau County police still have all the jewelry they took from the house in Bellmore and I can't get it back.

They believe that Benny won't come looking for me, but if he saw me he might put a finger on me. They also told me that Herbie probably would not go out of his way to find me. He's in jail for life and my death has no real value to him. As for the rest of them, they probably don't have the money to search me out. Those are big probablys to base your life on.

I do want to live. I'm only now beginning to understand what I've done to my life. I'm under psychiatric care and my doctor has helped me to see how destructive I've been. I'm drug free right now and trying to stay that way.

There are times when I get very paranoid. I haven't had a permanent address since we moved to this city. Every few months I change apartments, and I haven't had a telephone of my own in almost a year. Some mornings I'll get really scared and I'll just run around locking doors and pulling down shades. I've spent some days sitting alone in a quiet, dark house, afraid to go out the front door. At the suggestion of Drug Enforcement, I stay out of places the local mob is likely to go, like the dog track and baseball and football games.

I've often wondered if I did the right thing in cooperating with the government. But I did it for Louie, and that makes me feel good. People tell you whatever you want to hear to get you to testify and then apologize and explain they didn't have the proper authority to make such a promise when you look for the payoff. If anyone reading this book is ever asked to testify by a government agency, I would strongly advise them to contact an attorney they trust to represent them. Most important, get everything in writing. All I have left from my deal are a handful of empty promises.

I still miss Louie. I'm still in love with him. Those three years we spent together were the best years of my life. Good old Louie, he always made me laugh.

I never really understood him, though, that I know. There were at least three Louies: Louie the husand and father, Louie the mobster and Louie the lover—of other women. The problems we had came when Louie the mobster tried to be Louie the husband. Sometimes he got confused.

I know what I've done to myself, and my children. I know how I've ruined part of their lives. And now I'm trying, I'm trying very hard, to make it up to them. The best thing I can say about myself is that I never wanted to hurt anybody, I only wanted good things for everybody, including myself. I just wasn't tough enough to survive on my own. The bad thing is that I had to take other people down with me.

If Louie had lived, none of the kids would be using drugs. I'm positive about that. He had control, and he was tougher than I was. The only reason they started was they had me as an example. After he died, I got worse than ever. There was no discipline in my house after he was dead. I knew it, I cared, I just couldn't do anything about it.

I needed someone to tell me what to do, and I had nobody.

I know what Louie did to my life. I know he lied to me, and cheated on me, and used me. But he also gave me more than anyone else in my life. And knowing all this, knowing that I've turned out a family of potential drug addicts, if Louie walked into my life again, I'd marry him in one minute, without second thoughts. He was worth every bit of the misery I've lived through.

He took me on a long trip from Queens.